DSMC
COMPUTER STUDIES

COMPUTERS: INFORMATION AND DATA

COMPUTERS
INFORMATION AND DATA

Barbara and John Jaworski

NELSON

Thomas Nelson and Sons Ltd
Nelson House Mayfield Road
Walton-on-Thames Surrey KT12 5PL

51 York Place
Edinburgh EH1 3JD

P.O. Box 18123
Nairobi Kenya

Yi Xiu Factory Building
Unit 05-06 5th Floor
65 Sims Avenue Singapore 1438

Thomas Nelson (Hong Kong) Ltd
Watson Estate Block A 13 Floor
Watson Road Causeway Bay Hong Kong

Thomas Nelson (Nigeria) Ltd
8 Ilupeju Bypass PMB 21303 Ikeja Lagos

© Barbara Jaworski and John Jaworski 1982

First published by Thomas Nelson and Sons Ltd 1982
Reprinted 1982

ISBN 0-17-438126-3

NCN 200-3223-1

All rights reserved. No part of this publication may be reproduced, stored in a retrieval system, or transmitted, in any form or by any means, electronic, mechanical, photocopying, recording or otherwise, without the prior permission of the publishers.

Printed in Hong Kong

Phototypeset by Trident Graphics Ltd, Reigate, Surrey

Acknowledgments

The author and the publishers are grateful to the following organisations for permission to reproduce material.

Examples of standard forms
The Abbey National Building Society
The Open University

Examples of examination questions
The East Anglian Examinations Board
The Joint Matriculation Board
The London Regional Examining Board
The University of Cambridge Local Examinations Syndicate
The University of London University Entrance and School Examinations Council
The Yorkshire Regional Examinations Board

Cover photograph courtesy of Ferranti Electronics Ltd.

CONTENTS

Introduction *viii*

1 **What is a computer?** *1*
   A computer is automatic *2*
   A computer is reprogrammable *2*
   A computer is digital *3*
   A computer works with data *5*
   A computer is a processor *5*
   Summary *6*

2 **The ingredients of computing – Information and data** *9*
   The problems of collecting information *10*
   The connection between information and data *11*
   The importance of structure *12*
   The problems of collecting data *13*
   Summary *16*

3 **Representing data in a computer – Primary storage** *19*
   The structure of primary storage *20*
   How primary storage is organised *20*
   Representing data within a location *23*
   Computer words and bytes *33*
   Data structures *33*
   Storage of program instructions *38*
   Summary *39*

4 **The organisation of data – Files** *43*
   Data files *44*
   Locating data: record keys *45*
   The order of data in a file *46*
   Describing files of data *47*
   Linking data-items in files *49*
   Indexing files of data *53*
   Locating data: primary and secondary keys *55*
   Summary *56*

vi Contents

5 **Computer files – Secondary storage** *59*
Backing store *60*
Magnetic tape *61*
Magnetic disks *63*
Serial and direct access *66*
Summary *68*

6 **The machinery of a computer – Hardware** *71*
The CPU and peripherals *72*
Operation of the CPU *72*
Communication between the CPU and peripherals *77*
Types of peripheral *80*
Summary *90*

7 **The machinery of a computer – Software** *93*
Applications software and systems software *94*
An empty computer – the initial program loader *94*
Programming language translators *100*
Operating systems *107*
Other systems software programs *110*
Summary *111*

8 **Preparing a job for a computer – Systems analysis and design** *113*
Phases of system development *114*
Analysing the system *115*
Stating objectives *116*
Designing the system *117*
Designing the programs *118*
Testing *120*
Documenting the system *121*
Summary *123*

9 **Instructing the computer – Programming** *127*
The job of a programmer *128*
Describing the problem *128*
Developing the solution *129*
Coding the program *138*
Testing the program *140*
Documenting the program *140*
A note on languages *142*
Summary *143*

10 **Computer applications – Data processing** *145*
Examples of commercial DP *146*
Requirements of a DP program *147*
Data flowcharts *149*
The data processing cycle *152*
Computer personnel *161*
Summary *162*

11 Computer applications – Real-time systems *165*
　　Information retrieval *166*
　　Real-time working *166*
　　Databases *170*
　　Computer networks *173*
　　Other real-time systems *174*
　　Word processing *176*
　　Summary *178*

Appendix 1: Solutions to exercises *179*

Appendix 2: Examination questions *193*

Index *204*

INTRODUCTION

This is a book about computers. It describes what it is that computers do, why they are required to do these things and how they fit into the world around them.

Most important of all, it describes the principles behind the use of computers, rather than the details of their operation. Thus, it does not teach you to write programs, but it does teach the good habits of designing them properly. It does not teach much about the workings of disk drives, line printers and visual display units – rather it teaches about *why* they are designed the way they are, and what jobs they do best.

Because the book could well be used for a CSE or O-Level course in computer studies, many of the examples are slanted to discussion within a classroom; and there is at the end of the book an appendix containing some typical examination questions. To this end, we have given guidance with each exercise – *for discussion, practical* and so forth – indicating where we feel they should fit into class teaching. No teacher would be handicapped by ignoring this advice completely! Neither is the book restricted to this audience: we feel that it would be equally valuable to the beginning A-Level or Further Education student (although it would not be sufficient in itself), and to the interested individual reader.

The reader is expected to be familiar with binary arithmetic, which is used without formality throughout, although nothing more advanced than counting is required. It is also assumed that he or she is aware of computers and has some commonsense notion of the sort of work that they do. In some cases, it has been appropriate to refer to the BASIC programming language for illustration. It is never necessary to understand the details of BASIC in order to extract the most from this book.

There are some topics from current syllabuses of examinations at this level which will not be found in these pages. There is no *history of computing* because this is clearly becoming less and less relevant as time passes, and the current fashion is to omit this from such examinations. Similarly, *logic* – for which it is difficult at this level to relate what can be taught to what is required for an understanding of computer technology – is becoming less popular and should eventually wither away from examinations. The topic of *social impact of computers* is also missing, but for a different reason. We believe quite firmly that this is not a section of the syllabus, but rather an attitude to every other part of the syllabus. We should like to think that no technical topic is raised within these pages without some discussion of its effect on society. Thus, the student using this book will find a growing awareness of this social impact, as he studies the technical material.

This book will not do everything for you! There are two experiences in computing that we cannot provide in this book (or any other). For the fullest satisfaction, it will be necessary to do some practical computing and for this you will require a guide to a programming language available on a computer to which you have access, and a guide to the computer itself. Further, you will need to see computing in action, and for this it will be necessary to make visits to computer installations, computer users and other computer professionals.

Our thanks are in order to the many of our colleagues who have given advice and encouragement: we should like especially to thank Brian Jackson. The publishers' readers offered much advice that we have heeded and we wish to thank John Newton and Mike Johnston, even though they are anonymous. The publishers, in the guise of Elizabeth Johnston, Julia Denny and Andrew Nash, have been tirelessly optimistic throughout, and they too we thank. But our especial thanks have been reserved for Princess, our Labrador, for not eating the manuscript.

Barbara and John Jaworski
1981

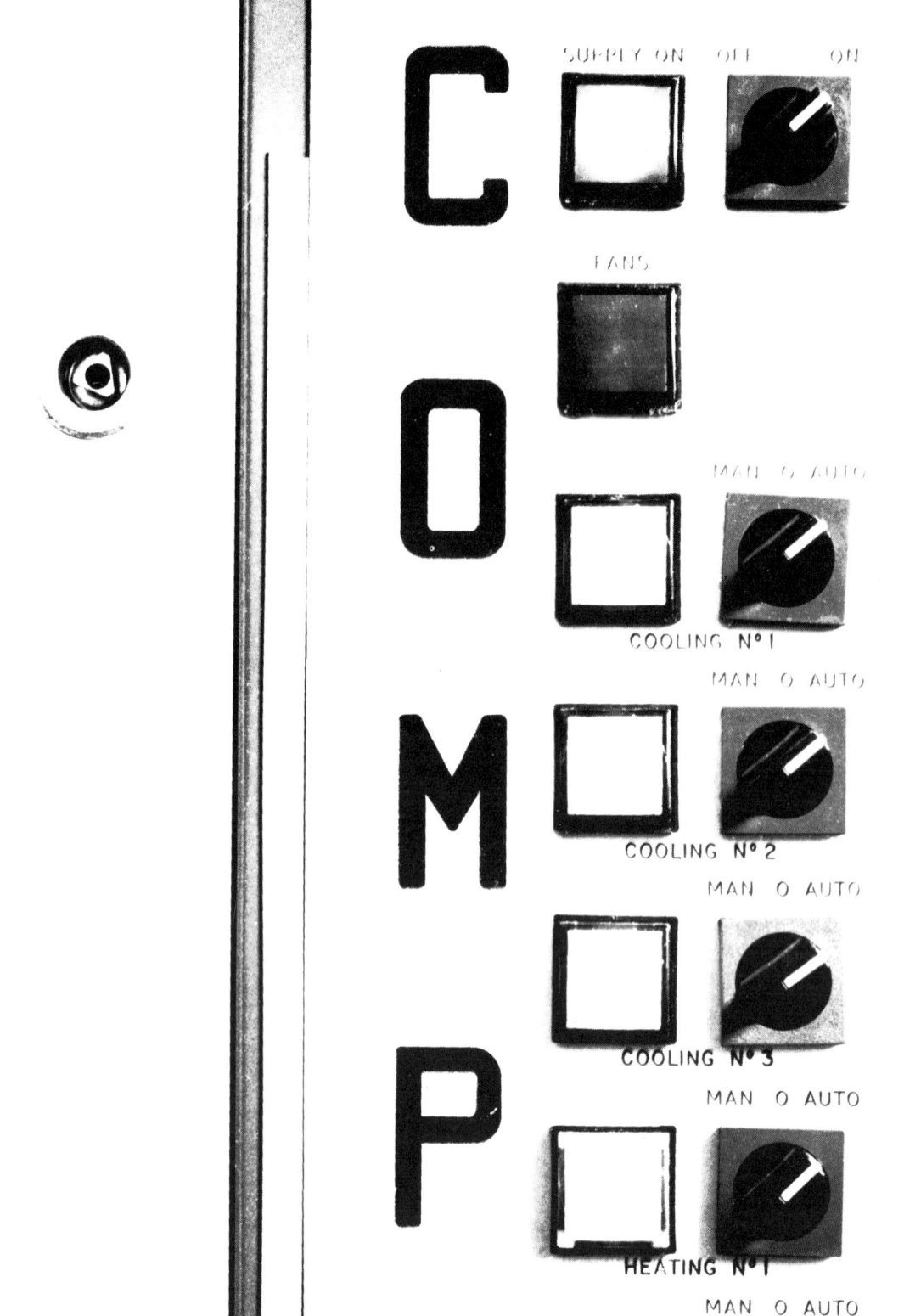

1 WHAT IS A COMPUTER?

A computer is an automatic, reprogrammable, digital data processor.

Computers have changed over the years. Where once there were valves, at the time of writing there are micro-electronic 'chips'. New pieces of technology are discovered, grow in importance, and then decline as yet newer technologies come to take their place.

Because computing is so changeable, it is important to have a definition of 'computer' that captures the essential things about computers, and nothing more. The definition above does this. It says very little about computers: just five things. There are many things it might have said, but didn't. *A computer is electronic*, *a computer uses binary arithmetic*, *a computer is fast*. These are all statements which are generally true about computers today, but which are not necessarily always going to be true. There have been computers working in denary (base 10) arithmetic; today's idea of 'fast' will be tomorrow's 'slow'.

But the definition above, by saying very little about computers, says what is most important about them.

A computer is automatic

Using a simple pocket calculator, it is possible to carry out many of the calculations performed by a computer – at least, the mathematical ones. But there is an important difference between the way we use a computer and the way we use a calculator. With the *computer*, once the user has pressed the START button, or typed RUN, or given whatever command is the appropriate one to start the computer working, the whole operation is carried out without further human intervention. The computer may come back to the user and ask for some figures – inviting the user to type in the next piece of information to be processed, perhaps – but this is always pre-planned and expected. The computer does *not* come back to the user and ask for instructions as to what to do next. From start to finish, the operation is completely automatic.

With a calculator, this is not true. The user keys in the numbers and the operations – add, subtract, multiply, divide – to be carried out on those numbers. Whenever the calculator finishes a calculation, it waits for the user to tell it what operation to carry out next.

Some calculators are more powerful than the one described above. They are *programmable* and allow the user to store a set of instructions in advance. The operations can then be carried out automatically. Whether this makes such calculators into computers is a matter of opinion. Certainly they are automatic. Whether or not they become computers depends on whether you feel that they satisfy the remaining conditions.

A computer is reprogrammable

This is really two ideas in one. To be *re*programmable, a computer must be *programmable*. This simply means that the computer stores its instructions within itself, so that it can automatically carry them out when required. If the instructions are to be repeated a large number of times, they need only be stored once. Most computers keep the instructions in a **store**, which can also be used for storing the values worked with – numbers to be operated on, for example. These values are called the **data**. A computer can be required to carry out a long and complicated set of instructions on just a very few items of data, or it can carry out just a few instructions repeatedly on a large collection of data. By using the same store for both data and instructions, a computer can be efficient, and not run out of storage for instructions when there is a lot of data storage left unused, or vice versa.

The collection of instructions is called a (computer) **program**. The art of designing a program is called **computer programming**. Later in this book, we shall look at how programs are written, as well as how they are stored in the computer.

But it is not just that the computer has a program of instructions held in its store. An important part of the definition of a computer is that these instructions may be changed. That is, the computer may be **reprogrammed**. This can mean that when you have finished using one program of instructions, you replace it by a completely new program to do an entirely different job – together with new data to work on. But it can also mean that a program is modified slightly to do a similar, but slightly different, task. A program to add one hundred numbers could be modified to add one thousand; a program to sort a list of names and addresses into alphabetical order could be modified to sort them into some other order, such as the order of house numbers.

Because computers may be reprogrammed, this usually means that the contents of the store can be changed at will. New instructions can replace existing ones, and because data and program share the same store, new data can replace existing data.

The idea of reprogramming is an important one in practical computing. Long before computers were available, it would have been possible to build machines to carry out the calculations. But these machines would have had the crucial drawback that they could perform one task only – the task they were built for. A true computer can be reprogrammed at any time to carry out new tasks. If a company buys a computer to handle its payroll – paying its employees – it need not worry that it should buy a new computer when the income tax rules change: it simply reprograms the computer to take account of the changes. Better still, if it finds that the computer is so efficient at the payroll that it is standing idle for half the week, the company can reprogram the computer to do some other task for the rest of the time.

A computer is digital

This is the hardest part of the definition to understand. But it is an important part, because it tells us a lot about how computers are designed. The word **digit** means 'one of the figures used in counting' – 1, 2, 3, and so on. It also means 'a finger' (there is an obvious connection, to do with counting on one's fingers). Ordinary arithmetic is **digital**, because it is to do with operations carried out on combinations of the digits 1, 2, 3, ...

We find ordinary arithmetic easy to understand (we may find it difficult to *do*, but that's a different matter!). We know that all arithmetic problems are made up of combinations of the basic digits, together with some operations to be carried out on those combinations. In turning through the pages of a science book, you may come upon the problem:

    1 598 726 + 2 840 228 = ?

You may never have seen these particular numbers before – but you can understand perfectly what is meant by them, and unless you are *very* bad at arithmetic, you are quite capable of adding them together to give you the answer, 4 438 954.

A computer is digital because it carries out operations on data that is made up of combinations of digits in exactly the same way. In a binary computer, the data is made up of combinations of the **binary digits** 0 and 1. Once you know this, you know that all computing problems are made up of combinations of 0's and 1's, together with some operations to be carried out on those combinations.

This does not seem to be a very powerful idea, but it is important, because once you know what the digits being used are, you know exactly what *sort* of data to expect. Of course, we shall want our computers to handle problems like 1 598 726 + 2 840 228; and to enable them to do so, we shall have to find ways of using binary digits to represent ordinary numbers. We shall look at how this is done in Chapter 3.

If you are prepared to extend the meaning of the word 'digit', you can see that many things are digital in nature. The words that make up this book are combinations of the 'digits' A, B, C, D, . . ., and some punctuation 'digits' like spaces, brackets and so on. This is an important idea, because it suggests (correctly) that a digital computer with a suitable program of instructions could operate on the text of this book. It could, for example, change every spelling of the word 'program' to 'programme'. So in Chapter 3, we shall also look at how text can be represented using the binary digits 0 and 1.

Not everything is digital, of course: a painting is *not* made up of combinations of digits – however wide we take our understanding of 'digit' to be. Music *could* be considered to be digital – it is made up of combinations of notes – but there are many subtleties of musical interpretation that make the difference between one performance of a piece of music and another performance of the same piece, so that we should probably conclude that music was *not* digital.

There is another sort of computer that should be mentioned here. We have not mentioned it before, because our definition rules it out! This is the **analog** (or **analogue**) **computer**. It has every characteristic we mentioned in our definition *except* that of working with digital data. Analog computers are almost always used for mathematical problems, and represent the numbers they work with by means of continuously changing quantities such as voltages, currents and so on. Two numbers may be added, by adding the appropriate voltages, for example. Because analog computers work with such a different type of data, their internal workings are so different that they would require an entirely separate book to describe them. This book is *not* about analog computers. Whenever you read the word 'computer' in this book, you may take it to mean a *digital* computer.

In ordinary arithmetic, we can do very powerful and advanced things with combinations of ten digits and a few signs, like decimal points. In digital computing, we can do equally powerful and advanced things with combinations of digits. Using digital computers is not a restriction – rather, it makes it simpler to design and understand the workings of the computer.

A computer works with data

We have used the word 'data' rather a lot in what has gone before. We have used it without saying clearly what it is! **Data** is what computers process. And because we know that computers are *digital*, we now know that data is simply the set of all possible combinations of the allowable digits.

That seems to say nothing, but really it says it all. It says that computers can process numbers (with a suitably well-designed program) because numbers are digital. Words (text) are digital, so they too can be processed by a computer. Paintings are not digital, so they cannot. Music can be, if we are prepared to ignore the subtleties of interpretation that we mentioned before (perhaps this is why computer-generated music has an 'unnatural' feel to it?). A game, like chess, can be handled by a computer because we can readily see that any chess position can be described by a combination of digits, as can any chess move: P–K4, for example. A game like football, at first glance, cannot be handled by a computer, because there is no obvious way to represent the play of it as a digital combination.

Of course, just being able to represent something as data for a computer does not mean that it can satisfactorily be processed in a computer. A suitable program of instructions has to be designed, and in some cases this may be literally impossible. Equally, something non-digital, such as a game of football, *may* be playable by computer if a clever digital coding scheme can be worked out.

A good and very natural example of this is the use of computers in controlling machinery. The positions of parts of a machine do not immediately seem to be digital. But by a suitable scheme of coordinates – such as distances from some reference position in each of three dimensions, together with the angle of a cutting head or similar measurement – an apparently non-digital situation can be turned into a digital one.

A computer is a processor

And here we come to the heart of our definition of a computer. We have already noted what characteristics a computer has; we have noted what it works *on*. Now we see what it is that a computer *does*.

A computer processes data. It is capable of accepting some digital data from outside the computer system. It manipulates that data in a way which is dependent both upon its own program of stored instructions and upon the data itself. As a result, it will output further digital data.

This **processing** of **input data** to give **output data** is what computing is all about. We can get a flavour of what computing is like by seeing what range of processing tasks computers typically tackle.

Some tasks use very little data, but involve a lot of processing. Most mathematical and scientific calculations fall into this category. For example, prime numbers are those like 7, 11, 13 and so on that do not divide by any other number. Testing to see whether or not a number is prime is essentially the process of dividing it by all numbers smaller than itself, to see if any divide into it exactly. There is very little input data – just the number to be tested – and not much output data – any divisors that have been found, or a message saying that there are no divisors.

Although a lot of processing might be involved in a program to test for prime numbers, the program may not be very large. It will probably be designed so that after trying one possible divisor, the same set of program instructions will be modified to refer to another possible divisor – the program will be arranged as a **loop** to be attempted any number of times. But even with a short program, the amount of *time* taken could be very large. The loop could be performed an enormous number of times. There is little connection between the size of a program and the length of time it takes to execute the instructions.

Alternatively, some tasks involve large amounts of data, but the processing involved is fairly trivial, and the use of a computer is only justified by the need for absolute reliability, and for speed in dealing with massive amounts of data. Most business applications of computing fall into this category. A payroll (mentioned above) is a nice example. It is not difficult (if a little boring) to produce one man's payslip, calculating the tax he should pay, his overtime, holiday pay, bonuses and so on. It is harder to do this with absolutely reliability, week after week, for tens of thousands of employees.

Surprisingly, most applications of computing do not involve lengthy and complicated processing. The great bulk of computer programs do fairly simple things – albeit to large amounts of data, and very fast indeed. But the popular picture of computers being used to guide missiles, play chess and compose music is just a small part of the picture. Most computers are happily whiling away their time doing quite simple jobs – preparing bills, keeping office records, sending out reminders, maintaining lists in alphabetical order, and so on. None of this makes computing less challenging and interesting – it makes it just a fraction less glamorous!

Summary

We have seen a definition of a computer which we can use to say whether or not any particular device is a computer. It is a simple definition, but captures all of the important features of a computer. A true computer is *an automatic, reprogrammable, digital data processor*. Whenever we use the word in future, this is exactly what we mean.

EXERCISE for discussion

1 The list below is of things that are not generally reckoned to be computers. How do they fail? Do you think that **b** *is* really a small computer?

   a A pocket calculator without programmable capabilities
   b A pocket calculator *with* programmable capabilities
   c An automatic washing machine
   d A digital watch
   e A central-heating thermostat
   f The electronic machinery behind a 'Space Invaders' arcade game
   g An automatic cash-dispenser in a bank
   h An electric typewriter

EXERCISE for discussion

2 An important part of our definition was the *digital* nature of the data processed by a computer. Which of the things on the following list are already in digital form, and which could easily be expressed digitally? Which are not digital at all? For the digital ones, do you know of any application that processes that sort of data?

   a Temperature
   b Words in a dictionary
   c Words as spoken in English
   d Words as spoken in French
   e Car registration numbers
   f The speed of a car
   g The position of the stars
   h A cookery recipe
   i Roman numerals
   j A map
   k A knitting pattern
   l People
   m A computer's program of instructions

EXERCISE for research

3 Make a list of uses of computers. There are several to be found even within the home: your gas or electricity bill, for example, is almost certainly produced by a computer. For each one, describe briefly what the computer is doing, what you would expect the input data to be, and what sort of output data is produced.

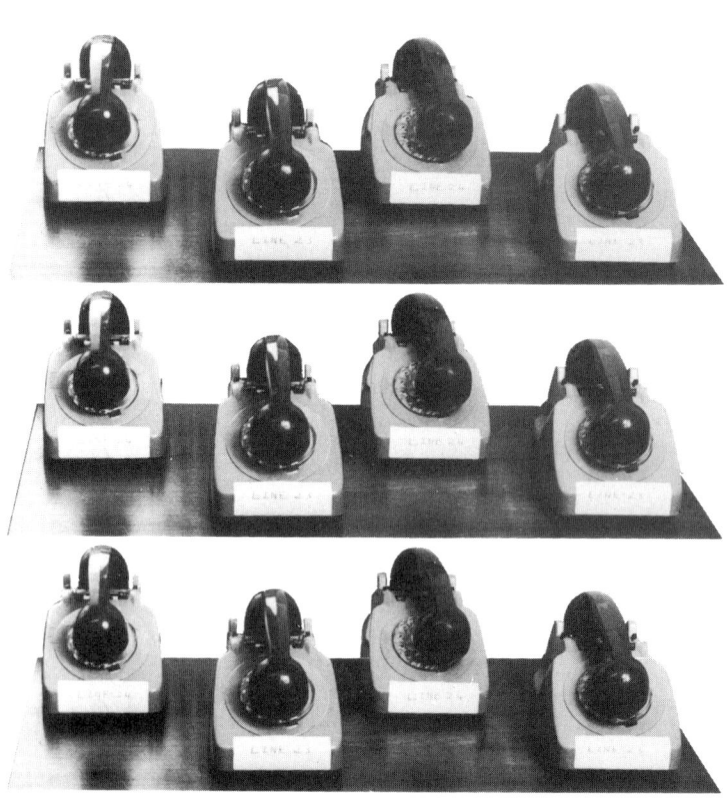

2 The ingredients of computing
INFORMATION and DATA

It is all very well being able to recognise a computer, as you have learnt to do in Chapter 1, but *using* a computer begins when you collect data for the computer to work with. In this chapter, we shall ask *you* to collect some data, so that you may see that there are problems even in an apparently simple task such as this.

We know from Chapter 1 that any data collected for computer processing must be in a digital form. The first problem is apparent as soon as we even glance at the world around us – the things we see are simply not digital. But this is an old problem, and has been with us since Man first began to write. We are used to expressing information about the world in the digits that make up the alphabet: combining them to make words, phrases and sentences. It is information in this form that is our starting-point in using a computer.

The problems of collecting information

In order to have some written information about the world, we shall begin by asking you to complete an exercise. It is an important one, and even though it is deliberately specified very vaguely, you are urged to tackle it in earnest.

EXERCISE for individual work

1 Think about yourself only, and write down a dozen or so pieces of information about yourself that might be required by someone such as a school secretary who had to keep records about you.
Do not discuss what you are writing, or ask any questions to make the exercise clearer.

You should now have a list of around a dozen pieces of information about yourself. But, by preventing you from discussing the exercise before you attempted it, we have probably caused a number of problems.

Some people, for example, might have written down things like 'name', 'address', 'age', 'sex' and so on. Others might have been thinking of the same things, but written down 'John Smith', '80 High Street', '15', 'male' and so on. Neither answer is wrong — the exercise didn't give you enough information on how to tackle the problem properly.

The first group, who wrote 'name', 'address' and so on, were talking about the **type** of information that they would collect, while the second group were talking about **examples** of that information.

To be a good and skilful user of a computer, it is vital that you are always aware, when talking about information, whether you are talking about its *type* or about specific examples of it.

Now let us look at another problem that might have arisen. Many of the pieces of information could have been written down in different ways. For example, a person's name could have been written as any of the following:

John Smith,
J. Smith,
Mr John Smith,
J. Smith Esq.,

and many other ways besides. This is hardly a problem for a human being, but for a computer (where this information may end up) a standard form of recording names will help to establish that 'John Smith' and 'Mr J. Smith' are one and the same person.

But there are other ways in which the same information could be recorded differently: one person may have used 'surname' and 'first name' instead of just 'name'. Another person might expect the answer to 'sex' to be 'male' or 'female'; yet another, 'boy' or 'girl' (or M/F, man/woman and so on).

We are now faced with a very important distinction in computing, and in many other activities where records are kept. This is the difference between information and data.

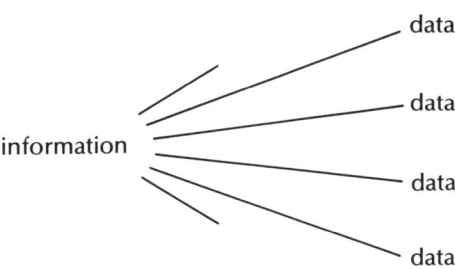

Figure 2.1 *One piece of information can be represented by many pieces of data.*

Information is quite simply what you know about someone: you know their name, their address, their sex and so on. But in writing it down, you were forced to make some choices about how to write it – and not everyone chose the same method.

In writing it down, you were representing it as **data**: in this case, combinations of the 'digits' of the alphabet, together with some numbers.

Information exists in the outside world, outside the records we wish to keep, or the computer programs that we write to perform data-processing. Whenever we write down some information, or code it in a form suitable for a computer, it becomes data. And we have to take time and care to ensure that our choice of data is the correct one for the information that we wish to record.

The connection between information and data

We have already seen that one piece of information, such as a person's name, can be represented in a number of ways as data. In fact, it is very difficult to write about information, because in writing about it, we automatically turn it into data. But we can talk about *types* of information, and then give *examples* of data.

But if one piece of information corresponds to many possible pieces of data, we also have the same problem in reverse. Consider the piece of data: 1/6/75. What does it mean? Written like this, it probably represents a date – somebody's birthdate, for example. So we should feel tempted to claim that this piece of data represented the information 'June 1st 1975'.

But in understanding this piece of data, we are making use of a lot of hidden knowledge. We know, for example, that it is customary to write dates in this way. We know that the '75' means 1975 and not 1875. All of this hidden knowledge, that we have to bring to bear on the data in order to extract information from it, is called **context**. In order to get information from data we must understand the context in which the data is written.

This is not just a trivial example. Our context for dates – day/month/year – is not the only one. In the United States, and some other parts of the world, dates are written month/day/year, so that the example we have given, 1/6/75 would be the totally different date – January 6th 1975!

Another context of some interest is year/month/day – a reversed form of the date. This has the advantage that if the data is now treated as a number, higher numbers correspond to later dates: at least provided that the data is structured correctly, as discussed in the next section.

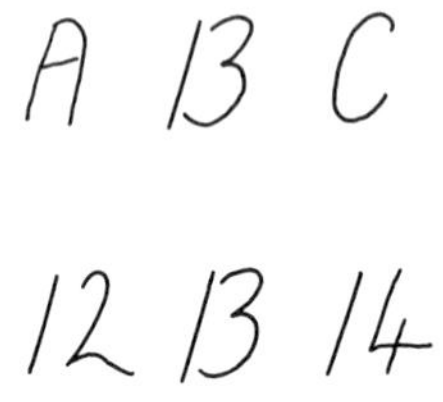

A B C

12 13 14

Figure 2.2 *The importance of context: in each example above, the badly-written centre figure is the same: context, or background knowledge, encourages us to read the same figure as a 'B' in the top line and as '13' in the lower.*

The importance of structure

Computer users tend to be misers: in writing down dates like 'December 25th 1981' they tend to worry about writing 25/12/81 (using the British context). The computer, they argue, doesn't need the extra '/' signs – it can equally well sort out what 251281 means, even if humans find this slightly harder on the eyes. This is a sensible point, but it causes problems with dates like 21183 – 21st of January 1983 or 2nd of November 1983?

To solve this problem, we must pay attention to the **structure** of the data. It is usual in computing to solve this particular problem by insisting that all dates are written with two figures for day and month, so that June the 1st 1975 becomes 010675. There is now no ambiguity about 21183: if January 21st is meant, it should be 210183, and if November 2nd, 021183.

This is another factor, to add to context, which must be taken into account in interpreting data in order to extract information from it. We can only get information from data when we are aware of the *context* of the data and the *structure* of it.

Information = data + context + structure

The six digits 010675, then, could be interpreted in a number of ways, depending on structure and context. Structured as 01/06/75, in the context of the British method of writing dates, the information we get is 'June 1st 1975'. Structured as 010/675 in the context of international telephone dialling codes, the same data represents the dialling code for Papua New Guinea!

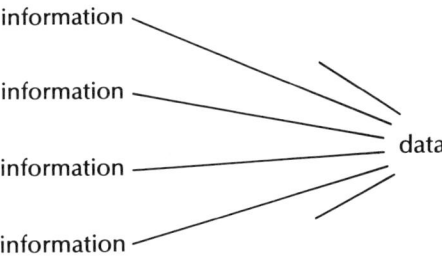

Figure 2.3 *One piece of data can represent many pieces of information.*

The problems of collecting data

It is now time to return to the exercise we began when you wrote down a dozen pieces of information about yourself. We have seen that there are many problems if this exercise is undertaken without some planning.

EXERCISE for discussion

2 Make a list of the *types* of information that you wish to collect in keeping records about people. For each type of information, give a description of how it is to be coded as data: include a description of the way in which the written data is to be structured, and the context in which it will be written. An example of a typical piece of data may be the best way of illustrating this.

EXERCISE for discussion

3 You may wish to collect this data from people who have not discussed it with you beforehand, and who do not understand the problems that their answers might cause. In what ways could you make sure that their answers were what you wanted?

Exercise 3 is an important one, because in collecting data it is important that the data you get is capable of being processed in the way you want. This may not always be computer processing. In a survey of people, we may ask them for the colour of their hair: some may answer 'brown' while others with identical hair-colouring answer 'medium-brown'. There are several possible answers to Exercise 3, and you may have thought of:

a Using trained interviewers, who have discussed the format of the data, and who will 'translate' the answers into the correct form before writing it onto paper; this may be very expensive.

b Making the person answering tick boxes or underline words in order to give answers, so that he is selecting from an existing set of 'good' answers.

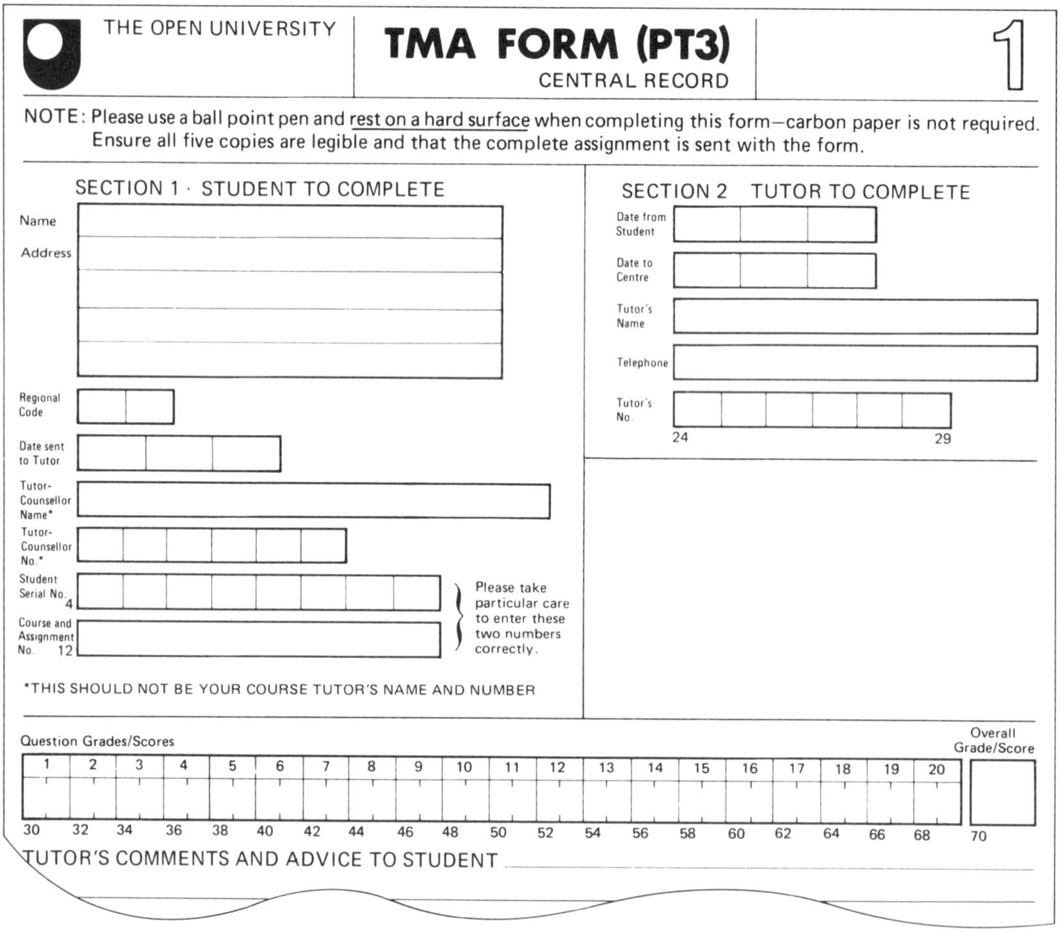

THE OPEN UNIVERSITY

TMA FORM (PT3)

CENTRAL RECORD

1

NOTE: Please use a ball point pen and rest on a hard surface when completing this form—carbon paper is not required. Ensure all five copies are legible and that the complete assignment is sent with the form.

SECTION 1 · STUDENT TO COMPLETE

Name

Address

Regional Code

Date sent to Tutor

Tutor-Counsellor Name*

Tutor-Counsellor No.*

Student Serial No. 4

Course and Assignment No. 12

Please take particular care to enter these two numbers correctly.

*THIS SHOULD NOT BE YOUR COURSE TUTOR'S NAME AND NUMBER

SECTION 2 TUTOR TO COMPLETE

Date from Student

Date to Centre

Tutor's Name

Telephone

Tutor's No.

24 29

Question Grades/Scores

1	2	3	4	5	6	7	8	9	10	11	12	13	14	15	16	17	18	19	20	Overall Grade/Score

30 32 34 36 38 40 42 44 46 48 50 52 54 56 58 60 62 64 66 68 70

TUTOR'S COMMENTS AND ADVICE TO STUDENT

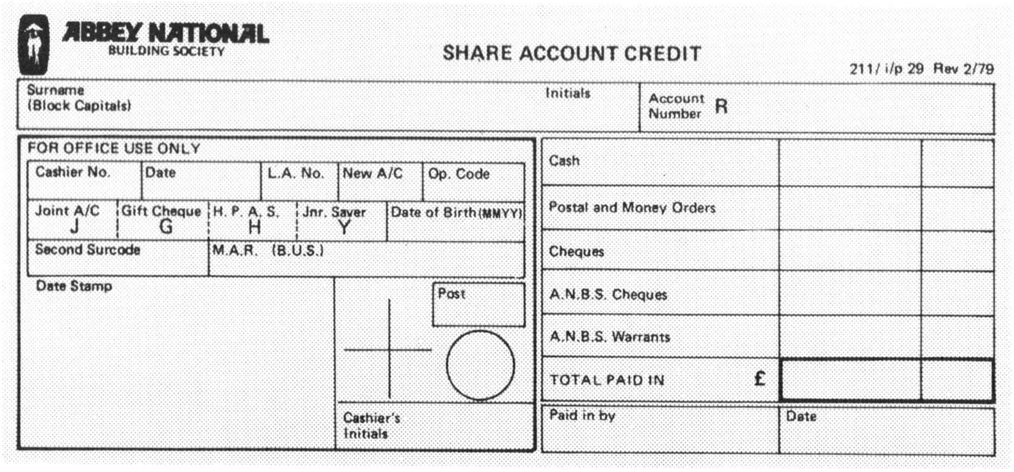

ABBEY NATIONAL BUILDING SOCIETY

SHARE ACCOUNT CREDIT

211/ i/p 29 Rev 2/79

Surname (Block Capitals) | Initials | Account Number R

FOR OFFICE USE ONLY

Cashier No. | Date | L.A. No. | New A/C | Op. Code

Joint A/C J | Gift Cheque G | H. P. A. S. H | Jnr. Saver Y | Date of Birth (MMYY)

Second Surname | M.A.R. (B.U.S.)

Date Stamp

Post

Cashier's Initials

Cash		
Postal and Money Orders		
Cheques		
A.N.B.S. Cheques		
A.N.B.S. Warrants		
TOTAL PAID IN £		
Paid in by	Date	

Figure 2.4 *Two examples of forms which encourage standard formatting of data*

c Using carefully-designed forms, like those in Figure 2.4, that encourage people to write what is required; notice that not all the problems are removed in this way, and that to make all the returned forms standard, someone will have to read each one and correct any inconsistencies.

EXERCISE for discussion or individual work

4 Design a form that can be used to collect the data that you have chosen in Exercise 2, without needing a trained interviewer on hand while the data is being written down. It is best to have a try at this exercise by yourself first, before discussing and possibly amending your form. A good data-collection form is not one that is designed by a committee; but everyone should be happy about the form before it is used.

ARE WE COLLECTING THE RIGHT DATA?

Before you go ahead and use the form you have designed to collect data, it is time for a last consideration of what you are trying to do. One way of making sure that you are collecting the right data might be to try a **pilot survey** on a small group of people and look at the results before going ahead. There may still be some ambiguities that you have not removed, or snags still to be ironed out.

Certainly, thinking about the survey before you carry it out will be a good thing. It may suddenly strike you that asking a person for his age may be a bad idea, because his age will change from year to year, while his date of birth will be something that doesn't change. In a boy's school, you may not have bothered to ask for the sex of the person answering the questionnaire. That will be fine provided that you are *sure* that you will never use the survey with any other group of people. In a similar way, if you designed the data-collection form thinking only about the people in one class at a school, you may not have asked for their class.

IS THE DATA CONFIDENTIAL?

We have not considered that the people we are going to collect data from may not be willing to give it. Most people will not object to giving information about their name, address and sex. In schools or colleges, people would probably not object to questions about age or pocket money. But there are groups of people who *would* object to some questions: the wages earned by people and whether or not they have been in prison are examples of information that most people are reluctant to supply; and it is often considered indelicate to ask people their age, or birthdate.

If the survey is really important, people may be persuaded to answer these questions or ones like them, if they can be sure that the data will be confidential, and that only a few people will see it. One way of ensuring this is to refrain from asking any questions that can identify the person – leaving out their name and address, for instance. If this is done, then the questionnaire must be designed to ask *all* the questions you want, first time. It won't be possible to go back to the person and ask for further information.

EXERCISE for discussion

5 This is your last chance to get your questionnaire correct before it is used. Are you asking the right questions? Will people be able to answer the questions easily? When you are sure . . . .

EXERCISE practical

6 Make copies of the questionnaire that you will use and distribute these for people to answer. Try to ensure that no one is bothered more than once, and that there are clear instructions that include what to do with the form when it is completed.

Summary

The *use* of a computer to process information begins at the stage of *collecting* this information: in this chapter, we have looked at the problems that can arise when information is wanted. We have seen that *information* must be represented in a digital form as *data*, and that some care must be taken over the way in which it is collected, or the resulting data will not be useful.

Information can be gained from data only when *structure* and *context* are also taken into account.

One means of collecting information is by forms or questionnaires, and these can be carefully designed so that the information provided by them can be converted accurately into digital data. We have seen that it is important to make clear what *type* of information is being sought, and this can be assisted by giving an *example* of the kind of answer which is wanted. The usefulness of such a form, when it has been designed, can be tested by subjecting it to a *pilot survey*. In most cases, those questioned will wish to have their answers treated confidentially; and in some cases, they may even remain anonymous, but it will not then be possible to check their information or to ask supplementary questions later.

The exercises in this chapter have taken us through the processes in designing a questionnaire. When these questionnaires are returned, you will have a large collection of data. The rest of this book is about how similar collections of data, large or small, are processed by computers.

EXERCISE practical

7 Design data-collection forms for recording daily readings of weather conditions. Some basic research into the information given in a daily newspaper may help.

EXERCISE practical

8 A short exercise that introduces most of the problems covered in this chapter would be to spend an hour or two collecting information about cars passing by, or aircraft landing at an airport. What do you wish to record, what forms will you need?

EXERCISE practical

9 Many supermarkets have labels on the shelves which describe the products: these are meant for the supermarket staff, not for customers. Can you decide, by comparing several of these labels, what information is being recorded here?

3 Representing data in a computer
PRIMARY STORAGE

In order for a computer to be useful in processing data it must have some place available where the data *and* the program of instructions for processing it can be held before processing takes place.

Early computers did not have such space available, and program instructions and data had to be fed into the computer as they were required, which made the process very slow. Computers as we know them today began with the invention of a machine (the 'electronic delay storage automatic calculator', EDSAC, built at the University of Cambridge) which had the capability of storing both the data to be processed *and* the program of instructions to control the processing.

There are several ways in which this storage is provided, but the one which we are going to look at in this chapter is known as **primary storage**.

The structure of primary storage

The main part of a computer is known as its **central processing unit** (or **CPU**), and a major part of this is the **main store**, often referred to as **primary** or **core store**. The last of these names refers to small ferrite rings, known as **cores**, of which the main store of many computers used to be composed. The cores could be magnetised in one of two directions by passing suitable electric currents through them, and were thus capable of holding data as combinations of binary digits. Most recently produced computers, at the time of writing, have a store which is composed of microelectronic elements.

Whatever the store is composed of, its elements must in some way be capable of representing data and program instructions. We are not actually very interested in the physical structure of the store or its composition, but much more in the way in which data and instructions are represented in it. We shall look first at the storage of data. In Chapter 2 we saw several examples of data and before we go any further it is worthwhile identifying the different types of data which would need to be stored.

EXERCISE for discussion

1 Using examples from Chapter 2 to help you, make a list of the different types of data which might need to be stored.

You almost certainly listed the numeric digits from 0 to 9 and the letters of the English alphabet from A to Z. Of course there are other alphabets, and plenty of other symbols that you might have listed – £, %, +, ?, /, for example. And what about numbers such as $\frac{1}{4}$ or π?

We shall be looking at all of these during this chapter.

How primary storage is organised

In order for an item of data to be stored there are two requirements. The first is a place to put it, and the second is some means of identifying that place so that the piece of data can be retrieved when it is required.

A convenient way of regarding the store is as a large array of pigeonholes or locations, each of which has an **address** dependent on its position within the array (Fig 3.1). This address is simply the number of the location, in exactly the same way as houses are numbered in a street.

When we draw diagrams of the store, it is actually more convenient to draw the pigeonholes in a vertical strip and write their addresses alongside for reference. The address of any location must be unique, otherwise confusion could arise between locations. Figure 3.2 is a diagram showing five locations of store with addresses from **115** to **119** inclusive.

1023	1024	1025				1029	
1123	1124						
1223							
1323			1326				
1623				1627			1630

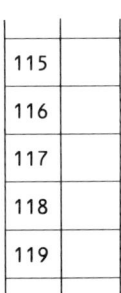

Figure 3.1 *A section of a large array of pigeonholes, each with an address depending on its position*

115	
116	
117	
118	
119	

Figure 3.2 *A linearly arranged diagram of storage locations*

We can think of pieces of data being placed in the pigeonholes or locations and staying there until a new piece of data is inserted, thus pushing out the original one. While a piece of data is in a location it can be copied for use in any processing for which it is required, but this will not remove it from the location. Even if it is not required for further processing, it will remain in the location until something else is put in its place.

IDENTIFICATION OF A PARTICULAR LOCATION

The computer identifies a location by its address in store. If an item of data is stored in a particular location, it can be retrieved by directing the computer to that location by giving its address. However, if a computer programmer has to remember addresses of locations in store for each item of data used, the process of programming becomes very complicated and errors easily occur.

Very often the programmer thinks of locations of store in terms of the data items which are stored in them. For example, if a particular location holds a number which is a person's height, the programmer will think of that location as the one which contains the height. If the location concerned has address 2000 in store, rather than thinking of '2000' when the data item is required, the programmer will think of 'height'.

For this reason a programmer will write the program and in it refer to the particular data item by the name `HEIGHT`, or maybe `HGT`, or simply `H`, whenever the item is required, leaving to the computer the job of remembering the address 2000. Such a name for a location is known as a **variable name** or **identifier**.

The use of variable names by a programmer makes the job of the computer more complicated, and we shall see in Chapter 7 how the computer 'remembers' which address is required when a particular variable name is used.

22 *Primary storage*

HOW A LOCATION IS ORGANISED

Any location of store in a computer will contain a number of the elementary components of which the store is composed. These elementary components can be thought of as switches which can have a number of positions. A computer in which these switches have just *two* positions is known as a **binary computer**. Other types are possible, but this is the most common.

A switch which has two positions (states) can be either 'on' or 'off' (Figure 3.3). Two such switches can have four possible patterns (Figure 3.4), three such switches can have eight possible patterns (Figure 3.5), and so on.

Figure 3.3   **Figure 3.4**

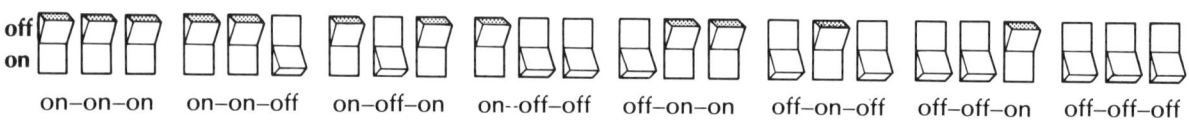

Figure 3.5

A more common way of writing down these patterns is to use the binary digits 0 and 1. Suppose that 0 is 'on' and 1 is 'off', then the pattern 'on–on–on' would be written as 000, and the pattern 'off–off–on' would be written 110. Binary digits are commonly referred to as **bits**.

A location therefore will be composed of a number of bits. Each bit has two possible states, which allows a variety of **bit patterns** to be formed within the location. Figure 3.6 shows all the possible bit patterns which can be formed in a location which has three bits: it corresponds to Figure 3.5.

Figure 3.6 *The eight bit patterns available with three bits.*

○ EXERCISE for discussion

2 We have observed that one bit may have 2 patterns, two bits may have 4 patterns, and three bits may have 8 patterns. How many patterns would you expect for four bits or for eight bits?

Test out your theory for four bits.

Can you extend this theory for any number of bits?

Representing data within a location

The different patterns which a location can have allow it to represent different items of data, and providing there is some way of associating an item of data with a particular pattern, the location can be thought of as 'storing' the data.

The question now is – how do we associate items of data with particular bit patterns? We shall answer this question by looking at the different types of data, such as were mentioned after Exercise 1 on page 20, in turn; and we shall start by looking at how numbers can be represented.

REPRESENTING NUMERIC DATA: INTEGERS

It is useful first to look at a number which is represented in a way with which we are familiar. The number 235 would be read by most people as 'two hundred and thirty-five' because we are brought up with the denary (base 10) number system and we are automatically familiar with the idea of 'hundreds, tens and units'. Sometimes however, we might read the number as 'two', 'three', 'five', and in this case the place values of the digits are understood rather than stated.

The number which we are discussing would look different if we wrote it in other bases: for example in base 8 (octal) it would be 353 and in binary it would be 11101011. It is important to realise that these are all just representations of the same number. A whole number of this sort without any fractional part is called an **integer**.

In a computer location which is composed of 8 bits, it would be possible to hold the binary pattern 11101011, and so one possible interpretation of this pattern is as the denary number 235. If this were the case then we could say that the location 'contained' the number 235.

When binary patterns in computer locations are interpreted as numbers in this way they are often referred to as **pure binary representations**. The binary pattern represents just one number for any location.

EXERCISE for individual work

3 The following diagram shows computer locations of 8 bits, each with a different pattern. If these patterns are *pure binary* representations of numbers, work out what data is stored in each location.

a	0	0	0	1	1	0	1	0
b	0	1	0	0	1	1	0	0
c	1	0	0	0	1	0	1	1
d	1	1	1	0	0	1	0	0

Figure 3.7

How would the numbers 5, 38 and 152 be represented in pure binary in 8-bit locations?

An alternative way to represent the number 235 would be to split it up into its separate digits and represent each of these individually as a binary pattern. In this way we should get the three patterns: 10, 11, and 101.

If we simply string these together we produce 1011101, a binary pattern of 7 bits. But how are we to distinguish the separate digits? This pattern could represent 93 in pure binary, or some alternative collection of digits such as 101, 1, 101, that is 515.

To represent separate digits in this way it is necessary to reserve a given number of bits for each digit. For digits from zero to nine, 4 bits would be sufficient (since 9 in binary is 1001). In this way, the number 235 would be represented as 0010 0011 0101. These three patterns could be strung together to fit in one location with a minimum of 12 bits, or would have to be split appropriately to fit into smaller locations.

This method of representing a number by using a binary pattern for each of its denary digits is known as **binary coded decimal** (or **BCD**).

These two ways of representing integers each have advantages and disadvantages. In the pure binary representation only one location is required for a number to be represented, but then the size of a number which *can* be represented is limited by the number of bits available in the location (see next exercise).

Alternatively, in BCD representation a number of *any* size can be represented, but it may possibly need several locations in order to do it.

EXERCISE for discussion

4 What is the largest number which can be held in pure binary representation in a location of   **a**   4 bits   **b**   8 bits?

Can you relate your answer here to your answer to Exercise 2?

EXERCISE for discussion

5 Using BCD representation and allowing 4 bits for a denary digit, show how the numbers 37 and 2496 would be represented in 8-bit locations.

Would it be possible to store these numbers in pure binary in 8-bit locations?

REPRESENTING POSITIVE AND NEGATIVE INTEGERS

In looking at how numbers may be represented in computer locations we have so far overlooked the fact that it might be necessary to store both positive and negative numbers.

In pure binary representation in locations of 8 bits we have noticed that it is possible to store numbers from zero to 255, as there are 256 different patterns available. However, if this is allowed, then there are no 'spare' patterns available to represent negative numbers.

Let us suppose that the number of available patterns is to be split equally between positive and negative numbers. This will of course halve the largest number we may store. The difficulty is in deciding how the available patterns are to be allocated to negative numbers.

There are obviously many ways in which this allocation can be done. Let us take a simple case and look at some of these possibilities.

We shall consider a location of just 3 bits, for which the possible patterns are:
000   001   010   011   100   101   110   111
If we are to have four positive and four negative numbers, the positive numbers which suggest themselves are: 000 as +0; 001 as +1; 010 as +2; 011 as +3. We notice that these all begin with a 0 and that the remaining patterns begin with a 1. A possible way to allocate these patterns is: 100 as −0; 101 as −1; 110 as −2; and 111 as −3. Figure 3.8 illustrates this.

+0	000	100	−0
+1	001	101	−1
+2	010	110	−2
+3	011	111	−3

Figure 3.8 *Allocation of 8 3-bit patterns to 4 positive and 4 negative numbers: 'sign and magnitude' representation.*

We see that, in each representation, the first bit represents the *sign* of the number (0 for + and 1 for −) and the other bits give its *size*. For this reason the representation is known as **sign-and-magnitude representation**.

One of the main disadvantages of sign-and-magnitude representation is the existence of plus and minus zero. We know that they are the same number, but the computer does not. The computer sees two different patterns and could arrive at either of them as the result of a calculation. So, in testing to see if a location contains zero, it would be necessary to test for both patterns. This could cause a lot of problems for the programmer.

Another disadvantage appears when we try some simple arithmetic with the patterns. When adding (+1) and (−1) we expect to get zero, but the patterns give (−2). See Figure 3.9. This would mean that some devious means would have to be devised for the computer to perform arithmetic with the patterns and arrive at the correct answer.

```
(+1) + (−1) = 0            (+2) + (−3) = (−1)

   001                         010
 + 101                       + 111
  ----                        ----
   110  = −2  ??              1001 = +1  ignoring the 'fourth' bit
                               ↑
                              this bit cannot be stored
```

Figure 3.9

26 *Primary storage*

Despite these disadvantages computers have worked with this representation. However, it is not common, so let us look at alternatives.

One alternative is to leave the positive patterns unchanged, and, to obtain the negative patterns, simply change each bit of the corresponding positive pattern. Thus as +2 is 010, −2 would become 101; and as +3 is 011, −3 would become 100. Figure 3.10 illustrates the full pattern set. However, the problem of plus and minus zero is still present, and arithmetic is no better as you will see if you try a simple addition. This representation is known as **one's complement representation** and again, despite its disadvantages, it has been used in computers.

+0	000	111	−0
+1	001	110	−1
+2	010	101	−2
+3	011	100	−3

Figure 3.10 *One's complement representation*

You may have already spotted the second alternative. If in order to avoid having plus and minus zero we 'move up' the negative patterns in the one's complement representation, so that 111 is −1; 110 is −2; and so on, we obtain the set shown in Figure 3.11.

0	000	111	−1
+1	001	110	−2
+2	010	101	−3
+3	011	100	−4

Figure 3.11 *Two's complement representation*

A quick test with simple addition shows that 'correct' answers are obtained. Whenever a 4-bit result is obtained it is necessary to 'chop' the most significant (left-most) bit in order for the pattern to be stored in 3 bits.

$(+1) + (-1) = 0$ $(+2) + (-3) = (-1)$

```
  001              010
+ 111            + 101
 ----             ----
 1000 = 0         111 = −1
 ↑
'lost'
```

Figure 3.12

Representing data within a location 27

It does look as if this at last is a satisfactory representation as it avoids the two previous disadvantages. However, one problem with this representation is that it is not immediately obvious what negative number a particular pattern represents. For example, it is not 'obvious' that 101 represents −3. The convention that a positive number begins with 0 and a negative number with 1 still applies, but translating the rest of the number is more difficult, especially when more than 3 bits are involved.

The following method of translation works, and you should not find it too difficult to explain why.

As an example, let us find the pattern which represents −6 in four bits:

Step 1   Find the binary pattern for +6.   This is   0110
Step 2   Change the bits in this pattern.   This gives 1001
Step 3   Add 1 to the result.   This gives 1010

So, the binary pattern representing −6 in four bits is 1010. We should check arithmetically that this is correct by adding it to +6 and satisfying ourselves that the answer is zero. We do this in Figure 3.13.

A bonus of this translation method is that it works exactly the same if we want to convert a binary pattern to obtain the corresponding negative number. Figure 3.14 shows how the pattern 1001 is translated to give −7.

```
(−6) + (+6) = 0

  1010
  0110
 ─────
 10000  = 0
  ↑
'lost'
```

Figure 3.13

```
                            1001
           change bits to get 0110
                 add 1 to get 0111
         convert to denary to get +7
           thus  1001  =  −7
```

Figure 3.14

This third representation is known as **two's complement representation**.

EXERCISE for individual work

6 Show how the number −5 would be represented in four bits in each of the three ways described. In each case check its addition with +5 and show that only the third method gives the answer zero.

EXERCISE for individual work

7 Using an eight-bit location, show how the numbers −10, −52 and −115 would be represented, using two's complement representation.

EXERCISE for individual work

8 If the binary patterns 10001100 and 11011011 are two's complement representations of negative numbers, work out what numbers they represent.

REPRESENTING NUMBERS WHICH ARE NOT INTEGERS

All the numbers which have been discussed so far have been integers, that is *whole* numbers. Arithmetic which works only with whole numbers is rather limited. For example, how could we write down the answer to 5 divided by 3? In everyday life we encounter non-integer numbers frequently — anyone who takes a size $5\frac{1}{2}$ in a shoe knows that neither 5 nor 6 will do; and if an alcove in your house is 6.35 metres wide, trying to fit a shelf that is either 6 m or 7 m would be pointless. So it is necessary to be able to represent such numbers in the computer.

This again raises the problem that for any number of bits in a location there is only a fixed number of patterns available. If the same method is to be used to represent both integer and non-integer numbers then either the range of numbers of each type is seriously limited, or there must be a clear way of distinguishing which type of number is represented.

The method of representing fractional numbers in denary is to place a decimal point after the units digit, and count the places after the point as tenths, hundredths and so on. In the same way, fractional numbers can be represented in binary by placing a bicimal point after the units digit and counting after the point in halves, quarters and so on. So, the number $5\frac{3}{4}$ could be written in denary as 5.75 and in binary as 101.11.

When we consider how this might be represented in a computer location, the difficulty is in what to do about the 'point'. As no spare binary digit is available to represent it, the point must be assumed to be at some specific position in the bit pattern. Fixing this position limits both the range of numbers which can be represented, and their accuracy.

To show what we mean by this, let us consider an 8-bit location which is to be used to represent fractional numbers by assuming the position of the bicimal point to be between the 5th and 6th bits. See Figure 3.15.

| 1 | 1 | 1 | 1 | 1 | 1 | 1 | 1 |

↑
assumed position of bicimal point

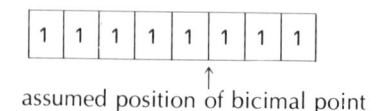

Figure 3.15

Now let us try to represent the numbers of $2\frac{1}{2}$, $22\frac{1}{2}$, and $6\frac{5}{16}$ in such a location. As each of these numbers is positive, the first bit in each case will be 0. Figure 3.16 illustrates the problem.

$2^{1}/_{2}$ = 10·1 | 0 | 0 | 0 | 1 | 0 | 1 | 0 | 0 | = $2^{1}/_{2}$
+ ↑

$22^{1}/_{2}$ = 10110·1 | 0 | 0 | 1 | 1 | 0 | 1 | 0 | 0 | = $6^{1}/_{2}$
+ ↑

$6^{5}/_{16}$ = 110·0101 | 0 | 0 | 1 | 1 | 0 | 0 | 1 | 0 | = $6^{1}/_{4}$
+ ↑

Figure 3.16

The first number, $2\frac{1}{2}$, can be stored without difficulty, but there are not sufficient bits to the left to store the $22\frac{1}{2}$, and not sufficient bits to the right to store $6\frac{5}{16}$ accurately. The best that can be stored in 8 bits is $6\frac{1}{4}$ (or $6\frac{4}{16}$) which is inaccurate by $\frac{1}{16}$.

An alternative to this type of **fixed-point** representation is known as **floating-point** representation. An explanation of this using binary numbers makes it appear unduly complicated, so we shall explain it by considering numbers in denary as the principles involved are the same.

Floating-point representation

Consider the following numbers:

  1234.5
  123.45 × 10
  12.345 × 100
  1.2345 × 1000
  12345 ÷ 10
  123450 ÷ 100
  12345000 ÷ 10000

With little calculation you will have realised that they are simply different representations of the *same* number. The usual way of writing the number is the first, but each of the others gives the same number quite unambiguously. In the last five representations the point can be 'floated' to its 'correct' position by the appropriate multiplication or division by a power of 10. We see therefore that we can in fact place the point in any position we wish, providing that we indicate the power of 10 by which the resulting number is to be multiplied or divided, to produce the number intended.

It is possible to decide in any number to write the number with the point in a given position provided that the appropriate power of 10 is supplied by which the written number must be multiplied. Two pieces of information are therefore necessary – the written number, with its point in a prescribed position, and the power of ten. These two pieces of information are often called the **mantissa** and the **exponent** of the given number. For example in the representation 12.345 × 100, the mantissa is 12.345 and the exponent is 2 because 100 is 10 to the power of 2.

EXERCISE for individual work

9 What are the mantissa and exponent in each of the representations above of the number 1234.5?

In order to represent numbers consistently, a standard form of mantissa must be chosen for use within a computer. The most usual is for the mantissa to be a number greater than or equal to 0.1 and less than 1. For example the numbers 0.456, 0.39625, 0.6789, 0.1, 0.99999, all fulfil these conditions.

Let us look at an example of this procedure. Suppose that we wish to express the numbers 1234.56 and 0.00098765 in the above standard form.

$1234.56 = 0.123456 \times 10000 = 0.123456 \times 10^4$
i.e. mantissa is 0.123456   exponent is 4

$0.00098765 = 0.98765 \div 1000 = 0.98765 \times 10^{-3}$
i.e. mantissa is 0.98765   exponent is -3

Writing a number in standard form in this way is known as **normalisation**.

EXERCISE for individual work

10 Express the following numbers in the standard form just described:
   a 42.57   **b** 5097   **c** 0.00265   **d** 0.852

Storage of floating-point numbers

When a number has been represented in two parts in this way, it can be stored in its two parts within the computer. The two parts would be represented as binary patterns as we have described for integer numbers. A computer location would thus need to hold not *one* number but *two*, and a number of bits would be allocated to each of the parts. In some computers two separate locations are used, one to hold the mantissa and one the exponent of a particular number. It is therefore often necessary when programming a computer to indicate whether a number is an integer or not. If this is not done, the computer would need to reserve space for both mantissa and exponent, whether or not this is needed.

A problem arises when a non-integer number cannot be represented exactly with the number of bits available. However many bits are allocated to storing the mantissa, there will be numbers which have to be approximated because not all their digits can be accommodated. This may be done by **truncating** the number (that is chopping off the excess digits) or by **rounding** it, but in either case the result is only an approximation to the true number.

Let us look at an example of this: suppose that the number

$0.123456789123456789 \times 10^{50}$

is to be stored, and only 10 digits of the mantissa can be accommodated. This means that the number stored will actually be

$0.1234567891 \times 10^{50}$

Thus,

$0.000000000023456789 \times 10^{50}$

quite a sizeable number, is lost!

When approximate numbers are used in arithmetic calculations, errors such as this can accumulate and the final result can be more seriously inaccurate than the individual numbers used. When the computer is being used for complicated calculations, great care must be taken in organising the calculation so that a minimum of error results.

When numeric data is to be stored it is obviously an advantage to distinguish between numbers which are integer or non-integer, as less store space is required for integers. Some computer languages allow this distinction to be made in a program, where some variables may be declared as representing integers and some as representing non-integers (or **real** numbers, as these are usually called). When this possibility is not available, all numbers are assumed to be real and the computer allows space for both mantissa and exponent regardless of the type of number.

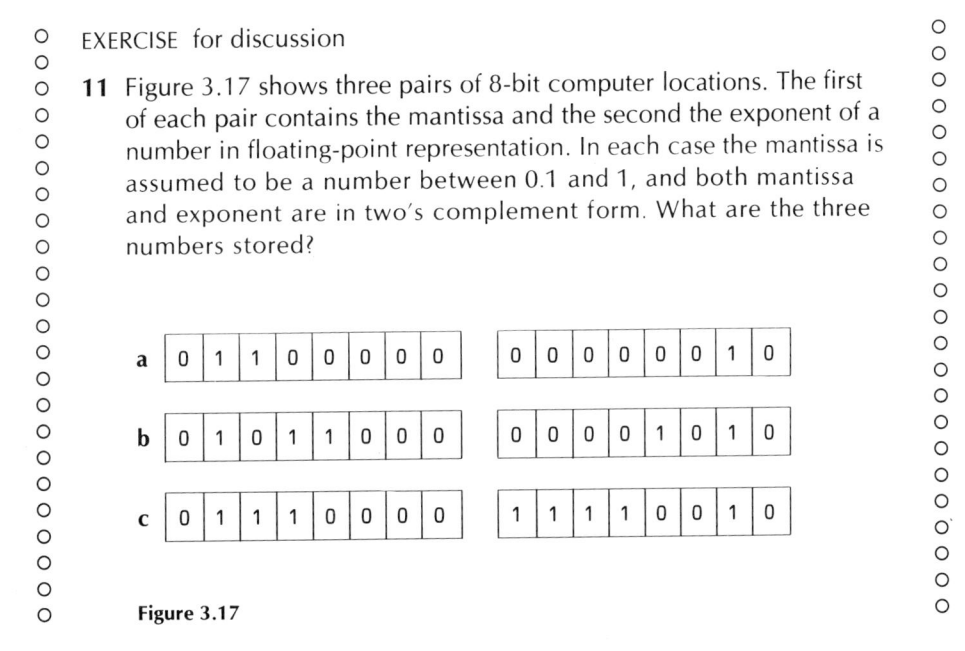

EXERCISE for discussion

11 Figure 3.17 shows three pairs of 8-bit computer locations. The first of each pair contains the mantissa and the second the exponent of a number in floating-point representation. In each case the mantissa is assumed to be a number between 0.1 and 1, and both mantissa and exponent are in two's complement form. What are the three numbers stored?

a | 0 | 1 | 1 | 0 | 0 | 0 | 0 | 0 | | 0 | 0 | 0 | 0 | 0 | 0 | 1 | 0 |

b | 0 | 1 | 0 | 1 | 1 | 0 | 0 | 0 | | 0 | 0 | 0 | 0 | 1 | 0 | 1 | 0 |

c | 0 | 1 | 1 | 1 | 0 | 0 | 0 | 0 | | 1 | 1 | 1 | 1 | 0 | 0 | 1 | 0 |

Figure 3.17

REPRESENTING ALPHANUMERIC DATA

When we wrote down different types of data earlier we saw that there are many characters that might need to be stored which are not numbers; letters of various alphabets, for example, and other symbols. Often a piece of data consists of numbers mixed up with these other characters. Data of this type is commonly known as **alphanumeric data**.

In order to represent alphanumeric data in the computer store, each of the characters involved must be uniquely represented by a binary pattern, and so there must be enough patterns available for all of these characters. As we saw earlier in the chapter, an 8-bit location can contain 256 possible patterns and this is enough for most practical purposes. However, allocation of patterns to characters can cause a problem if this is different for every computer which is manufactured. To avoid this, some standard allocations have been made which computer manufacturers have agreed to follow for reasons of uniformity. The most common of these in current use is known as the **ASCII** (American Standard Code for Information Interchange) code, and we show a section of this in Figure 3.18.

ASCII character	Denary code	Binary code (7 bits)	ASCII character	Denary code	Binary code (7 bits)
NULL	0	0000000	2	50	0110010
CTRL-A	1	0000001	3	51	0110011
CTRL-B	2	0000010	:		
:			8	56	0111000
CTRL-H	8	0001000	9	57	0111001
TAB	9	0001001	:	58	0111010
:			;	59	0111011
CTRL-Y	25	0011001	:		
CTRL-Z	26	0011010	A	65	1000001
:			B	66	1000010
:			C	67	1000011
SPACE	32	0100000	:		
!	33	0100001			
"	34	0100010	M	77	1001101
:			N	78	1001110
:			O	79	1001111
%	37	0100101	:		
&	38	0100110	:		
:			Z	90	1011010
0	48	0110000	:		
1	49	0110001	DEL	127	1111111

Figure 3.18

Notice here that the digits from 0 to 9 do *not* have the expected binary patterns, because of punctuation and control characters which precede them; and that letters of the alphabet have a pattern which relates to their position in the alphabet. Thus A, the first letter, has the pattern for 65; and N, the fourteenth, the pattern for 78 (i.e. 65 + 13).

Most alphanumeric data consists of groups of characters 'strung' together in some way. One example is the car registration number, which has the following format in this country:

ABC 123 W

For printing, this consists of nine characters, as the spaces are significant. The way in which this would be stored in a particular computer would depend on the size of the storage locations and the organisation of the store. In a computer with 8-bit locations, which holds one character per location, nine locations would be necessary. Figure 3.19 illustrates this. We suggest that you check with the ASCII table in Figure 3.18 that the patterns are correct.

A	0	1	0	0	0	0	0	1
B	0	1	0	0	0	0	1	0
C	0	1	0	0	0	0	1	1
▽	0	0	1	0	0	0	0	0
1	0	0	1	1	0	0	0	1
2	0	0	1	1	0	0	1	0
3	0	0	1	1	0	0	1	1
▽	0	0	1	0	0	0	0	0
W	0	1	0	1	0	1	1	1

note: ▽ is a symbol which often means 'space'

Figure 3.19

Computer words and bytes

In this chapter so far we have talked about computer 'locations', but in fact the most commonly used term for a location is a computer **word**. A word is the smallest unit of the main store which can be individually addressed. It is composed of a number of bits which may differ from one computer to another. This number of bits is referred to as the **word length** of the computer and is usually fixed by the manufacturer, although some computers do allow variable word length. One word can often hold several characters, and the bits which hold a single character are called a **byte** of store. It is possible for a word to be only one byte in length, in which case it can then hold only one character. Each byte is then capable of being addressed, and a computer which allows this is sometimes called a 'character' machine.

Data structures

The data which is to be stored in a computer very rarely occurs in the form of individual numbers or characters. Very often the numbers or characters are grouped together in some way and this grouping is important in the interpretation of the data. When you write your name, for example, you do it by linking a set of alphabetic characters together. When you say or read your name you rarely think of the individual characters of which it is composed. However, when these characters are stored in a computer they are in fact stored separately, each one in a byte of store, so that to recognise them as a group, the computer must have some additional information about their structure.

A telephone directory is another example of structured data. Anyone who has ever searched for a telephone number can imagine what this task would be like if the telephone directory had its entries arranged randomly rather than in strict alphabetic order of names. Without the structure it would be almost impossible to locate a particular number.

It is possible to recognise many different data structures and to identify ways in which storage of the data in the computer allows the structure to be preserved. Some of these are very complex and beyond the level of this book, but we should like to describe just two of them, which are commonly known as **strings** and **arrays**.

STRINGS Your name is an example of a 'string'. So is a car registration number, or a date of birth written 8/8/80, or an industrial part number SJ352.

The characters of a string would each be stored in a separate byte of store, so it would be necessary to inform the computer that the contents of these bytes are linked together to form a single item of data, so that they can be retrieved together when required.

The computer needs two pieces of information when a string is to be stored. The first is simply the fact that the characters to be input do form a string, and the second is the number of characters of which the string is composed. The first piece of information is often given by using a special type of variable to identify the string to the computer, and the second by 'clearing' a certain amount of space, or a given number of bytes, for the characters in the string.

When the string is stored, the computer 'remembers' the address of the byte in which the first character is stored, as well as the number of characters, so that in order to retrieve the string it is only necessary to call it by its variable name and the computer will do the rest.

For example, to store the car registration number ABC 123 W as a string, the computer would need to reserve nine consecutive bytes of store and remember the address of the first of these. Suppose that this data item was to be identified by a variable `CARREG`, whenever the 'value' of `CARREG` is required, the computer would print out the contents of the byte whose address is remembered, followed by the contents of the eight successive bytes. Figure 3.20 illustrates the storage of this string in a group of nine bytes of store starting at address 300.

299	
300	A
301	B
302	C
303	▽
304	1
305	2
306	3
307	▽
308	W
309	

Figure 3.20

EXERCISE for discussion or individual work

12 Your address is likely to consist of several lines of which one is the STREET, another the TOWN, and another is the POSTCODE. Suppose that you wish the computer to store your address, holding each line as a separate string, what information would you need to give the computer in order that each line of your address may be identified, and sufficient storage space reserved to contain it?

Data structures 35

EXERCISE for discussion or individual work

13 Different versions of the BASIC language have different ways of instructing the computer as to how much space must be reserved for the storage of strings. Find out how this is done on a computer system to which you have access, and write the appropriate lines of BASIC to reserve sufficient space for:

a the car registrations mentioned in the last section,

b your own address as outlined in Exercise 12.

ARRAYS It very often happens that, in order to make some information clear, the information is presented in the form of a **list** or **table**. For example, a netball team, consisting of seven players, would be most likely to be written down in the form of a list consisting of the names of the players, one beneath the other, in the order of the positions in which they play. The football league results after Saturday's matches are likely to be presented in the form of a table with the name of the home team, followed by the number of goals which it scored; then by the name of the away team followed by *its* goals scored, on each row of the table. Figure 3.21 illustrates sections of a list and a table.

K SMITH
J ROBINSON
C JONES
D PATEL
P BROWN
A ELLIS
C TATE

Arsenal	1	Ipswich	1
Birmingham	3	Sunderland	2
Liverpool	0	Leeds	0
Stoke	2	Coventry	2
Bolton	1	Blackburn	2
Newcastle	0	Derby	2
Oldham	1	Grimsby	2

Figure 3.21

In the two examples given, the structure of the data as a list or table is important in order to enable the whole set of data to be seen at a glance with each individual item related to the other items. However, it is also important to be able to single out any particular item for independent attention: for example in the football league results, as well as seeing the table as a whole, you would most likely want to notice especially the result of any team which you support.

We can see from these examples that in storing lists or tables it is important to preserve their structure, but also to enable individual items to be easily obtained. The name usually given to a list or table when stored in the computer is an **array**: a list is referred to as a **one-dimensional array**, and a table as a **two-dimensional array**, for fairly obvious reasons. Each array as a whole is identified by a single variable such as TEAM or just T, and individual items of the array are identified by attaching a subscript to the variable, for example T(4) would refer to the 4th item of the team (i.e. D. Patel in our netball team).

In both of the examples given, individual items of the arrays could be in the form of a string. Because of the requirements for storing strings, arrays which contain strings are quite complicated to handle, and indeed some computer systems do not allow arrays with strings to be stored. For this reason we shall confine ourselves to examples of numeric arrays in order to describe the way in which arrays are handled by the computer.

L

1	-2
2	0
3	41
4	15
5	60
6	36
7	-28

T

	1	2	3	4	5	6
1	3	6	-2	29	0	1
2	86	50	3	-15	8	77
3	100	42	63	-4	104	20
4	13	-5	22	48	-62	51

Figure 3.22

In Figure 3.22 we have a list of 7 numbers, and a table of 24 numbers, arranged in 4 rows of six items each. Let us identify the list as L and the table as T. The individual items of the list will be identified as L(1), L(2), L(3), ... L(7); while the individual items of the table will each need *two* subscripts for identification. For example the item in the fourth position of the first row will be identified as T(1,4) and that of the second position of the fourth row as T(4,2). So, referring to the diagram, T(1,4) holds 29 and T(4,2) holds −5.

In storing the two arrays, the computer needs to be told which type of array to expect and how many entries are to be stored. It will then store the items in sequence, remembering the address of the first location of store which is used. In storing the table, the sequence will be in order of rows: all of the first row in sequence, followed by the second row, then the third row etc.

Figure 3.23 illustrates the storage of the two arrays, using in each case a section of store starting at location 501.

In order to retrieve an individual item of either array, the identifier of that item will be sufficient to direct the computer to the item required. For example, in the two-dimensional array, if the item 32 is required, its identifier which is T(2,3) will instruct the computer to count nine items starting with the first at location 501. The nine items consist of the first row of six items, and the second row of three items. So the item 32 will be found at location 509.

Data structures 37

a

500	
501	-2
502	0
503	41
504	15
505	60
506	36
507	-28
508	

b

500	
501	3
502	6
503	-2
504	29
505	0
506	1
507	86
508	50
509	3
510	-15
511	8
512	77
513	100
514	42
515	63
516	-4
517	104
518	20
519	13
520	-5
521	22
522	48
523	-62
524	51
525	
526	
527	

Figure 3.23

EXERCISE for individual work

14 Referring to Figure 3.22 rather than Figure 3.23, *work out* as the computer must, the addresses of the following items of the two arrays, assuming that only their identifiers are given:

a List: 15,   0,   60
b Table: −5,   29,   104

You can use Figure 3.23 to check your answers.

As we have already said, string arrays are rather more complicated to handle, and when they are allowed, they are often treated differently from one system to another. If you are interested in the way your particular system deals with string arrays, we suggest you consult your own system documentation.

In this section we have looked at one- and two-dimensional arrays. It *is* possible to have arrays of higher dimensions but they become rather difficult to visualise and are certainly not used so frequently as the ones we described.

Storage of program instructions

Everything so far in this chapter has been about the storage of data, and we have not yet considered how the instructions of the program which controls the data might be stored.

In many respects this is not different to the way in which data is stored. The instructions occupy the same locations as the data, and are represented in the same way – as bit patterns. In fact the bit pattern representing an instruction will not appear to the computer different from one representing any item of data. It will however be interpreted differently so long as the computer 'knows' that it is to be treated as an instruction.

The instructions which are represented by bit patterns are known as **machine instructions** and are usually much more simple than the sort of instructions that might be written in a language such as BASIC. If the computer is to perform a calculation which would contain the operations of addition, subtraction and multiplication, the instructions for each of these operations must be given separately, with information as to where in the computer store the data to be used will be found. For example the instructions 'add 4', 'multiply by 5', and 'subtract 7', would require three separate machine instructions which must include the addresses of the locations at which the numbers 4, 5 and 7 can be found. Figure 3.24 illustrates this.

```
ADD       396
MULTIPLY  399
SUBTRACT  394
```

394	7
395	
396	4
397	
398	
399	5

Figure 3.24

We can see from this example that a machine instruction consists of two parts. These are usually referred to as the **operation** and the **address**. The operation refers to *what* is to be done, and the address directs the computer to the location of store *where* data is to be found or sent.

The binary pattern representing an instruction is correspondingly split into two parts, the first representing the operation and called the **operation code** (or often the **instruction code**) and the second representing the address. In most computers the manufacturer decides how many bits to allocate to each part. In some computers the entire instruction is contained in a single word, and in others it is split into several words or bytes. Whichever of these is the case, the manufacturer has to make two important decisions in allocating the bits.

The first of these decisions is how many operation codes the computer is to have. It will need one code for each operation which it is to perform, and each of these will need to be represented by a unique binary pattern. Thus if 8 bits were allocated to an operation code, it would be possible for the computer to cope with 256 different operations.

The second decision, how many bits to allocate to the part of an instruction specifying the address of data in store, actually depends on the number of locations which the store contains. A location of store is only useful if it can hold data, and the data can only be put there as a result of an instruction which gives the address of the location. It is therefore necessary to be able to address every location of store.

If the pattern representing an address consists of eight bits then only 256 locations of store will be possible, as it will be impossible to address any more. Thus if a computer is to have 1000 locations of store, the bit pattern representing an instruction must contain at least 10 bits. In fact with 10 bits it would be possible to address 1024 (2^{10}) locations. For this reason, the number of stores which a computer contains is usually some power of 2. The number 1024 or 2^{10} has become a unit of storage which is denoted by the letter **K**. A store capacity 8K has 8×2^{10} locations, or 8192 locations.

In Chapter 6 we shall be looking at machine instructions in more detail when we discuss the movement of data within the computer and the way in which the computer performs operations.

Summary

The *main store* of the computer consists of locations known as computer *words* or *bytes*, which are composed of binary digits – *bits*. All data and instructions are represented as binary patterns within the store. The number of binary patterns available depends on the number of bits in a location – if the number of bits is 'n', the number of patterns is 2^n.

Data can be classified as *numeric* and *alphanumeric*. Numeric data can be stored in *pure binary* form, or in *binary coded decimal (BCD) form*. In pure binary form, numbers can either be *integer* or *real*, and each type can be either positive or negative. Positive and negative numbers are represented using the *two's complement* representation, and real numbers by the *floating-point* representation. Alphanumeric data is stored by representing individual characters by a binary pattern so that each character occupies one byte of store. A word of store may consist of one or more bytes and may thus hold one or more characters.

Instructions consist of two parts, each represented by a separate binary pattern. The first part is the *instruction code* and the second part is the *address*. Each location of store has an address which uniquely identifies it and each address, as part of an instruction, must be contained in a location of store. Thus a word of store must contain sufficient bits to hold the binary pattern of any store address. For this reason the number of locations of store is usually a power of two, and the unit of store is 2^{10} or *K* locations.

Two simple data structures which occur frequently are *strings* and *arrays* which consist of numbers and characters grouped in a specific way. These are stored in the computer in an appropriate number of words or bytes so as to preserve their structure.

EXERCISE for individual work

15 What is the difference between the *pure binary* and the *binary coded decimal* representations of an integer in a computer store? Use the integer 129 to illustrate your answer, for a computer which has 8-bit locations.

EXERCISE for individual work

16 Explain what is meant by *numeric* and *alphanumeric* data.
From the following examples, decide which would be numeric and which alphanumeric for computer storage:

a A car registration number
b A date of birth
c A person's height
d An address
e A shoe size
f An industrial part number
g A map reference

EXERCISE for individual work

17 Explain why non-integer numbers in general require more storage space than integers.

EXERCISE for individual work

18 Distinguish between the three representations of negative integers and give examples.

a Sign-and-magnitude
b One's complement
c Two's complement

What *advantages* does the two's complement representation have over the other two representations?
Does the two's complement representation have any *disadvantages* in comparison with the other two representations?

EXERCISE for individual work

19 a The following binary patterns represent integers in two's complement form in 8-bit computer locations. What denary numbers do they represent?

   i) 00110101   iii) 10001010
   ii) 10111101   iv) 10000000

b Show how the following integers would be represented in two's complement form in 8-bit computer locations:

i) 53
ii) −112
iii) −3

EXERCISE for individual work

20 A pair of 8-bit computer locations contain the binary patterns:

01010000   11111001

When asked to interpret this data, three students answer as follows:

a These are two separate integers, the first positive and the second negative.

b This is the floating-point representation of a real number. The first eight bits represent the mantissa and the second 8 bits the exponent or power of 10 by which the mantissa must be multiplied.

c This is an instruction. The first four bits represent the instruction code and the next twelve bits the address at which data is to be found.

Assuming that each of these interpretations is possible, what information would be contained in the locations according to each student?

EXERCISE for individual work

21 If you wanted to store the name of your favourite pop group in a computer, starting at location 500, what information would the computer have to be given? Draw a diagram of store to illustrate your answer.

EXERCISE for individual work

22 If the current football league table of team name, matches played, wins, draws, etc. were to be stored in the computer, what information would the computer have to be given? Take part of a real league table from a newspaper and draw a diagram of a section of store to show how the storage would take place.

Suppose you wanted the computer to print out the *points* for the team which is fourth in the second division, what information would be necessary for the computer to locate the correct piece of data for printing?

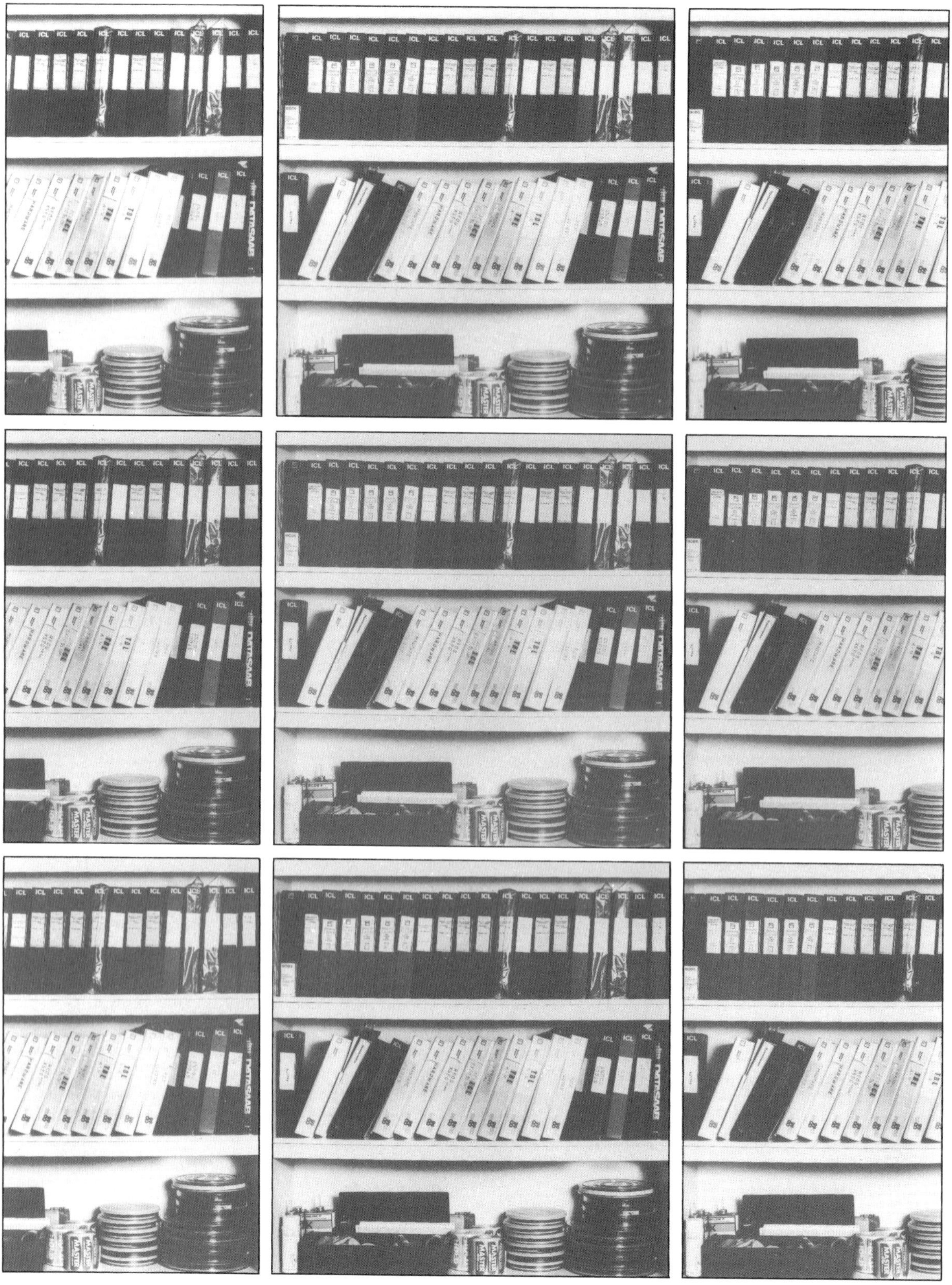
ICL
DATASAAB
MASTER

4 The organisation of data
FILES

Just having data by itself is not always enough. A list of the names of people with telephones and a separate list of telephone numbers would be of no use at all if we wished to ring someone up. The most important thing about a telephone directory is that it links the names with the corresponding numbers (by printing them together on the page).

So, if computers are to be useful to us, we must find ways of representing information about the links between data-items. Chapter 2 talked about getting data from information, and Chapter 3 followed this up by showing how data could be represented inside the computer. This chapter is paired with the next in the same way; in this chapter, we talk about what links are necessary – in the next about how these links are held in the computer.

Data files

Let us go back to the exercises in Chapter 2. There you were asked to collect some information, and to turn it into data. We suggested that you could collect information about people. You might have the following, for each person:

Name	Weight
Address	Sex
Telephone number	Method of transport to school (or work)
Date-of-birth	Form/class/set in school
Colour of eyes	Class teacher's name
Height	

... and so on. There are many other pieces of information that you might have collected, but these will serve to make our point.

Before there were computers, you might very well have stored this kind of information on a filing card. Two possible examples of a card are shown in Figure 4.1.

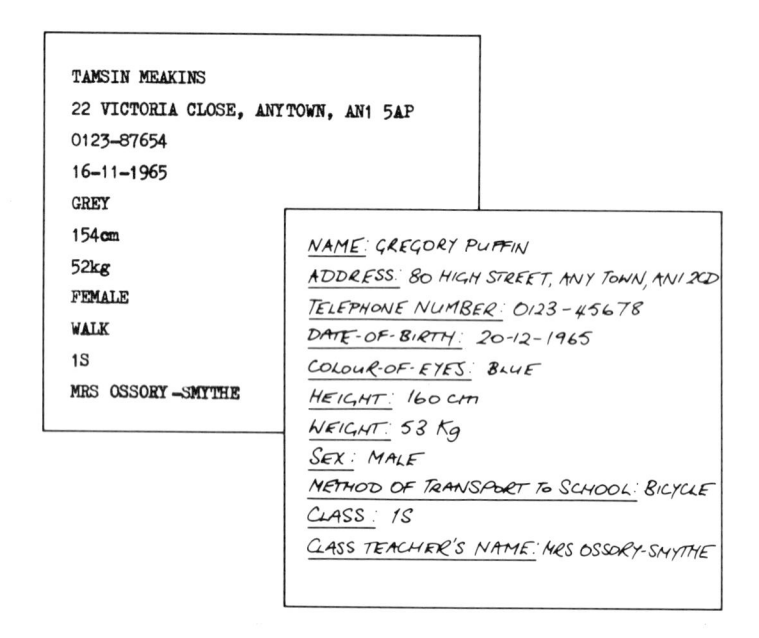

```
TAMSIN MEAKINS
22 VICTORIA CLOSE, ANYTOWN, AN1 5AP
0123-87654
16-11-1965
GREY
154 cm
52 kg
FEMALE
WALK
1S
MRS OSSORY-SMYTHE
```

```
NAME: GREGORY PUFFIN
ADDRESS: 80 HIGH STREET, ANY TOWN, AN1 2CD
TELEPHONE NUMBER: 0123-45678
DATE-OF-BIRTH: 20-12-1965
COLOUR-OF-EYES: BLUE
HEIGHT: 160 cm
WEIGHT: 53 Kg
SEX: MALE
METHOD OF TRANSPORT TO SCHOOL: BICYCLE
CLASS: 1S
CLASS TEACHER'S NAME: MRS OSSORY-SMYTHE
```

Figure 4.1 *Two possible filing-cards*

The front card is the sort of thing you would get *very* tired of writing out over and over again — especially if you had a lot of cards to write! It simply isn't necessary to write out the words 'name', 'address', 'height' and so on, over and over again. You can tell what the data represents, simply by its position on the card. The second card is just as understandable, provided that you know what each piece of data stands for.

There are a number of words which are commonly accepted in describing collections of data like this. The collection of all the filing cards together, with the information from everyone who answered the questionnaire, is called a **file**. (That is why they're called filing cards!) Each single card, with all the information for one person, is called a **record**. And on each card, each separate piece of data is called a **field**.

So a file is made up of records, which contain fields.

Usually all the records in a file are the same — that means that they have the same layout, and contain the same fields, in the same order on each card — and if you had some more cards of a different layout, you would make a new file of them. But you might, for example, have a special card at the start of the file, to show you the layout of the fields on the cards which followed; and you might have a title card at the very start, to tell you what was in the file.

Locating data: record keys

A lot of the information on the record cards will be the same. Because there are only two possible things to put in the 'sex' field ('male/female', 'm/f', whichever you have chosen to code), there will clearly be many cards with each. We usually say that the field has the **value** 'male' or 'female'. Similarly, many of the other fields will have the same values. Two people can well have the same birthdate, or height. But if the file is to be at all useful, there must be at least one field that is different on all the cards. In our example, it will be the name field. Every single card must have a different name. If that wasn't the case, it would be more difficult to use the file sensibly. If you want John Smith's details, it would be useless to find that the file had records for two John Smiths, because you wouldn't know which one you required.

Each record must have a field which uniquely identifies the record. This field is called the **record key**, or simply the **key**. In our example, the record key is the name field.

EXERCISE to tackle before reading on

1 If the record key in a very large file (such as the file of all people holding driving licences, which is held on a (computer) file at the Driver and Vehicle Licensing Centre (DVLC) at Swansea) were the name field, holding the name of a person, it would be very likely that there would be two or more records with the same key. This cannot be allowed to happen. What can be done about it? Looking at a driving licence may give you some ideas.

The name field by itself cannot be allowed to be the key. Something must be added to the field so that it is different for every record. On a driving licence, you can see that as well as the name field, which is *not* used as a key, there is a 'driver number'. This is made up of the first five letters of your surname, then a 'scrambled' version of your date of birth. By itself, this is not sufficient to provide a unique key, as twins, for example, will have the same driver number up to this point. So another part is added, making a sixteen-digit code number which *is* unique, and which can serve as a key. It is cleverly designed, since you can work out the first eleven digits just by knowing your name and birthdate. If you cannot remember your driver-number (because you have lost your licence, perhaps), the DVLC can look at the relatively few records that have keys beginning with those eleven digits, and pick the correct one (by looking at the address, for example). Scrambling of the birthdate was a delightful feature, designed to avoid embarrassment: it is so easy to unscramble, however, that it isn't very much use as a method of ensuring secrecy. See if you can unscramble a few drivers' numbers!

Other possible solutions are: giving every record a number, and using that as a key instead of the name (this is done, for example, with the National Insurance numbers given to everybody who works). Or adding some suffix to a name to make it unique: this is often done in the USA – Oscar Hammerstein I and Oscar Hammerstein II, for example; or adding an extra initial – James A. Murray and James B. Murray.

The most important thing is that the field that is used as a key *should be unique*.

MULTIPLE KEYS A record need not just have a single key. The telephone directory file is a good example. Both the name-and-address field and the corresponding exchange-and-number field uniquely identify the record. Both are keys to the record (which doesn't have any other fields when it is printed in a directory, but may have other information held in the Post Office's own file). There are some complications, because some people have two telephones, but it is probably simpler to forget this when making the point.

Because a record may have several keys, it may be possible to place it in several sensible orders – the natural order of each of the keys. For example, although it is not published, the Post Office holds a copy of the directory in telephone number order.

Because a file can be held in several different orders, programs which sort files are especially important in computing.

The order of data in a file

One use of the key field is that it may be used to put the file in order. We would probably keep our example file in alphabetical order, as that is the most natural ordering of the name field. It is not essential to do this, and we could store the records in any order. They could, for example, be stored in the order in which the questionnaires came in, or in no particular order at all. Or, whenever people consult the file, they may remove a card, obviously allowing the file to close up, and then replace the card at the end, or anywhere in the middle.

While it is not *essential* to store files in order, it is almost always desirable to do so. Think of a big collection of data – a telephone directory, for example, which is just a printed file of records of telephone subscribers, made up of fields such as name, address, exchange, number – it would be practically impossible to find any particular record, unless the file were in order. Without order, we should simply have no alternative but to look through every single entry until we came to the correct one.

Keeping a file in order is not only helpful in finding records, it is also helpful in deciding whether we have a particular record or not. Because we know where a record *should* come in an ordered file, we also know when we have *passed* the position where it should be.

EXERCISE to tackle before reading on

2 A telephone directory is a file of data. The records are the entries for individual subscribers. What is the key field? Think carefully!

Strictly speaking, the key is not a single field, but two fields – the name *plus* the address. Sometimes this is called a **concatenated key** ('concatenated' means 'put together'). We use the telephone directory by searching for the correct name, and once we have found the correct names, then we look at the addresses. There are other examples of this situation. Neither the destination nor the time of departure is sufficient to identify uniquely a particular train, at least not in a large station. But the combination of time and place is (usually) sufficient, although in Europe it is common to give each train a number as a sort of 'artificial' key.

Describing files of data

Computing is an area where good habits are particularly important. If you have a file that is poorly organised, or badly documented, it may not matter much while the file is small. But as soon as the file gets large, poor organisation and documentation get in the way of smooth easy working.

A very good habit in handling files (and this applies as readily to card files outside the computer, as to computer files like those of the next chapter) is carefully to document the structure of your files. That is, to describe the records in the file, the fields contained in each record, and the order in which the file is held. This may not seem very important while you are working on building up the file, but if you need to go back to a file that you haven't touched for a year or two, or if someone else wants to see what is in your file, this sort of documentation can be crucial.

In Figure 4.2, you can see how this documentation might be carried out in the computer programming language COBOL. This is just a short fragment of a COBOL program that handles records containing the same information as the eleven data fields discussed earlier. It is not necessary to understand COBOL to find this instructive. If you look at the printout, you will notice the following points.

```
            RECORD NAME IS PERSONAL-DETAILS
               01 NAME PICTURE A(25) IS RECORD KEY
               01 ADDRESS
                  02 STREET-ADDRESS    PICTURE A(25)
                  02 POST-TOWN         PICTURE A(15)
                  02 COUNTY            PICTURE A(15)
                  02 POST-CODE
                     03 OUTWARD-CODE   PICTURE AA99
                     03 INWARD-CODE    PICTURE 9AA
               01 TELEPHONE-NUMBER     PICTURE 9(10)
               01 DATE-OF-BIRTH
                  02 DAY               PICTURE 99
                  02 MONTH             PICTURE 99
                  02 YEAR              PICTURE 99
               01 COLOUR-OF-EYES-CODE  PICTURE 99
               01 HEIGHT               PICTURE 9(3)
               01 WEIGHT               PICTURE 9(3)
               01 SEX                  PICTURE 1
               01 TRANSPORT-CODE       PICTURE 99
               01 CLASS-NAME           PICTURE A(3)
               01 CLASS-TEACHER        PICTURE A(25)
```

Figure 4.2 *Describing the structure of a record in the COBOL programming language*

Every field in the record has been given a name – ADDRESS, DATE-OF-BIRTH, and so on. The record as a whole has also been given a name, PERSONAL-DETAILS. This means that if we wish to, we can talk about all the data in the record as a whole, by referring to the PERSONAL-DETAILS record; or we can talk about an individual data-field, by giving its own name, ADDRESS, HEIGHT etc. These names describe the *type* of data (see page 10).

Each field in the record has been described on a separate line. The line begins with a number, 01, 02 or 03, which is the *level* number, and we'll describe that later. The field is then named, and there follows a PICTURE of what the data looks like. The PICTURE for NAME is A(25) which means that this field is made up of 25 alphabetic characters. Other records are made up of numbers, not characters, and they have pictures like 9(3) which just means any three numeric digits (a 9 stands for any numeric digit). The PICTURE for the SEX field is just 1 which means that a binary value will be stored here: say, 1 for male, 0 for female. Notice that some pictures mix alphabetic and numeric digits – PICTURE AA99, for example. Notice also that there is a choice between describing (say) a numeric field as PICTURE 999 or PICTURE 9(3) – both mean exactly the same.

The description in Figure 4.2 uses the level numbers to show how some data fields are broken up into smaller **sub-fields**. For example, DATE-OF-BIRTH is a field at the top level, level 01. It is shown as being divided into three separate fields, DAY, MONTH and YEAR – each with PICTURE 99 as it happens. There is no PICTURE for DATE-OF-BIRTH, since this can be worked out from the PICTURE of each of the three items at level 02. Again, this means that if we wish to talk about the date of birth as a single entity, we can do this, by calling it DATE-OF-BIRTH, but if we wish to refer to the day, month and year separately, this can be done by those names at level 02. The ADDRESS part of the description takes this even further. An ADDRESS is made up of four items, one of which is POST-CODE. But a POST-CODE, in turn, is made up of two parts. Thus the post-code NN12 7PQ is made up of the OUTWARD-CODE, NN12 (used by the sorting office in the town where the letter was posted, to decide where to send the letter to), and the INWARD-CODE, 7PQ (used by the delivery sorting office to decide which postman's walk to sort the letter into).

Taken together, the COBOL record description tells you quite a bit about the structure of a record. It gives names to the various fields, it tells you how much space they each take up, and it says which order they come in. This is the very least you should write down in describing a record in any sort of file. COBOL has other descriptive facilities too – for describing how many records might be expected, for example – but we shan't discuss these here.

Linking data-items in files

We are usually concerned with using space economically. This is just as true in a computer as on a filing card. We have already seen that it is a waste of space to write the field-names on to each card, because the position on the card tells us all that we need to know – and the same sort of job is done by the COBOL record description.

There is another way of saving space. In our example, part of the data was the class name, and the class teacher's name. But once you know what the class name for a particular pupil is, then you probably know the teacher's name as well. The class name and teacher's name always go together. To write both of them on to each card is a waste of space. An alternative way is to record just the class name, and have a separate file that contains class names and the corresponding names of teachers.

To find out all the details of any particular pupil, we have to read from two files – one file to get all the pupil details, and another file to find out the name of the class teacher.

Is this an advantage? It certainly seems more complicated. On a handwritten filing-card, there would probably be enough space anyway, but in a computer it could be a valuable saving of space. Like so many things in computing, it depends on whether space is more important than time. Let us look at the advantages and disadvantages.

Advantages

It takes less space. In a file containing details of 1000 pupils in 30 classes, we would save the space used for the teacher's name (that is, 25 characters) 1000 times over. We should also have to have a new file with 30 times the class names (90 characters) and 30 times the teacher's names (750 characters). We should save, in all 25 000 − (90 + 750) = 24 160 characters.

50 *Files*

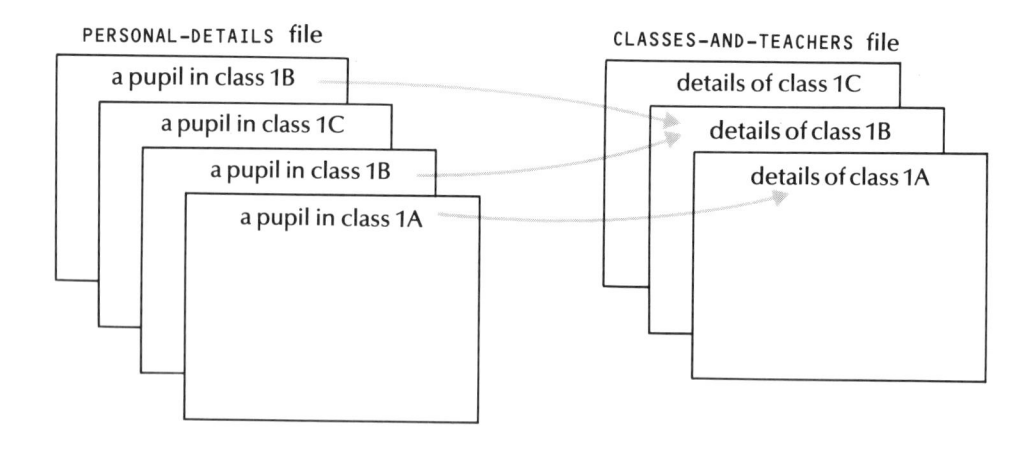

```
PERSONAL-DETAILS file                CLASSES-AND-TEACHERS file
    a pupil in class 1B                   details of class 1C
      a pupil in class 1C                   details of class 1B
        a pupil in class 1B                   details of class 1A
          a pupil in class 1A
```

Figure 4.3 *Imaginary pointers linking two files together*

Disadvantages

Every searching for a record now becomes longer because the data is not all in the same place. Exactly how much longer depends on how records are stored in the computer.

○ EXERCISE to tackle before reading on
○ **3** There is another very important advantage, that hasn't been mentioned above. Can you think what it is?

If the class teacher changes (perhaps because it's the end of the school year, and the pupil moves into a new class, or because a class teacher leaves), then every pupil record must be examined and the teacher's name changed where required. Under the alternative scheme, if the teacher changes, it is only necessary to alter *one* of the records in the CLASSES-AND-TEACHERS file, and it is not necessary to look at the pupil files at all. If the pupil is changing classes, one need change only one piece of data on his record, not two.

Sometimes, too, there can be problems if the computer is taking the long way round and changing all the pupil records, and it is interrupted before it has changed all the records. Some pupils will have the old teacher's name, and some the new.

Also, because we have saved so much space, we could store some more information about the class — which their form room is, how many seats there are in it, their assembly point in case of a fire drill, and so on. All of this is information about the *class*, and need be stored only once.

One important thing about splitting data to save space, like this, is that the pupil's PERSONAL-DETAILS record must contain one field that is then used as the record key in the CLASSES-AND-TEACHERS file. If the pupil record doesn't contain this key, then we cannot find the correct record in the second file.

PERSONAL-DETAILS file

MEAKINS	T.	1S
WILLIAMS	J.P.	1B
PUFFIN	G.	1S
MAJOR	S.J.	1A
HIGGINS	J.	1A
PATEL	J.	1C
HILL	J.O.	1S
THOMAS	P.G.	1B
ANTONIONI	M.	1A
ROBINSON	B.W.	1C
SMITH	W.	1S

CLASSES-AND-TEACHERS file

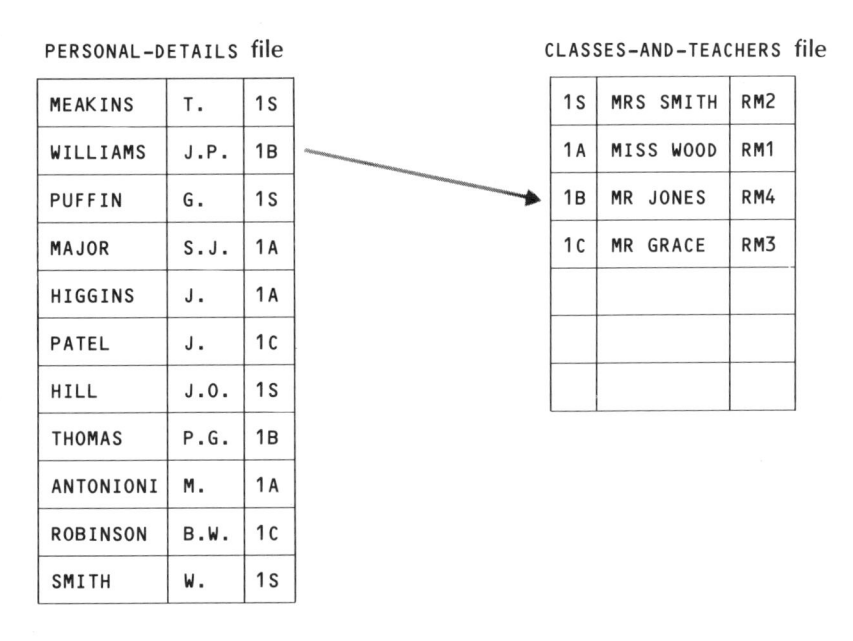

1S	MRS SMITH	RM2
1A	MISS WOOD	RM1
1B	MR JONES	RM4
1C	MR GRACE	RM3

Figure 4.4 *How pointers really happen: each record in the PERSONAL-DETAILS file contains the pupil's class (Williams is in class 1B). The class is the key to a record in the CLASSES-AND-TEACHERS file. The arrow shows the link.*

One very useful way of picturing this is shown in Figure 4.3. A record in the PERSONAL-DETAILS file, can be thought of as having a **link** or **pointer** (shown by the arrow) that *points to* one of the records in the second file. In Figure 4.4, we show how this is made to happen. Each record in the first file contains a field that is a key field in the second file.

LINKING BACKWARDS

In our school records example, as we have modified it to save space, every pupil record contains a link to the details about the class and teacher. But it isn't easy to select those records for pupils all in the same class. The design of our file makes it easy to go one way, but not the other. Another system of links can make it almost as easy to work the other way as well.

Each class record in the CLASSES-AND-TEACHERS file contains a single link, to the *first* pupil in the class (this record is in the other file, the PERSONAL-DETAILS file). The first pupil's record contains a link to the *next* pupil's record (in the same file); that is, to the next pupil in the same class, not necessarily to the next pupil in order. Figure 4.5 shows how these links join together all the pupils in one class into a chain. All of the other class-and-teacher records have similar links into a similar chain of all the pupils in the class. In Figure 4.6, we show how this chain is represented in a computer file. To make it easier, each pupil has been given a reference number.

52 Files

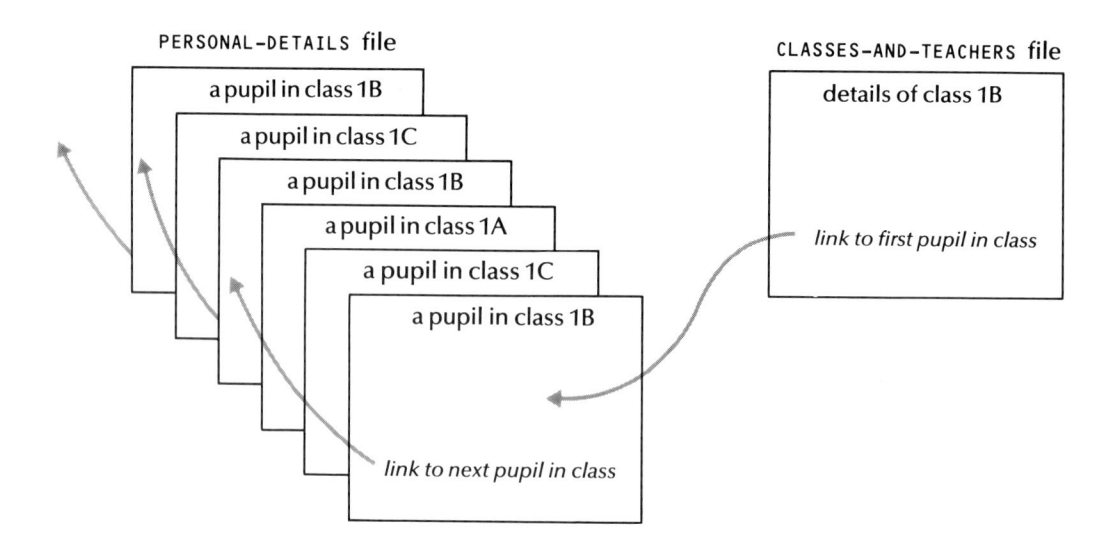

Figure 4.5 *Using pointers to link pupils in the same class: this diagram shows the beginning only of the chain for class 1B. Classes 1A and 1C are also arranged into chains, and there would also be pointers from each pupil record to the* **CLASSES-AND-TEACHERS** *file. With all these arrows, the diagram would be unreadable!*

PERSONAL-DETAILS file

1	MEAKINS	T.	1S	3
2	WILLIAMS	J.P.	1B	8
3	PUFFIN	G.	1S	7
4	MAJOR	S.J.	1A	5
5	HIGGINS	J.	1A	9
6	PATEL	J.	1C	15
7	HILL	J.O.	1S	11
8	THOMAS	P.G.	1B	13
		M.	1A	12

CLASSES-AND-TEACHERS file

1S	MRS SMITH	RM2	1
1A	MISS WOOD	RM1	4
1B	MR JONES	RM4	2
1C	MR GRACE	RM3	6

pupil reference number

pointer to next pupil in same class

pointer to first pupil in that class

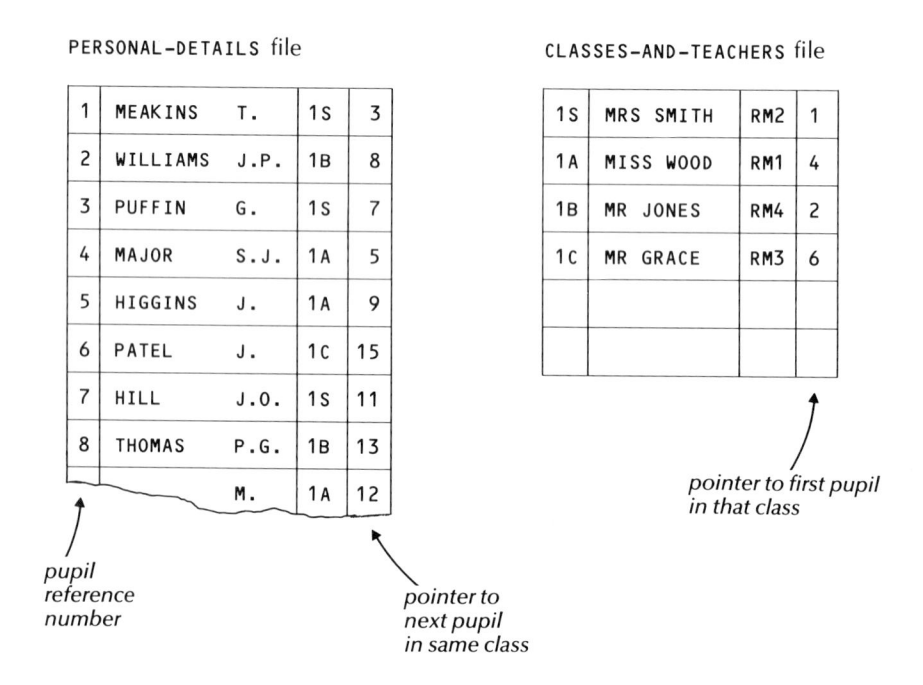

Figure 4.6 *Linking classes: giving each pupil a reference number means that pointers can be stored simply as numbers.*

We have already introduced the idea that some pieces of data to be stored in each pupil record are not data which were collected, but are linking data concerned with organising the file efficiently. Links do not usually take up much space, and they save on the space used in repeating data (such as teacher names) so they are usually a good idea. In real-life computing, most files have as many links as 'genuine' data items, if not more! We can easily see that it could be useful to have a link in every pupil record to his maths teacher, his French teacher and so on, and there would be links chaining the maths sets and the French sets and so on.

○ EXERCISE to tackle before reading on

4 What would be the advantages and disadvantages of using links as described to allow us to find out, starting with a pupil record, which set he was in and its teacher for each one of his timetabled subjects?

The advantages would be that it would save an enormous amount of space as compared to storing this information in each pupil record. Even the relatively small amount of space saved by not having to store the teacher's name in every record would be multiplied by 1000 (pupils) and then multiplied again by every subject. We would, of course need a lot of links. In practice, we would probably not even think of starting such a wasteful task without using links, so that using links like this could be said to be enabling us to do something that wasn't possible before.

The principal disadvantage is that every reading of the file consists of following a lot of links, and this clearly takes a lot of time. In the sort of example we've described, using a computer, following links would be worthwhile as it would be relatively fast. It can even be faster, as there will be less repeated redundant information to be skipped over in the pupil records, but this depends on how the file is actually organised in the computer.

One disadvantage that is often overlooked is that the structure of the file is now a lot more complicated. If it was a card-index file, a human would probably find the task of following links to new files too difficult to manage; so this is very much a computer technique, rather than a manual one.

Indexing files of data

We've seen before that a file may be built up of records with more than one record key. In storing data about books, both author's name and title are fields that we would want to have as record keys. That is, given either the author or the title, we would want to be able to find the full record for that book. Clearly, we cannot arrange the file into two different orders at once, so it doesn't seem possible to have two different record keys.

However, by clever use of links, this can be possible. There are two ways. One is a method that we've actually seen in use already in our school example, that is to link the records into two chains, in different orders. Figure 4.7 shows how this could be done. Starting with the author link, we can follow the chain of links putting the books into author order, and similarly with title. As well as the links, we need to store two new items: the starting points of the two chains. Such a start link is usually called a **header**. It wasn't necessary to store it separately in the school example, because there was a place for the header information in the teacher record.

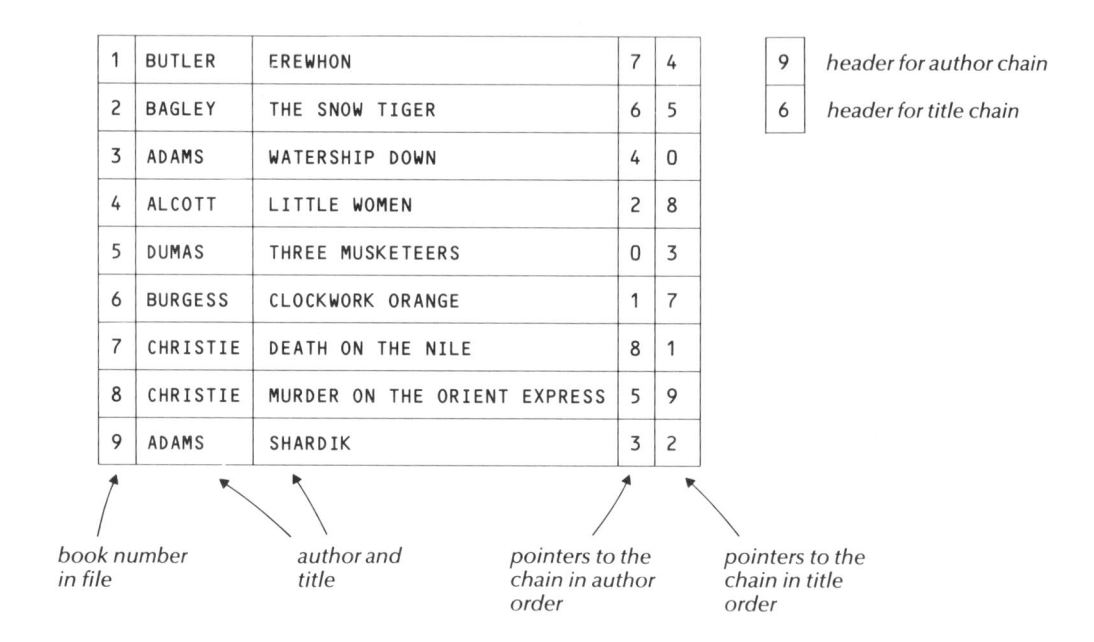

1	BUTLER	EREWHON	7	4
2	BAGLEY	THE SNOW TIGER	6	5
3	ADAMS	WATERSHIP DOWN	4	0
4	ALCOTT	LITTLE WOMEN	2	8
5	DUMAS	THREE MUSKETEERS	0	3
6	BURGESS	CLOCKWORK ORANGE	1	7
7	CHRISTIE	DEATH ON THE NILE	8	1
8	CHRISTIE	MURDER ON THE ORIENT EXPRESS	5	9
9	ADAMS	SHARDIK	3	2

| 9 | header for author chain |
| 6 | header for title chain |

book number in file / author and title / pointers to the chain in author order / pointers to the chain in title order

Figure 4.7 *Two different orders at once. Notice how a pointer-value of 0 is used to show the end of the chain. The book file is not held in any particular order.*

Using headers and links for the book example also means that the file need not be stored in any particular order, and new books can be added at the end, rather than sorting them into some other order. The chain of links keeps the order correct for us.

Sometimes even this is too cumbersome, it now being necessary to follow what may be a long chain of links. A second solution is to keep **indexes**. Each record will be stored in the file, and given a reference number. This reference number could simply be its position in the file – 1st, 2nd 850th, and so on – so it need not be stored, and will not take up space. Then we make up a number of subsidiary files, called indexes. The author index will be stored in author order, and each record in the index will contain just the author's name and the reference number of the book record. Figure 4.8 shows how it can be used. Similarly the title index contains just the title and reference number. Using an index or indexes is only valuable when there are a lot of data-items in the book record that are *not* record keys. Indexes use more space, because they store the record keys in the index as well as in the book record.

Title index

CLOCKWORK ORANGE	6
DEATH ON THE NILE	7
EREWHON	1

Author index

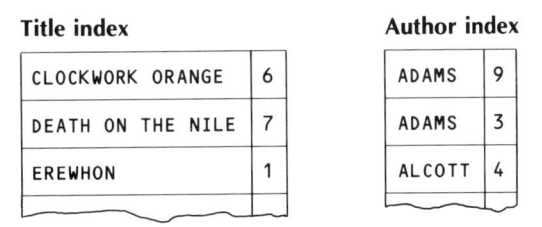

ADAMS	9
ADAMS	3
ALCOTT	4

Figure 4.8 *The beginnings of two indexes for the file in Figure 4.7*

SWINGS AND ROUNDABOUTS

You are probably beginning to get a picture of designing files in particular, and of computing in general, as a process of carefully weighing up alternatives. This is absolutely correct. In designing computer programs and structuring the data they work with, there is a continual trade-off of time against space. Usually, methods that work fast use more space than slower ones, and those that economise on space take longer to use. The correct solution for any problem depends on the costs that are current at the time the decision is made, and also on the likely changes to those costs in the future. The simplest solution is not always the best!

Locating data: primary and secondary keys

Now that we know something about how record keys are used in finding data and how links are used in structuring data, it is time to correct a minor false impression. We have said quite strongly that a record key should be unique (else we can't find the record!). That's only partly true, and now that we know about indexes, we can see why this is so.

Think again about the book example. Some authors have written more than one book, so it is wrong to talk about the author field being a record key. But, of course, it is very important to have an author index. Well, we *can* have an author index, even though the author field is not unique. We actually have two sorts of key. One is a **primary key**, that uniquely identifies a record. Every record should have at least one primary key, otherwise it is true that we couldn't find the record we wanted; in the example, the reference number was the primary key. But other important fields, that might not be unique, can be used as **secondary keys**. We would look these up in the index, and find several records, each with the appropriate secondary key. We would then have to choose the correct one by examining the records. It is in this way that we can deal with books both by Adams and by Christie.

A primary key is the unique value that identifies each record. A secondary key is an important value that may not be unique, but which is *helpful* in finding a record. We always need some other information to pick out the record we need, but we can use an index based on a secondary key to get us closer to the record we want. In the book example, author was a sensible secondary key, but price would not be. A price index wouldn't be worthwhile.

Summary

We have seen that the structure of data is often as important as the data itself. Knowing which class a school pupil belongs to – that is, where he is placed in the structure of the school – can be as important as simply knowing that he belongs to the school. Where things are in a particular order – position in class, alphabetical order, etc. – this can be the *only* important thing.

In a computer, related data is kept in *files*: each entry forms a *record*; each part of a record is a *field*. To assist in *documenting* the file, each field is given a *name* which describes the *type* of data it holds.

Data in a file is usually kept in a particular *order*, since this makes it easier to locate particular fields and hence the data which they contain (their *values*). Because you know where data should be, you also know when you have passed that point, which saves time in searching.

It is frequently useful to have *links* or *pointers* between items of data: such links may provide *chains* of data-items, each being related to the item before and the item after it. Additional information about the start of a chain may form a separate *header* record.

It must be possible to identify each record in the file *uniquely*, by means of one or more fields: the *record key*. *Multiple keys*, *concatenated keys* and *indexes* may help to save storage space, to locate data quickly and to facilitate updates.

EXERCISE for individual work

5 Look back at the data you collected in the exercises in Chapter 2. It should be possible to divide the data into

a data about the person, and

b data about his class in school,

in exactly the way that we have been describing in this chapter. There may be other divisions that you can make, which would save space if this data were stored in a computer file. Write brief notes describing how and why you have divided the data.

EXERCISE for individual work

6 Give a formal description of the way you have divided your data (as in Exercise 5) by writing a COBOL-type record description. It is not necessary to know any COBOL – Figure 4.2 is enough of a guide. Remember that each type of record needs to be given a name (this is equivalent to giving a name to each different type of filing card) and then each field needs to be named in order, together with a PICTURE saying how much space the data will take up.

EXERCISE for individual work

7 Make a list of the data that you might wish to keep in a file about books that you own. Is the list different from the data that a bookseller or a publisher might keep?

EXERCISE for individual work

8 Write out a COBOL-type record description for your answer to Exercise 7. Consider only books that you own and the data that you might wish to keep about them. It should be possible to split the data up, and your COBOL-type record description should show this, by having a number of different types of records that would be stored in different files.

EXERCISE for individual work

9 Re-read the section on indexed files. Why is it necessary to 'waste' space by repeating the record key (which is already in the index) in the actual book record? After all, we *know* what the record key is, because we have just used it to look the book up in the index – why not just store the items which are *not* record keys?

HOLD
DATE
JOB
FILE NAME
GEN No.
REEL No.
COMMENTS
TBL
CONTROL DATA TOTAL SERVICE TAPE
000143
ALPHA PHI
6250

5 Computer files
SECONDARY STORAGE

The examples of the last chapter – telephone directories, card files of pupils in a school – were all *large* collections of data. For these to be stored in a computer, a *large* amount of storage space would be required. We shall see in this chapter that for various reasons the space available in main store is generally too limited for this purpose. In considering the solution to this problem, we shall find it convenient to think of the data in terms of the records and fields into which it is structured, rather than the bits, bytes and words of which main store is composed.

Backing store

Let us consider the idea of a file, which was discussed in Chapter 4. This is a useful form for a collection of data which is composed of a number of records which in turn are subdivided into fields. If a computer is to be used to get information from a file, the file must first be stored in the computer.

In Chapter 4 we discussed a file of data which was concerned with the personal details of pupils in a school. Each record of the file consisted of data about an individual pupil, and the fields of the record were described in Figure 4.2 (see page 48). Let us suppose that we want to store this file in the computer so that we can use the computer to get information from it.

EXERCISE for discussion

1 The only place that we have discussed so far for storing information in the computer is the main store. Can you think of the advantages and disadvantages of keeping the pupil records file in the main store of the computer?

The size of the main store of a computer is usually limited, for two reasons. The first is that the maximum number of store locations is determined by the space allocated in the address part of an instruction (see page 39). The second is expense. The components of main store are expensive and should not therefore be used unnecessarily. A file is often very large, and it may even be physically impossible to hold it all in main store. Even if this were possible, it would be a very bad use of main store to keep the file there – it would take up valuable space that could be used for other programs and data in current use. Even when the file itself is in use it is not necessary to hold it all in main store. Often only one record at a time can be used and so only this record need be in the main store, although in practice it can be more convenient to hold several records at a time, as we shall see shortly.

If the file is not going to be held in main store, where will it be stored? The answer is in some form of **secondary storage**, often known as **backing store**, which is less expensive, and is capable of holding a larger amount of data. This is usually slower in providing data for processing, as it is outside the CPU of the computer.

This secondary storage must be linked to the computer so that data stored there can be readily transferred into main store for processing. The most common materials or **media** used for this storage are **magnetic disks** and **magnetic tapes** or **cassettes**, although others such as **magnetic drums** or **cards**, and **punched paper tape** or **cards**, can be used. Whatever the medium, there must be an associated machine or unit, which can be linked to the CPU of the computer in order to **read** data from main store or **write** data from main store to medium. Such a unit is often referred to as a **peripheral unit**, or sometimes just a **peripheral** for short. Thus we have **magnetic tape units**, **magnetic disk units**, **paper tape readers**, etc.

○ EXERCISE to tackle before reading on
○
○ **2** A file of records could be held on a magnetic cassette of the sort
○   which is used in domestic cassette recorders. Can you think of any
○   advantages of this, other than the saving of space in main store?
○

The cassette holding the file can be kept in any convenient place and can be transported easily to *any* computer. Of course it is important that any such computer stores data in the same way, which is why the character codes mentioned in Chapter 3 are so important. It is also an easy matter to copy the cassette, either to provide a copy for someone else, or as a spare copy in case the original is lost or damaged in some way.

Despite the apparent number of media for backing store, they all fall into two categories: those which are similar to magnetic tape, and those which are similar to magnetic disk: so we shall discuss the main similarities and differences between the two.

Magnetic tape

Magnetic tape is physically similar to that used on domestic tape recorders, although wider and stronger, and is recorded in only one direction. The magnetic tape unit has two spools for holding the reels, read and write heads for the transfer of data, and a driving mechanism (see Chapter 6). Data is recorded on the tape magnetically, but we shall be much more interested in the way it is *organised* on the tape than the way it is recorded.

A file is stored on magnetic tape by writing it field by field, record by record along the tape, so that as the tape is read, the second field follows the first, the third field follows the second, and so on.

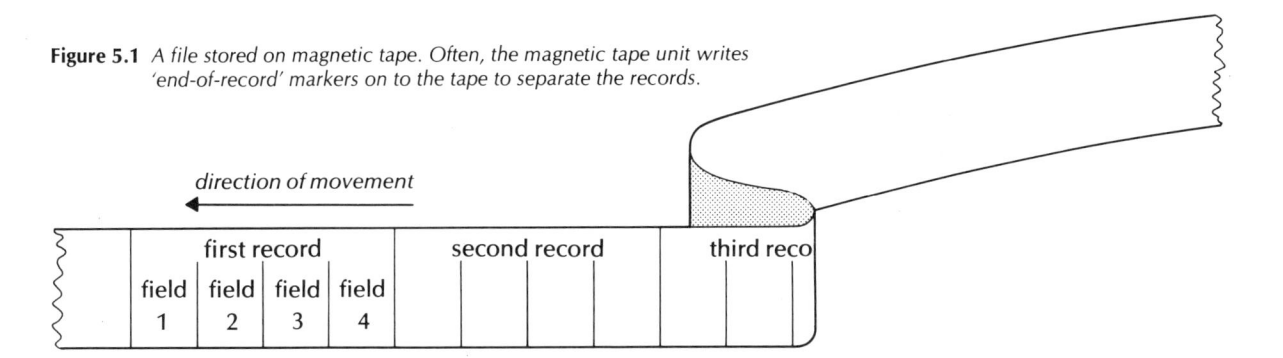

Figure 5.1 *A file stored on magnetic tape. Often, the magnetic tape unit writes 'end-of-record' markers on to the tape to separate the records.*

This has a very important consequence on the way that the file stored on tape may be used. If some information is required from the third record, the computer must pass over the first and second records before the required record is reached. Once these records have been 'passed over' it is hard to return to them, so it is essential to look for the required records in the same order as the records on the tape: the tape would otherwise have to be read through several times to find all the required information.

In practice, although the records are examined by the computer one by one to see if they are required for processing, taking them into main store one record at a time for examination makes a very slow business of reading the file. To speed up the process, they are actually transferred in groups known as **blocks**, where the number of records in a block usually depends on the size of the records. The records are actually arranged on the tape in blocks with a gap between successive blocks called an **inter-block gap**. The purpose of this gap is to allow the motion of the tape to stop between the reading of each block. The space in the gap is just sufficient to allow the tape to slow down to a stop and then to accelerate again to the speed required for reading records, known as **reading speed**.

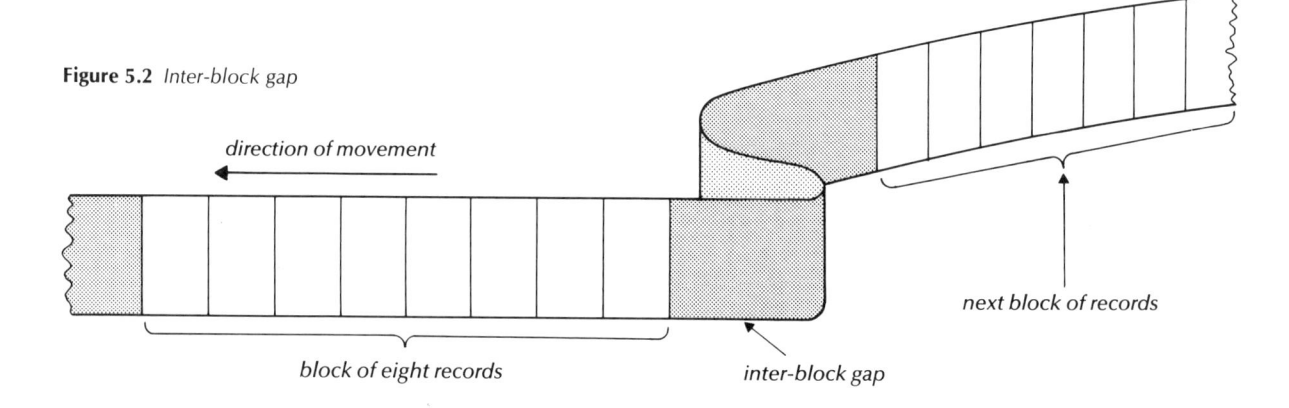

Figure 5.2 Inter-block gap

direction of movement

block of eight records

inter-block gap

next block of records

FIXED AND VARIABLE LENGTH FIELDS

When a block of records has been read into main store and the computer starts to examine them, starting with the first field of the first record, how does the computer determine where one field ends and the next begins? In the example which you saw in Chapter 4 (Figure 4.2) this would not be a problem, as the length of each of the fields – and therefore of the records – was clearly defined. For example, 25 alphabetic characters were allowed for the NAME field, so that the computer should know that the 26th character is the start of the next field. Of course, if the name were SMITH a lot of those 25 characters would be spaces. This doesn't matter if plenty of space is available for the file; but if space is limited, this waste might prove very significant with regard to fitting the file into this space. If this is the case then it might be necessary to make the lengths of fields and records vary according to what information they contain. Thus SMITH would require less space than ROBERT-SON. But then there is the very real problem of making it clear to the computer which character is at the end of a particular field. In this case what is required is some marker at the end of each field to identify the **end-of-field** state. This would be done by some special character which would be reserved for this purpose. In a similar way the **end-of-record** and **end-of-file** positions could also be marked with other reserved characters. These reserved characters

```
┊ |SMITH....................|ROBERTSON...............|BATTENBERG-WILLIAMS......| ┊
```

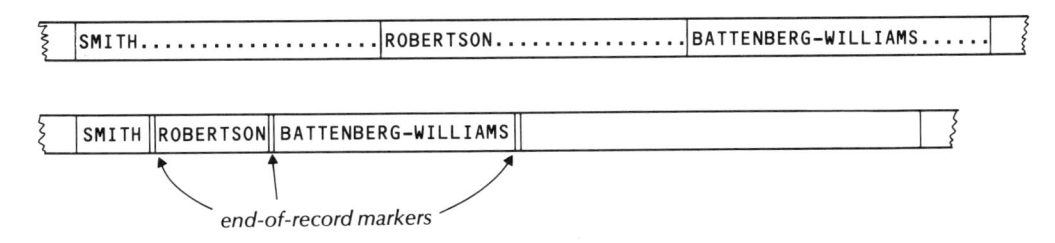

```
┊ |SMITH|ROBERTSON||BATTENBERG-WILLIAMS|           | ┊
```
end-of-record markers

Figure 5.3 *Fixed- and variable-length records on tape: the upper, fixed-length storage which uses 25 characters for each name is wasteful of space, but it is not necessary to read each character to see when a new record begins.*

must be represented by bit patterns which are not used to represent any of the standard characters, such as numbers or letters. Looking back to the table on page 32 should convince you that there are likely to be some available, particularly among the **control characters** which have been included in the code for just this sort of purpose.

Alternatively, each field could be preceded by a count of the number of characters in that field, as shown in Figure 5.4.

```
┊ |05|SMITH|09|ROBERTSON|19|BATTENBERG-WILLIAMS|           ┊
```

Figure 5.4 *Using field-lengths for variable-length records: The five characters used for SMITH are noted immediately before the first character: to skip the field, we look at the sixth character thereafter. Often the complete count for a whole record is inserted before the count for the first field so that the whole record may easily be skipped. As the record will be in main store when processed, this can save time.*

In our school pupil records file, suppose that it is required to use that file to print out labels for end-of-term reports for the whole school. In this case each record of the file has to be accessed, since each pupil needs a label; and there is obviously no virtue in taking individual pupils out of order. So, if the file were held on magnetic tape, it would be an easy matter to run through the file, record by record, printing out the address field from each record in turn. If it is known that this is the main use of the file, then some thought should be given to the initial storing of the file in form order, so that form tutors could receive their labels in form order without someone first having to sort them.

Magnetic disks

Some of the disadvantages of magnetic tape will have been made obvious in the previous section. The need to read through the records in the sequence in which they are stored can be a great disadvantage if only one particular record is required and this is toward the end of the file.

For example, again looking at our pupil records file, suppose the secretary of the school wishes to use the file to find out the telephone number of the parent of a pupil who is ill and needs to be sent home. To have the computer read through the file, record by record until the correct record is found, is obviously a waste of computer time if not of the secretary's time. What is desirable is for the computer to go straight to the appropriate record and supply the required information. Thus a file stored on magnetic tape would be inconvenient in this instance, but the use of magnetic disks as secondary storage would allow exactly this sort of **direct access**.

A magnetic disk usually has two recording surfaces, and recording is done on concentric tracks rather than on a spiral groove. Magnetic disks for large computer systems usually come in **exchangeable disk packs**, that is a pack, or cartridge, consisting of a number of disks physically grouped together, which can be fitted into a magnetic disk unit. The unit is designed so that the packs can be exchanged to allow the use of different packs within the unit. In microcomputer systems the disk may come singly rather than in packs, and the fact that they are often made of a flexible plastic has given them the name of **floppy disks**. The tracks of a disk's surface are divided up into **sectors** or blocks, usually eight to a track, which can each hold one or more records of a file.

The physical structure of the disk lends itself to a system of **addressing**. That is, each sector can have an address depending on its position within a track (say, sector 5), the position of the track on a surface (track 12), and the position of the surface with respect to the other disks within a pack (surface 4). Thus if a record of a file is stored on disk, it could be located by an address such as 4:12:5, the address of the sector in which it is held. This sector would then be searched for the required record. This is obviously much faster than searching through all previous records of the file, as the reading head can move directly to the required track and only a short wait is necessary until the sector comes round under the head.

When a file is stored on disk, an empty disk would present no problems. The file could be stored track by track and surface by surface, or on the same track on successive surfaces in a disk pack: the latter is commonly known as using a **cylinder** of a disk pack (see Figure 5.6). However, when a disk has been filled with files and some have been deleted, the space available together in any single section of the disk may not be sufficient to hold all of the file now to be stored. In this case the file must be split into different parts of the disk, so that successive records may not be physically positioned next to each other. When this happens, the 'links' between records of a file become very important. Each record needs to have a field which links it to the 'next' record in the file, and providing that this link exists, it does not matter where on the disk that record is positioned. All that is actually needed is the position of the first record of the file and thereafter the other records can be found in sequence by following the links.

The links will simply be disk addresses like 4:12:5. In fact the first record will not be a 'real' record at all, like the other records of the file, but rather an introductory record or **header** providing information about the other records.

Figure 5.5
Two reading heads, one for each surface of the disk, are positioned a few millimetres from each surface. As shown, they will read from (or write to) data on the track shown as the outer dotted path. To access data on another track, such as the inner dotted one, the pair of heads move together inwards until positioned over the track.

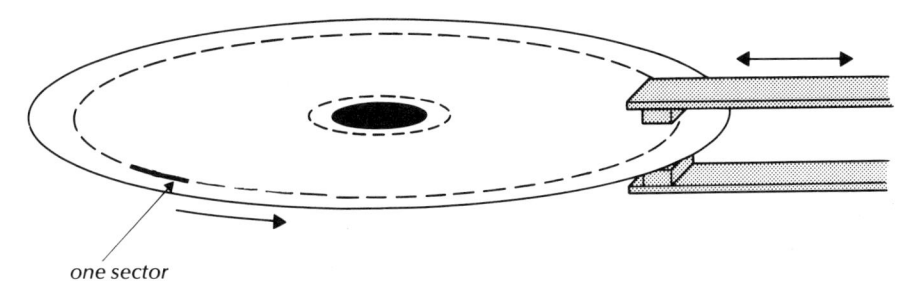

one sector

Figure 5.6
An exchangeable disk pack: there is one read/write head for each surface, and the complete set of heads moves together. At any one time, without moving the heads, any one track from a 'cylinder' of tracks, one above the other, may be read. For protection, it is common for the outer surfaces of the top and bottom disks to be unrecorded and read/write heads are then not necessary.

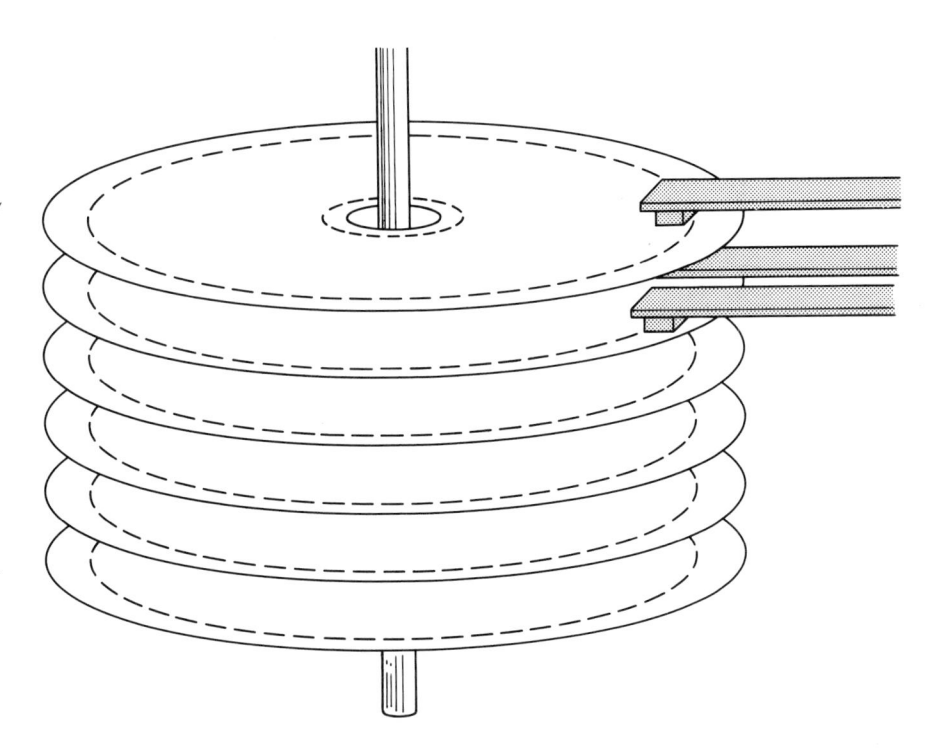

The information contained will include the number of records in the file and the address at which the first real record is to be found, as well as other information such as the name of the file, its version number (if more than one version is kept for security purposes), and other details which might prove necessary about the use of the file.

The information in this header record could be even more detailed in the case of fixed length records which are stored with a fixed number to a block. If the number of the first record in each block is stored, any record can be located by first finding its sector address from the header record. In fact, the header record in this case would contain an index to the file.

PHYSICAL AND LOGICAL LINKS

We have just seen that a large file may need to be split into several portions, stored in different places on the disk, and linked together by the use of sector addresses. This linkage is rather like that which we described in Chapter 4, where the links or pointers between records enabled us to save filing space, and also to keep the order of our file up to date. But we actually have two very different uses of links here, and it is well to be absolutely clear about what they are.

We begin with the 'real' data in our file (names, addresses and so on). This is the data that we need to be able to retrieve from the computer when required: everything else that we do is intended to make it easy to retrieve this data.

We saw in Chapter 4 that links can be added in order to organise our data (to save space, or to keep indexes, or to arrange it into alphabetical order). These links can be stored together with the data, but in computer storage of these links, only the computer needs to know about them – the user, asking for details of a name and address, does not even have to know that they exist. They are links invented by the computer programmer, and used by the programs in order to meet the principal objective of making it easy to retrieve the 'real' data.

But now we have a file consisting of some 'real' data and some 'hidden' links. Although the links are hidden to the user, they are not imaginary – they take up storage space, and on the disk they will look identical to real data. When the data comes to be stored on disk, all the data, links included, are treated in the same way. So, when the part of the computer running the disk – the **disk controller** – finds it necessary to split up portions of a file, it is not concerned that the data that are being divided in this way include some pointers. When the disk controller splits a file, the links which it inserts to keep track of what goes where are different from those we've seen before. This time, the links are even hidden from the computer programmer, who need not worry about how his file is split up.

The links used by the disk controller are sometimes called **physical pointers** or **physical links**. They are addresses of sectors on the disk and depend on the particular disk drive in use. Neither the user of the program (who wants only real data) nor the computer programmer knows about these links.

The links used by the computer programmer are sometimes called **logical pointers** and refer to positions within the file. They are reference numbers of records, or key values linking to another file. They are hidden from the user, but not from the programmer.

Serial and direct access

Although the two methods of accessing records on secondary storage devices come about because of the physical nature of the devices themselves, they have an important effect on the way we process data with computers. It is generally true that magnetic tape is cheaper than magnetic disks, so for a file where the records occur in one natural sequence and where *all processing of these records* will be in that sequence, magnetic tape storage is perfectly adequate. This is known as **serial** or **sequential access**: records are accessed one after another in strict sequence.

○ EXERCISE to tackle before reading on
○ 3 What sort of files will be suitable for serial access?

Any computer application where something has to be done to every one of a series of records (such as printing a label, or updating the running total) is a suitable application for serial access files. Master payroll files, stock files, customer files are all good examples, and the sort of information held as data in these files is discussed in Chapter 10.

An interesting example of a serial file is one holding the text of a computer program before it is translated (see Chapter 7). As translation is accomplished by dealing with each statement in turn, the file holding such a program could well be organised for serial access.

However, as we have seen, not all applications can afford to wait for the time it would take to reach the required record in reading through a serial access file. This would be rather like forcing yourself to start at the beginning of the telephone directory and reading every entry in order, even where you know that it is the entry for 'Williams' that you are seeking.

It is in cases such as these that **direct access**, as used on disks, becomes important. Provided that we know *where* on the disk a record is held (and it is the job of the various pieces of computer software to keep this information for us), it can be retrieved after a very short waiting time – the time taken to move the reading head over the correct track, if it is not already over the correct one, *plus* the waiting time until the correct sector rotates under the head. Although in computer terms this time is enormously long, compared with access times in main store, it is very much faster than the equivalent time on a tape.

The terms 'serial access' and 'direct access', while principally applying to secondary storage, can also be used to describe other features of a computer. Thus, main store is a direct access component, because any one of the store locations can be accessed directly, without having to read the data in any other location at all. Paper tape, on the other hand, is a serial access method of data input.

The ability of a direct access device to go to any record, chosen at random, without having to take records in a serial order, results in the term **random access** being used, equivalent to direct access. Do not be confused: there is nothing random or unpredictable about the method, for which reason the name 'direct access' is far preferable.

SORTING RECORDS We saw in Chapter 4 that a system of links could be used to keep a file in several different orders at once. These links are logical links, and they will have no effect on how the file is actually stored on backing storage. If the medium in use is magnetic tape, then these logical links are not particularly helpful to us. In the serial processing of data, it is important to get the file into the order required before you start any processing. It is for this reason that computer sorting is so important, and many books have been devoted to this topic alone. We shall see computer sorting in use in Chapter 10.

If a serial access file is required for use with two different programs, and is required in a different order for each one, then two copies will probably be made, one in each order. The original file will be copied, and the copy sorted, or a method of sorting will be used to prepare a tape in one order from the original directly. As soon as two copies of the data exist, we have problems! If the data changes (if someone moves house, for example) then it will not be possible to alter both copies at the same time. For a period of time, no matter how short, there will be two different copies of what is supposed to be the same data. In that period of time, a computer program may use one value and produce different results from a program working with the new updated value.

For this reason, files of data that are likely to be required in different orders are most often held on disk. In Chapter 11, we discuss so-called 'databases', where the links described in this chapter are used to help avoid this problem of duplication of data.

Summary

In this chapter, we have seen that a computer usually requires some storage outside of main storage, either because of cost or because the data to be held is too large to fit into main store. Although all processing of data is carried out in main store, *secondary* or *backing storage* is necessary. There are many *media* available: those used principally are *magnetic disks* (including *floppy disks*) and *magnetic tapes* (including *cassettes*). *Magnetic drums*, *magnetic cards*, *punched cards* and *punched paper tape* are also available. Each medium needs a *peripheral unit* to *read* and to *write* data.

Tapes and disks have very different characteristics. Tape allows only *serial* or *sequential access* to files stored on it, and while this is adequate for some data files, it would be prohibitively slow for other applications: for these, *direct* or *random access* methods are required, and are provided by disk storage.

Tape is divided into *blocks*, between which there are *inter-block gaps* to allow the tape to adjust to the correct *reading speed*: markers are used to identify *ends-of-fields*, *ends-of-records* and *ends-of-files*. Disks are divided into *sectors* which can be accessed individually by the *disk controller*: this uses *physical links* or *physical pointers* to connect together the parts of any file it has to split.

EXERCISE for individual work

4 A microcomputer uses magnetic cassettes as backing store. Cassettes with tape of various lengths are available – in particular, it is possible to buy tapes which run for 12 minutes, and others, which are relatively cheaper, for 60 minutes. In using these tapes to store files, what are the advantages and disadvantages of the long and short tapes?

EXERCISE for individual work

5 Explain the differences between direct and serial access to computer files, and why some media are more suited to one or other of these types of access.

EXERCISE for individual work

6 Many decisions on computing are a trade-off between time and space available. What are the advantages and disadvantages of fixed and variable length records with regard to time and space?

EXERCISE for individual work

7 Figure 5.7 shows three files to be stored on a disk. Copy and complete the table to show where you would put these files. Use a sector address of `0:0:0` to mark the end of a file, which doesn't therefore need to be linked to another sector.

Files to be stored

FILEA – 2 sectors
FILEB – 4 sectors
FILEC – 6 sectors

Vacant sectors

4:12:5	2:11:5
4:12:6	2:11:6
4:12:7	2:8:4
3:9:8	2:8:5
3:8:5	2:4:1
3:7:1	2:4:3
3:7:2	2:4:7

Disk storage table

FILEA: SECTOR	1	LINK:	
START:	2	LINK:	
FILEB: SECTOR	1	LINK:	
START:	2	LINK:	
	3	LINK:	
	4	LINK:	
FILEC: SECTOR	1	LINK:	
START:	2	LINK:	
	3	LINK:	
	4	LINK:	
	5	LINK:	
	6	LINK:	

Figure 5.7 *Disk storage*

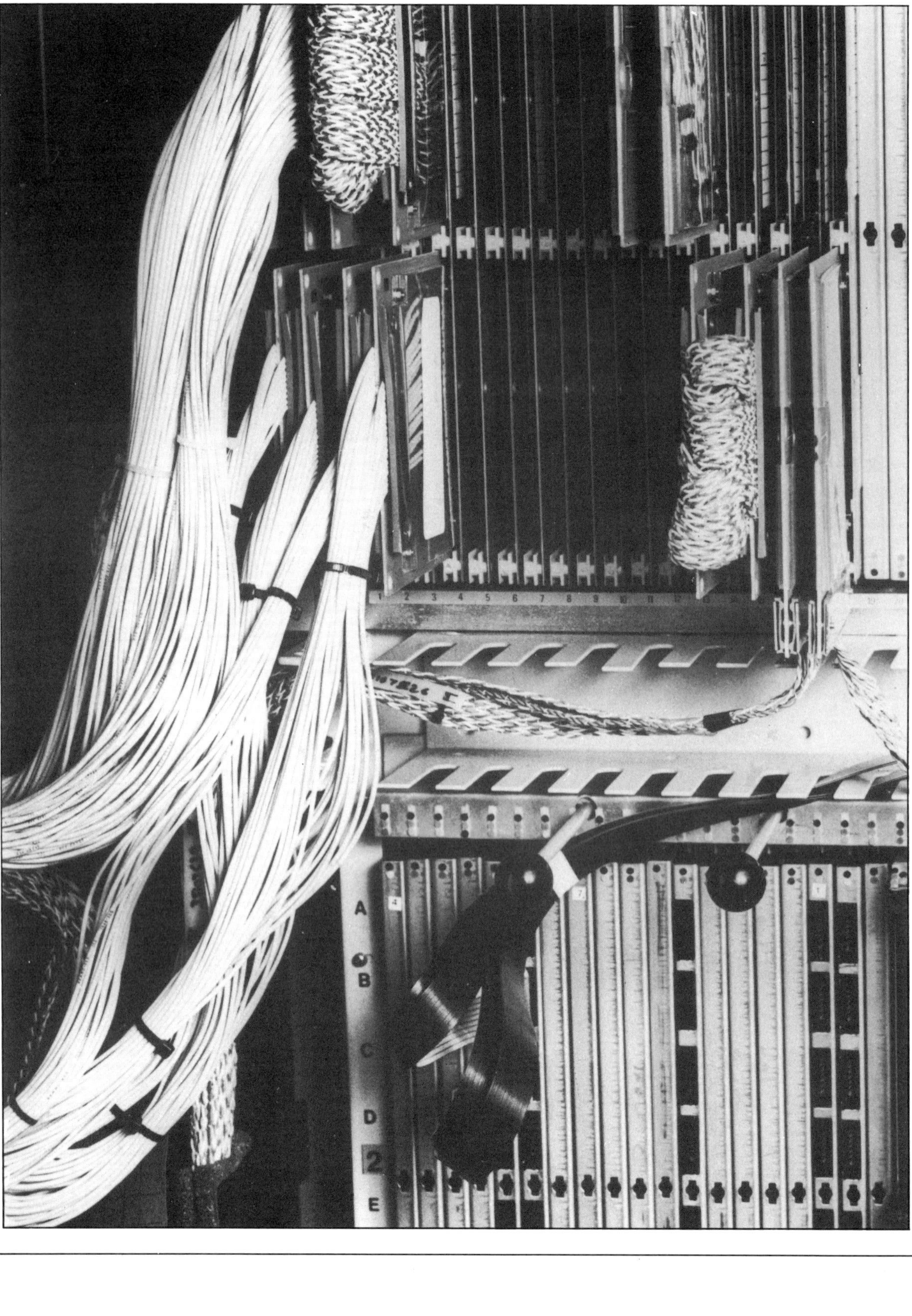
A
B
C
D
E

6 The machinery of a computer
HARDWARE

In this chapter and the next, we are going to look at how a computer is put to work: that is, how many of the computer operations we have already discussed are made to happen.

The operation of a computer depends on two separate, but complementary, parts of the system. First, there are the electronic circuits, the mechanical devices and other pieces of equipment. Together, these are called the **hardware**. The hardware of a computer system is what you can see and touch.

By itself, hardware is of no use – it requires the other vital part of the system: instructions to make it work. The instructions (computer programs, that is) are known as the **software**, and this is discussed in Chapter 7. This chapter is about hardware.

The CPU and peripherals

If you were to examine a computer system – a very large one, or a small microcomputer – you would soon spot that each piece of hardware falls into one of five groups:

input devices: things like keyboards, card readers and so on;

output devices: line printers, card punches, paper tape punches and so on;

secondary storage: magnetic disks, drums, tapes and so on;

supporting devices: power supplies, air-conditioning and so on;

a central processing unit.

The last of these, the **central processing unit**, or **CPU**, is the heart of the computer system. It is there that instructions are executed, that tests are made and decisions taken, and the whole system coordinated. And it is inside the CPU that we shall begin our tour of a computer.

The remaining devices are also of great interest. We shall not be interested in power supplies, air-conditioning or other supporting devices, but the others – the input and output devices and the secondary storage – are usually called **peripherals**, because they are attached to the outside, or the periphery, of the system.

Operation of the CPU

Different manufacturers describe their computers in different ways, but all computers have CPUs and inside all CPUs you will find the following, even though the names may be different.

Control unit It is the control unit which is responsible for the execution of program instructions, in charge of retrieving the next instruction from store, recognising the instruction code, and setting the circuits of the computer to enable that instruction to be carried out. Most instructions involve a piece of data, and the control unit ensures that the correct data has also been retrieved from store, and is available when it is required.

Arithmetic unit While many computer instructions simply involve moving data around, or examining it and testing it, an important class of instructions are those that carry out arithmetical operations – adding two numbers, dividing them and so on. These operations are carried out by the arithmetic unit, under orders from the control unit.

Main store It is here that a program, and the data it needs, are stored while the program is being executed. Instructions are taken from main store, and the control unit inspects them to decide what is to be done. If the instruction needs data, as most instructions do, the data is fetched in turn from the store. Some instructions write data into the store.

Special registers These are a number of store locations, like those in main store, that are used by the control unit and the arithmetic unit. Some registers are used to hold data temporarily, while the control unit decides what is to be done with it. Others are used to hold the results of an arithmetic calculation, until another instruction indicates whether the result is to be stored, or have a further operation carried out on it. One very special register keeps a track of which instruction is to be executed *next*, so that the control unit doesn't lose its place!

THE CONTROL UNIT AND THE FETCH CYCLE

There is a rhythm to the operation of a computer. First, the control unit fetches an instruction from store and decodes the instruction, so that it knows what it has to do and prepares itself for the actual execution of the instruction. This is called the **fetch cycle**. Then, the instruction is executed. Exactly what happens will depend on the nature of the instruction: the **execute cycle**, as it is known, will be different for each different instruction. Some execute cycles will involve the arithmetic unit, some will only put things into store. But for every instruction, the fetch cycle is exactly the same. And this rhythm continues all the while that the computer is working: fetch–execute, fetch–execute, fetch–execute, ... Let us watch a fetch cycle on a typical computer. A great deal happens in a short period of time. To understand it, you need to have a 'map' of the computer, and you can see this in Figure 6.1.

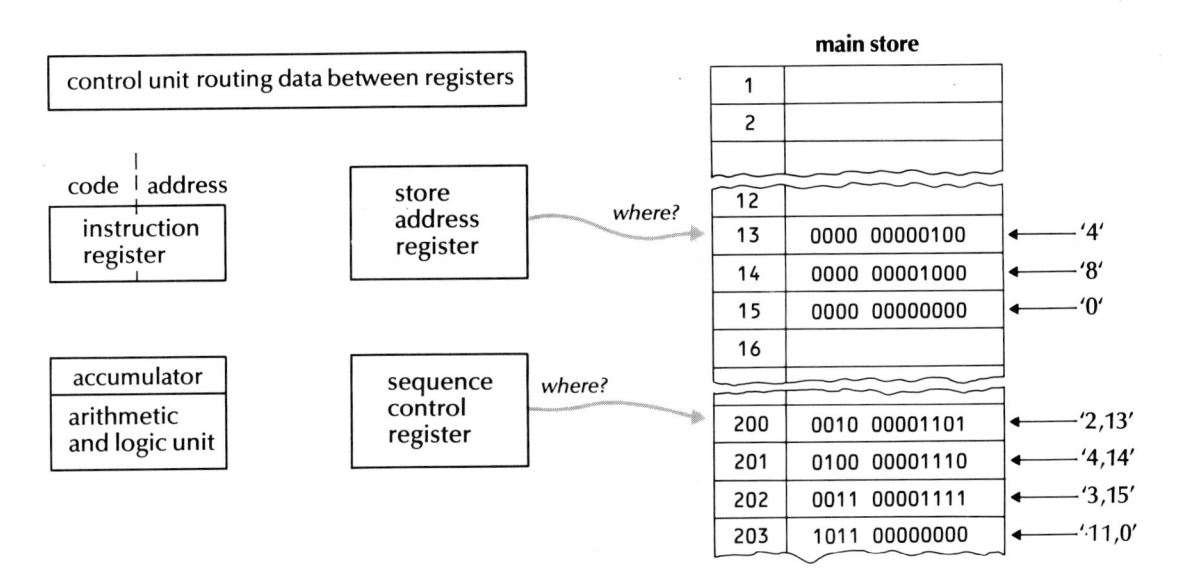

Figure 6.1 *Special registers in the CPU: the short program in locations 200–203 manipulates the data stored in locations 13–15. Just by looking, we cannot tell which is data and which is program, as both are stored as binary patterns.*

74 Hardware

The instruction that we are about to fetch is the one that is stored at present in store location 200 in main store. It is stored in binary, and is simply the twelve bits 001000001101. This could mean anything at all! We need to know that in the computer we are considering, instructions are split up as follows:

```
┌──────┬──────────┐
│ 0010 │ 00001101 │
└──────┴──────────┘
```

instruction   address
code $00001101_2 = 13_{10}$
$0010_2 = 2_{10}$

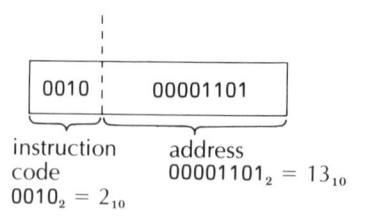

Figure 6.2 *The format of instruction 200*

so that this instruction is the one with instruction code 0010, referring to address 00001101. In denary notation, this is instruction code 2, and this refers to address 13.

Instruction	Description	Operation code Denary	Binary
OUTPUT	Copy a value from store to output	0	0000
INPUT	Read a value from input, and place it in store	1	0001
LOAD	Copy the contents of store into the accumulator	2	0010
STORE	Copy the contents of the accumulator into store	3	0011
ADD	Add the contents of store to the contents of the accumulator	4	0100
SUBTRACT	Take the contents of store from the contents of the accumulator	5	0101
MULTIPLY	Multiply the contents of the accumulator by the contents of store	6	0110
DIVIDE	Divide the contents of the accumulator by the contents of store	7	0111
GOTO	Continue with the next instruction from the given store	8	0000
BRANCHZ	If the contents of the accumulator are zero, treat this as a GOTO, otherwise do nothing	9	1001
BRANCHN	If the contents of the accumulator are negative treat this as a GOTO, otherwise do nothing	10	1010
STOP	Stop processing	11	1011

Figure 6.3 *Operation codes for some machine-code instructions*

We also need to know what instruction code 2 stands for. Of course, this varies from computer to computer. In our computer, there are 12 possible instruction codes, shown in Figure 6.3. Code 2 is the code for a LOAD instruction. That is, some data is to be taken from store, from the location specified by the address part of the instruction, location 13, and is to be loaded into one of the special registers called the **accumulator**. The fetch cycle is *not* going to do the loading, it is simply going to get everything ready for the loading to be done. As we watch the fetch cycle at work, we shall see what most of the special registers are for.

First, the control unit looks at the register called the **sequence control register** (or **SCR**: other names for this include *program counter, instruction address* *register* and *next instruction register*). The SCR keeps a record of the address in main store from which the next instruction is to be taken. In this case, it holds 200, telling us that the next instruction is the one in location 200. We shall see later how the 200 got into the SCR.

Next, the control unit takes the instruction from location 200, and puts it temporarily into another register, called the **instruction register**. As it does so, it splits the instruction up into its two main parts – the address and instruction code – so that each may be looked at separately.

At this stage, the fetching is done, but there are two other jobs to be done in the fetch cycle. The execute cycle, which follows next, will do something to store location 13 (*we* know that it will take something out, but another instruction *could* put something in). So the control unit makes the main store ready for an operation involving location 13, and it does this by putting 13 – the address part of the instruction register – into the **store address register** or **SAR**. After this, when the execute cycle refers to the main store, it will automatically refer to location 13.

And finally, the fetch cycle attends to the SCR. This still holds 200, the address of the instruction that we have just fetched. Unless it is changed, the next instruction to be fetched will be the same one again. So the control unit changes 200 to 201, which it expects to be the next instruction required. Later on, we shall see how this sequence from one instruction to the next can be varied. The fetch cycle simply assumes that it will be the instruction after the current one.

When all these steps have been carried out, the fetch cycle is complete, and the control unit switches into the execute cycle.

THE CONTROL UNIT AND THE EXECUTE CYCLE

Each execute cycle is different. Our computer has 12 instruction codes, so there will be 12 execute cycles, stored in the control unit. Our particular instruction has code 2. The execute cycle for code 2 tells the computer to take data from store (it will come from location 13 automatically, because of what we did in the fetch cycle) and put it into the accumulator. It is likely that the next instruction will do something further with this value, but we cannot know this without inspecting the program, and the control unit certainly doesn't know, because it hasn't yet fetched the instruction in location 201.

EXERCISE to tackle before reading on

1 Act out the job of the control unit in executing the program shown in main store, starting at location 200. Continue until you meet a STOP instruction.

In doing the exercise, you will have found that the computer has added 8 to 4, getting 12, and has put the answer back into store location 15. More accurately, the program has added whatever data was in location 14 to that in location 13 and put the result in location 15. If the data in locations 13 and 14 were different, the solution would be different also.

INSTRUCTIONS WHICH DO NOT AFFECT STORE

The last instruction in the program, STOP, was rather special. Obviously, it caused the computer to stop executing the program. It did this by holding the computer back from the next fetch cycle. If it had been allowed to continue, the next instruction to be fetched would have been some rubbish that happened to be in store location 204.

But the fetch cycle has set up two registers that weren't used. The SCR has been altered to 204, even though no instruction will ever be retrieved from location 204. And the store address register has been set to 0, because the fetch cycle treated 00000000 as an address, and prepared the store for an operation referring to location 0. This little bit of extra work doesn't matter. We·shan't fetch any instruction from location 204, and we won't refer to location 0.

There are other instructions that do not affect store, even though they set up the store address register just as if they were going to. One important one is the GOTO instruction with code 8.

EXERCISE to tackle before reading on

2 Write down the values that the control unit will have placed in the store address register and the SCR after fetching the instruction 8 200 from location 77.

You should have found that 200 has been placed in the store address register and 78 in the SCR. The execute cycle of instruction 8 is going to treat both these values in an unusual way, however. A GOTO instruction means that we want the next instruction to come out of sequence: *not* from location 78, as we might expect, and as the fetch cycle has prepared us for, but from location 200.

The execute cycle of a GOTO instruction then, takes the address part of the instruction (200) and puts it into the SCR, overwriting the value already there (78). The execute cycle can take its value (200) either from the instruction register, or from the store address register; it doesn't really matter which.

The GOTO instruction thus changes the SCR. In future, unless another GOTO instruction is met, instructions will come from locations 200, 201, 202 and so on in order. Although the main store was made ready for a reference to location 200, the reference never came, and the address part of the instruction was used for the new SCR value instead.

There are other sorts of GOTO instruction. Code 9, for instance, is that for a BRANCH IF ZERO instruction. If the accumulator has a zero in it, it acts just like a GOTO, resetting the SCR. If the accumulator isn't zero, it does nothing at all. It is a valuable instruction, because it can be used to end a loop. If you want to do something ten times, you keep a count, set initially at 10, and each time around the loop you subtract 1 from the count. To test if you have finished or not, you load the accumulator with your count and make use of BRANCH IF ZERO to send you off to a STOP instruction if you are done, and if not to carry on with the program.

EXERCISE for individual work

3 Write out a machine-code program to add up ten numbers. Store your program in location 50 onwards. Use instruction code 1 to get the numbers. You will need a `COUNT` as described above, and also a `TOTAL`.

Communication between the CPU and peripherals

Figure 6.3 showed the 12 instructions available on our computer. A real computer would have had many more than these 12. But even with these 12, a great deal of realistic computing could have been done. But one area where our computer instructions are very deficient is in the area of transferring data between the CPU and the peripherals we mentioned before. And to continue our tour of the computer's hardware, it is these peripherals that we must look at next.

Our table of instructions in Figure 6.3 was too simple for a real computer, because we have ignored the problems caused by having more than one device to take input from or send output to, and also because we cannot just send data to a peripheral device without understanding something about how it works.

Let us consider the computer system shown in Figure 6.4; as you can see, it has three output devices, a printer, a VDU and a magnetic tape unit. When we want to send some output, it will be necessary to let the system know which of these three we wish to send it to.

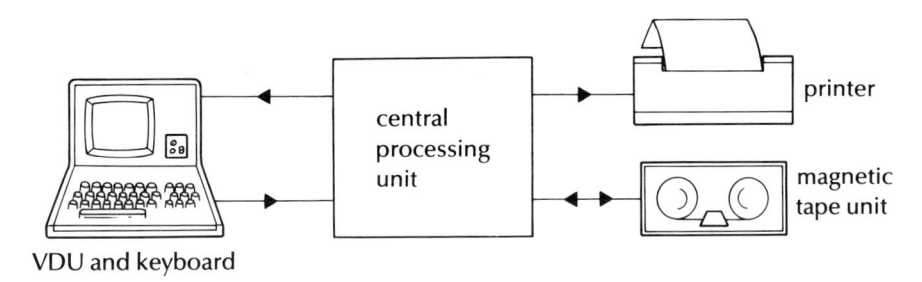

Figure 6.4 *A typical small computer system*

Suppose we want the word `COMPUTER` to be printed on the printer. The printer is rather like a typewriter, but without a keyboard, and it is connected to the computer by a large number of wires — usually these wires are made up into a flat strip, and you can see similar strips connecting many parts of the computer together. Some of these wires will be used to send the pattern of bits corresponding to the letters C-O-M-P-U-T-E-R one after the other. If our computer is using an 8-bit code for characters, then there will be eight wires for the data, one for each bit.

What do the other wires do? Firstly, there's the problem that the eight data-wires will *always* have some data on them, even if it's eight zero bits. The printer will need to know when the data on the data-wires is real data intended for printing, and when it's just 'noise'. So one wire will have a signal that means 'it's OK to print this'.

Next we have to realise that a printer works very slowly indeed compared to the CPU. If the CPU simply sent the characters COMPUTER off to the printer as fast as it could, the R would have arrived before the printer had even begun to print the C. So some of the other wires are used to control this. When the printer has begun to print the C, it will put an 'engaged' or 'busy' signal on one of the other wires and the CPU will continually test to see if the printer has finished printing C yet. When it has, when the 'busy' signal has gone, it will be time to send the O. And in turn, the remaining letters. The other wires all have to do with timing and control in similar ways. The C, for example, must be left on the data wires for long enough for the printer to respond and begin typing it, so it may not be removed too soon.

OTHER ASPECTS OF USING PERIPHERALS

The printer we described printed out words one character at a time. Not all devices do this. A **line printer** collects characters until it has a complete line of them, and then prints the whole line in one go. So the CPU can send a full line of characters very fast indeed but must then wait until that line is printed before sending any more.

The peripherals used in a computer system are not always purchased from the same manufacturer as that of the CPU. Different manufacturers use different codes for characters. So it may be necessary to translate from the code for C used by the manufacturer of the CPU into that used by the manufacturer of the printer.

Input peripherals cause different problems again: if someone is typing COMPUTER at a keyboard, the characters can only be read while the key is actually depressed. There is plenty of time for this, as the human finger is so slow compared to the CPU, but even so, the keyboard must be looked at before too long, or else the data will be missed.

Parity checking

Any transfer of data is a risky business, because the data may get distorted on the way. This is especially a problem when the peripheral is a long way away from the CPU, and is perhaps communicating over telephone lines. (Think of how many times you get crackling, interference or crossed lines when making telephone calls!) One solution to the problem is to do some **parity checking**. An extra bit is added to the bits making up the data. This bit is set to '1' or to '0' depending on whether the number of '1' bits in the real data is odd or even. In this way, the character that is actually sent down the wires always has an even number of bits (called **even parity**) or always has an odd number of bits (**odd parity**). Characters that already have an even number of '1' bits (in even parity checking) are left unchanged with a '0' sent as the spare bit, while those that have an odd number of '1' bits have the spare bit set to '1' so that the total is even. (Of course, everything is reversed with odd parity.)

In this way, the peripheral can refuse any data-item that has the wrong sort of parity, sending a control signal back, asking the CPU to try sending it again. This will not catch all the mistakes, but it will allow the detection of some.

Echoing back

Another way of checking that the data received is the same as the data sent is to send the data back again! One place where this is often used is where the user is actually typing at a keyboard, with a printer attached. When the user types the letter C it does not automatically appear on the printer – he can't in fact see what he has typed. Instead, the CPU notes the arrival of a C and as well as recording it, sends a C back to the printer. If all is well, the C appears on the printer, and the user has hardly noticed the time-delay.

But suppose that the C is corrupted – into the code for D perhaps. Then the CPU will receive a D and send it back to the user's printer. There *is* a slim chance that the D on its way back is corrupted back into a C, but this is a *very* slim chance – it's more likely to be corrupted into something else. So if the user sees anything except a C he can be certain that there has been a failure somewhere, and may be able to do something about it. And if he sees a C, he can be almost certain that the CPU has received a C as well.

This **echoing back** is also sometimes used with magnetic tape units where the character just written is read back again, to see if it's the same. If not, the tape unit rewinds and tries again.

Interrupts

Often, particularly with large, powerful computer systems, it is convenient to let the peripherals work by themselves, and let the CPU get on with something else. So instead of the CPU having to keep checking the printer to see if it has finished printing and is no longer busy, one of the control wires linking printer and CPU will be an **interrupt** wire, and the CPU will send the character to the printer and then continue with other processing. When the printer is ready for the next character, it will place a signal on the interrupt wire, and the CPU will sense this, and stop whatever it was doing and deal with the printer.

The CPU detects the interrupt signal by looking at the interrupt wire during the fetch cycle. It looks for an interrupt before it alters the SCR, so that if it has to deal with an interrupt, when it next gets back to the execution of the program it was working on, the same instruction will be retrieved, and none are missed.

Interrupts are especially valuable in using *input* peripherals. Instead of having to waste time looking to see if the user has typed anything, the CPU does something else until it is interrupted by the keyboard to say that there is a character to be read.

Usually, all the interrupt wires come together, so that during each fetch cycle, the CPU checks only that there *is* an interrupt somewhere. It then has to look at each peripheral in turn, to see which is causing the interrupt. But this is very, very much faster than looking at each peripheral every time.

Power-fail interrupts

One very impressive demonstration of the speed of a computer is the use of interrupts to deal with power failures. If there is a sudden power-cut, many nasty things can happen to a computer. The disks may stop spinning, and the heads may crash onto the disk surface, causing much damage, costing thousands of pounds, and losing the data stored on the disks. As some computers can have literally hundreds of disk units, this is no small problem. Also, the main store will usually lose its data during a power-cut, as will registers like the SCR and the accumulator.

This problem is tackled by arranging for special power failure detection apparatus that causes an interrupt. The CPU detects the interrupt, finds that it comes from the power-fail detector, and has just enough time to whip the reading heads off the disks into a safe position clear of the surface, write the contents of the CPU registers into special storage and sit back and let the power-failure do its worst!

Types of peripheral

We have seen that understanding the hardware of a computer requires you to know a lot about how peripherals work – that a line printer needs a line of characters before it can print any of them, that a keyboard only passes signals to the CPU if the CPU is looking for them, and so on. We finish this chapter by describing briefly the commoner peripherals, how they work, what they are used for, and any special problems that they have. We do *not* give details of sizes, speeds and so on, because it is not necessary to know these. The principles behind peripheral devices will be with us for a long time, but new technology means that speeds and capacities will increase year by year.

KEYBOARDS

Figure 6.5 *Keyboard*

Most computer keyboards are laid out in the same arrangement of letters as on a typewriter. For this reason, they are sometimes called 'QWERTY' keyboards, after the first six letters on a typewriter. As each key is pressed, a coded signal corresponding to the character is sent out. Some problems are that the key may 'bounce' if it is struck strongly, and the same character may be sent twice. Keyboards are designed to eliminate this. There are usually more characters on a computer keyboard than on a typewriter, including some special control characters which do not have visible characters corresponding to them. Lower-case (small) letters are not always possible.

PRINTERS Serial printers are those that receive each character in turn and print it. Line printers collect a line of characters and print them all together. Serial printers use one printing head that moves across the paper, while line printers may require a head for each position across the page. Early printers used a typewriter-like head, with characters embossed in reverse, and made their mark by printing through an inked ribbon. As printing is slow and messy in this way (you have to move the ribbon as well as the head, for example), there have been many developments in this field. **Ink-jet printers** spray a finely-controlled jet of quick-drying ink on to the paper, actually drawing the letter on the page. **Dot-matrix printers** use an array of fine wires to make letters out of dots. Both these printers have the advantage that the actual set of characters allowed can be changed easily, possibly under the control of a user's program. The program to draw $ with an ink-jet can be amended to draw £, for instance.

Some printers require special high-grade (and expensive) paper. Indeed, some computer paper is of such high quality that it can be recycled to make paper again (ordinary grades of paper can only be used for making cardboard or packaging when recycled).

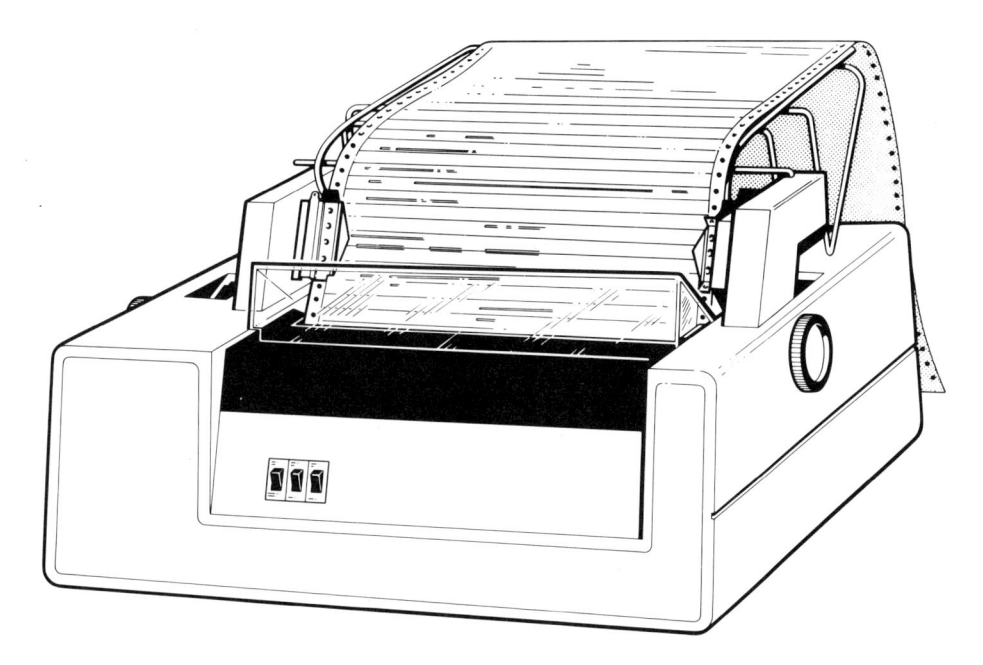

Figure 6.6 *Printer*

82 Hardware

Figure 6.7 *Graph plotter*

GRAPH PLOTTERS Although rough graphs and other pictures can be plotted by printing an * or an X on a VDU screen or using a printer, these results can be very crude, and there is often a need for specialised equipment.

There are many variations in the way that such **graph plotters** work. On a **flat-bed plotter**, a large sheet of paper lies under a moving pen. The pen (or possibly pens, allowing several colours to be used) moves across the paper reponding to signals from the computer. These same signals will indicate when a pen is to be raised or lowered, in which direction it is to move and when the drawing is complete. On a **drum plotter**, the pen can move only across the paper, and movements in the other direction are accomplished by moving the paper which is wrapped around a drum.

Some plotters (**x–y plotters**) treat the paper as if it is ruled into squares as with graph paper, and the signals from the computer take the form of 'go to the point with coordinates 253, 82'. Other plotters (**incremental plotters**) respond to commands of the form '3 steps East, 5 steps North'.

High-quality results are usually obtained when the graph plotter is working slowly, and in any case it works very much more slowly than the CPU of the computer that is driving it. For this reason, graph plotters are often used **off-line**: a magnetic tape of plotter instructions is recorded, and this tape drives the plotter without further reference to the computer.

PAPER TAPE READERS AND PUNCHES

Data is stored on **paper tape** as a series of round holes punched along a narrow tape. The holes corresponding to one character run across the tape. Usually a parity hole (see page 78) is added. Reading tape can be done by passing it under a set of probing needles which detect where there is paper and where there is a hole, or more rapidly by passing it between a light source and a row of photocells, one for each hole position. This is faster, as the tape can move continuously. With mechanical sensors, it may need to come to rest momentarily, and hence moves in a series of jerks. Paper tape is punched by a set of sharp needles with cutting edges.

Errors made in punching a tape cannot easily be corrected, and the usual code of holes for 'nothing' is to punch all the holes across the tape. Thus a character punched can be 'rubbed out' by altering the hole-code already punched to one with holes across the full width of the tape. A correct character cannot easily be inserted, however.

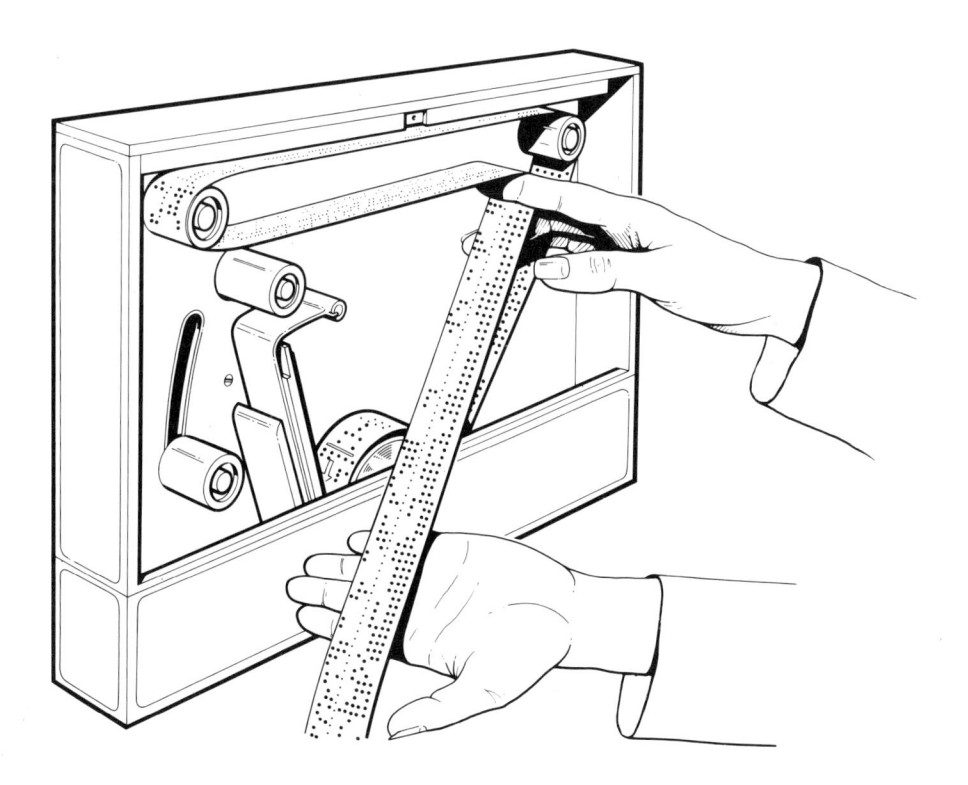

Figure 6.8 *Paper tape reader and punch*

CARD READERS AND PUNCHES

Punched cards are similar to paper tape, in that they must be punched mechanically, and are read either by photocells or by some mechanical sensing mechanism. It is not possible to correct a mis-punched character on a card, but it is a simple matter to repunch the whole card and throw away the faulty one. One disadvantage of cards as compared to paper tape is that the full width of the card must be read, even where there is a large number of blank columns. A tape uses a special character to mark the end of a line, and hence only characters actually present on a line need to be recorded on the tape.

It is frequently said that the punched card is 'dead', its days being over. It has few advantages, admittedly – using expensive card, needing expensive reading mechanisms – but nevertheless, each year more and more punch cards are sold!

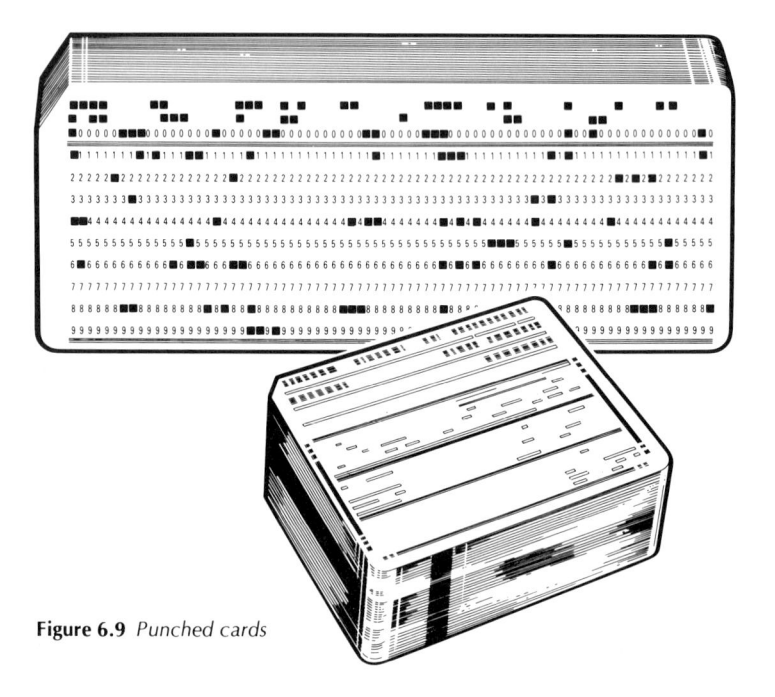

Figure 6.9 *Punched cards*

VISUAL DISPLAY UNITS

A **visual display unit** (**VDU**) has a screen somewhat similar to a television set, and works on a similar principle. Special software, which is often found in the VDU itself, generates a TV picture with the outlines of the characters at positions on the screen. Indeed, some computer systems do use an ordinary television set.

The simpler VDUs allow characters only at a limited number of positions over the screen. More sophisticated VDUs allow some sort of graphics. This can simply be the plotting of blocks of colour to make simple pictures (so-called **low-resolution graphics**) or it may be the plotting of individual points (**high-resolution graphics**) to form pictures. With very high-resolution graphics, it may be possible to draw characters – allowing the user to program the use of foreign alphabets (Russian or Chinese perhaps).

This capability should be compared with line printers or teleprinters, where the character set is fixed when the device is manufactured. A dot-matrix printer (see above) allows a degree of software control similar to that of the more sophisticated VDUs.

The price of these increased graphics capabilities is always speed and computer power – it uses more computer time, and takes longer to tell the VDU how to draw a Greek letter than it does to send a signal to the VDU telling it to plot an X on the screen, where the instructions for drawing the X are part of the TV-type circuitry of the VDU.

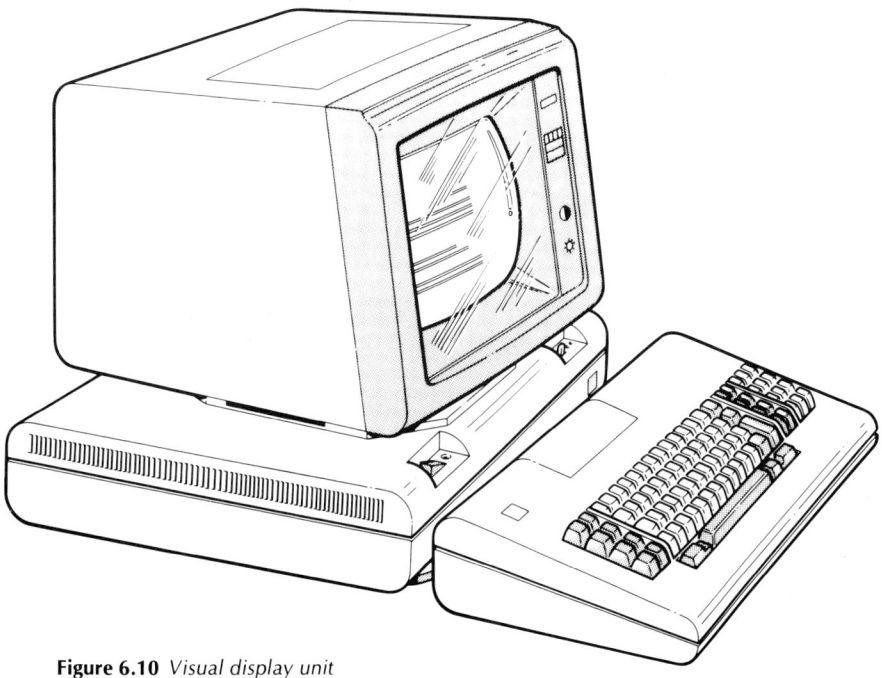

Figure 6.10 *Visual display unit*

Light pens

A **light pen** is used in conjunction with a VDU, and is basically just a single photocell at the end of a pen-like wand (replacing the nib, as it were). As such, it is rather simpler than the photocell readers necessary in an optical paper tape or punched-card reader. What gives the light pen its power is the software associated with it.

The user presses his light pen against the screen of the VDU and when he is sure that he has the position he wants, he presses a button on the pen, or presses on the pen tip, causing a switch to sense the pressure. This switch signals to the computer that the position of the pen on the screen must now be worked out. The computer first passes a horizontal band of light from the top of the screen to the bottom. Somewhere in its travel it will cross the photocell at the tip of the light pen and a signal will pass to the computer indicating that the photocell has 'seen' the band of light. The time delay between the computer starting the band and the detection of light by the photocell indicates to the computer how far down the screen the pen is placed.

Similarly, a vertical band passed from left to right enables the computer to detect how far across the screen the light pen is placed. In this way, the computer can determine the coordinates of the place at which the pen is pointing.

This information can be used in several ways. The user could be selecting from a **menu** of options on the screen – choosing what he wants the computer system to do next, for example; or he could be interacting with a graphics program which draws a line to the point chosen. Or again, he could be selecting an area of the screen that he wishes to have magnified for closer study.

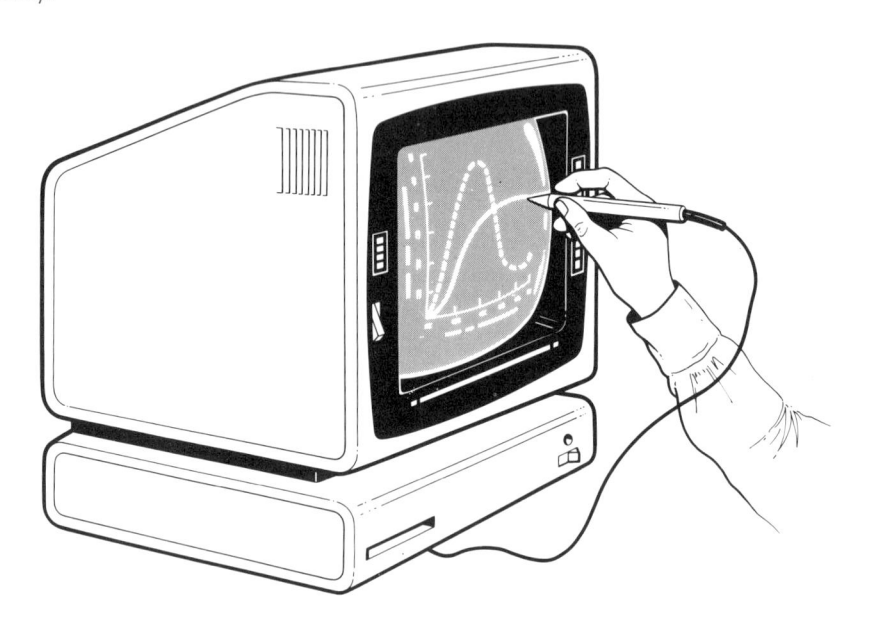

Touch-sensitive screens

Another way of using a VDU screen, as an input device rather than as an output device, is to embed fine wires in a grid pattern across the screen, so that when the user touches the screen with a finger, the presence of the finger can be detected electronically or by pressure. This is rather like the light pen, but coarser.

BAR-CODE READERS A device used often in public libraries and increasingly in supermarkets is an **optical bar-code reader.** The book, or the can of beans or whatever, is marked with a bar-code like that shown in Figure 6.12. This is read by a light pen, or sometimes a laser beam, and the resulting binary pattern passed to the computer, which thus knows the number of the book being borrowed, or the product being bought.

Figure 6.12 Bar-coding

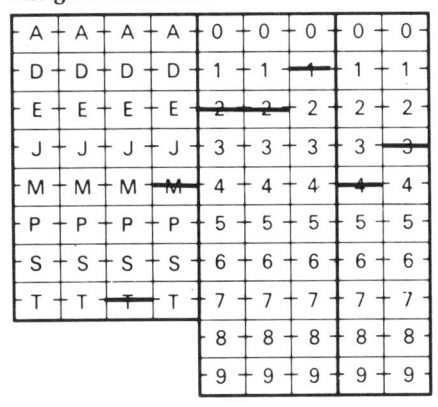

Figure 6.13
A section of a mark sense form: the assignment number, TM22143, has been coded in dark pencil. Everything except the pencil marks would be printed in 'drop-out' ink.

MARK SENSE READERS

Many of the devices we are listing here are attempts to avoid the necessity for complicated and expensive machinery when a user prepares data for input to a computer. One example is **mark sense** reading. The user – who might be a salesman taking orders from a customer, a meter-reader recording a reading, a student submitting answers to a test and so on – uses a specially-designed form like the one in Figure 6.13. Some information, to help the user know what his marks mean, is printed in a carefully chosen colour of ink that will be invisible to the automatic reader, which is deliberately designed to be 'colour-blind' to this colour of ink – called **drop-out ink**. The user makes marks using another colour, usually a dark pencil, and when the document is passed through the reader, which has an array of photo-cells, something like an optical punch-card reader, only the pencil marks are read. Down the margin, a series of reference marks are printed in solid black, called a **clock track** or **timing track** so that the computer knows which row of the document is being read at that instant.

MAGNETIC TAPE UNITS

Computer **magnetic tape** is essentially the same material as that used in an ordinary domestic tape- or cassette-recorder, although it can come in rather wider sizes. Data stored on tape can only be read by the computer, so magnetic tape devices are an example of secondary storage – a cheap but slow means of keeping data in a computer system. Programs (which are, after all, only another sort of data!) can also be stored on tape, particularly on cassettes used in microcomputer systems.

88 Hardware

In understanding the uses of magnetic tape, it is important to realise one very obvious fact – that tape comes wound on a reel, and to read or write something in the middle of the tape it is necessary to pass over all the tape before the required piece. This process of locating data, which is known as **serial** or **sequential access**, is acceptable provided that this is how the data is to be treated. Chapter 5 – on files in the computer – has already discussed this method of access to data, together with the method suited to our next device, magnetic disks.

Before leaving the subject of tape, however, it is worth mentioning that some shops use a cash register that can read short strips of magnetic tape which have been fixed to the goods being sold, in much the same way as light pens read the bar-codes mentioned above. Such methods of data collection are discussed further in Chapter 10.

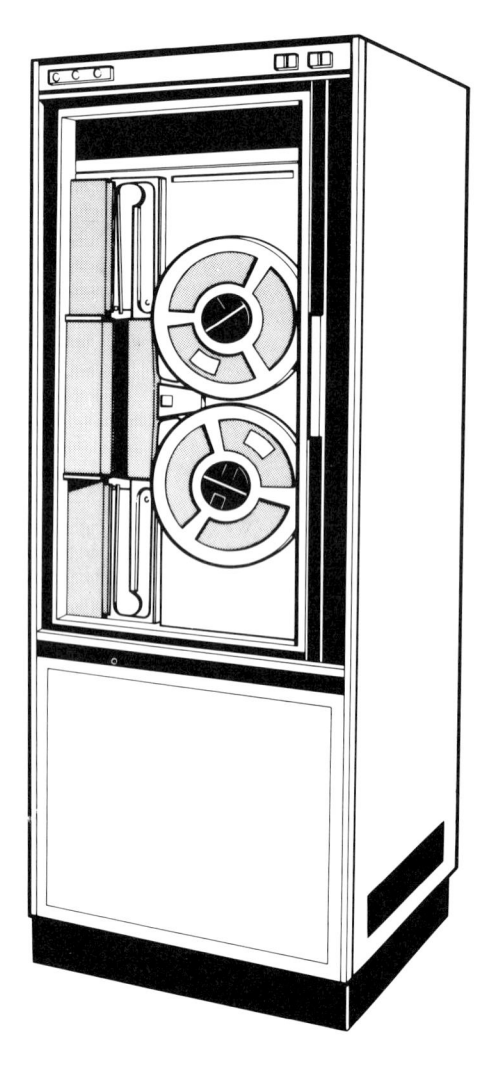

Figure 6.14 *Magnetic tape unit*

MAGNETIC DISK UNITS

Recording data on **magnetic disks** uses the same physical principles as recording on magnetic tape. But because the reading or writing head is free to move across the surface of the disk there is no need to access the data in any particular order. This is called **random** or **direct access** to the data – meaning that you can read directly any piece of data chosen at random, without having to read any other data first. Of course, there will be a waiting time – small by human standards, very long by computer ones! – while the head moves mechanically to the right place on the spinning disk, and while the disk spins for the correct piece of data to appear under the head.

It is usual to mount a number of disks on a common spindle to form a **disk pack**, and to have a stack of reading/writing heads, one for each disk surface. As was explained on page 64, each surface is divided into tracks, and each track into sectors. A sector forms the smallest part of the disk which may be accessed directly, and thus it is largely the size of sectors which determines the **access time** taken to locate a particular piece of data.

Figure 6.15 *Magnetic disk pack and unit*

While most disks are rigid, many small computer systems use **floppy disks** which are small plastic disks, coated in the same way as the rigid disks. In use, the high rate of spinning effectively renders them rigid. They are, however, light and flexible enough to stand up to the rigours of being posted.

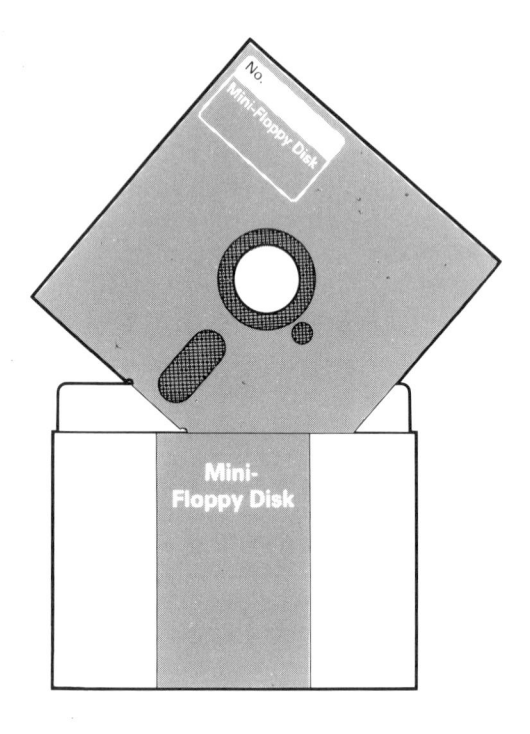

Figure 6.16 *Floppy disk*

Summary

In this chapter, we have looked at the *central processing unit (CPU)*, and at its constituent parts – *control unit*, *arithmetic unit*, *main store* and *special registers* (*accumulator, instruction register, store address register* and *sequence control register*). We have seen that the *fetch–execute cycle* is the basic organising force of the computer, and that the rhythm of this cycle drives all the activity in the computer.

We have looked also at some *peripheral devices*, and at the way in which *communication* between these and the CPU can be monitored by *parity checks* and *echoing back*, or can be *interrupted*. To understand how major uses of the computer are possible, it is necessary now to look at the other part of a computer system – the software. We do this in Chapter 7.

EXERCISE for individual work

4 Using the machine-code instructions given in Figure 6.3, write short programs to carry out each of the following tasks:

   a read a number N and use that number to control a loop that adds together 1 + 2 + 3 + ... + N;

   b if the number stored in location 100 is 50, then branch to location 200; if not, to location 300.

EXERCISE for individual work

5 Our main store in Figure 6.1 was arranged into storage locations each capable of holding one word, or one instruction. Some computers use smaller amounts of storage, called *bytes*. An instruction might then occupy *two* bytes, one for the operation code and one for the address, or only a single byte for an instruction such as STOP which does not have an address part. How will this affect the fetch–execute cycle?

EXERCISE practical

6 Investigate a computer system that you have access to, making a list of the pieces of hardware you find. For each one, describe the part it plays in the whole system, who uses it, and what job it does.

EXERCISE for discussion

7 What peripheral devices would you require if you were designing a computer system for a school? For a library? For a gas board?

You will find that these questions are deceptively simple. You will need to discuss which jobs the computer is required to, what data it has to store, what input and what output is likely.

This exercise, designing a system, is the subject of Chapter 8.

6 7 0 1 2 3 4 5 6 7 0 1 2 3 4 5
DATE
JOB
FILE NAME
REEL No.
GEN No.
COMMENTS
HOLD
TBL
00225
CONTROL DATA
TAPE
TOTAL SERVICE
400
800
1200
1600
2000
0 1 2 3 4 5 6 7 0 1 2 3 4 5 6 7

7 The machinery of a computer
SOFTWARE

It is no good having all the *hardware* of the computer, described in Chapter 6, or all the means of storing data described in Chapters 3 and 5, if we cannot do anything with the data.

The processing of data is carried out under the control of computer programs. In Chapter 8, you will learn how to *design* a computer program, and in Chapter 9, how actually to *write* a program. This chapter is about how the programs fit into the computer, how the computer is made ready to accommodate them, and how various pieces of hardware, such as printers and disks, are made available to a program.

Applications software and systems software

The physical pieces that make up a computer system are called the **hardware**; the programs that make the system process data are called **software**. This profusion of names ending in *-ware* seems a little like an epidemic; some people refer to the operators and programmers who work a computer system, as the **liveware**, and **firmware** is term used for software that is permanently built into main storage. Remember that one of the key features of a computer system is that programs can be changed – the computer is *reprogrammable*. So the parts of a computer that aren't changed (the physical parts) are called hardware; the parts that are changed, like programs, are called software; and firmware is something between – programs that aren't changed!

There are two types of software, even in the simplest of computer systems. First, and most obvious, there are the programs that the user has written (these are the sort of programs that are discussed in Chapters 8 and 9). These are programs to process data, and they include programs like payrolls, stock control programs, games, mathematical programs – in fact almost anything at all. They are generally known as **applications programs**, because they are programs designed for one particular application of the computer. If we need to be very specific, the type of programmer who writes an applications program is known as an **applications programmer**.

It might seem as if every computer program fell into this category, but there is an often-forgotten group of programs that are known as **systems programs**. These are the programs that the system needs to have in order that it can actually run. Rather than try to give you a formal definition of what systems programs are, we shall describe in this chapter those programs that you might find as part of **systems software** (written by **systems programmers**).

An empty computer – the initial program loader

If you bought a computer, it would probably arrive from the manufacturer absolutely empty. Because the way we have of sorting data in a computer means that every pattern of bits means something, the computer cannot really be empty, but what is in it will be perhaps a lot of zero bits, all the way through the store: or worse, random 0's and 1's meaning nothing at all to the user. Let us suppose that we have written out on paper a simple program using the machine code.

Why machine code? Well, we know that the computer has no programs in it, so there certainly won't be a program to translate a program written in a high-level language like BASIC or FORTRAN (exactly what 'high-level' means will be described later in this chapter).

We know that our program would do something useful if we could store it in the computer, and the first problem is how to get it in. One way that can be used only works when your computer has a front panel like the one shown in Figure 7.1.

An empty computer – the initial program loader 95

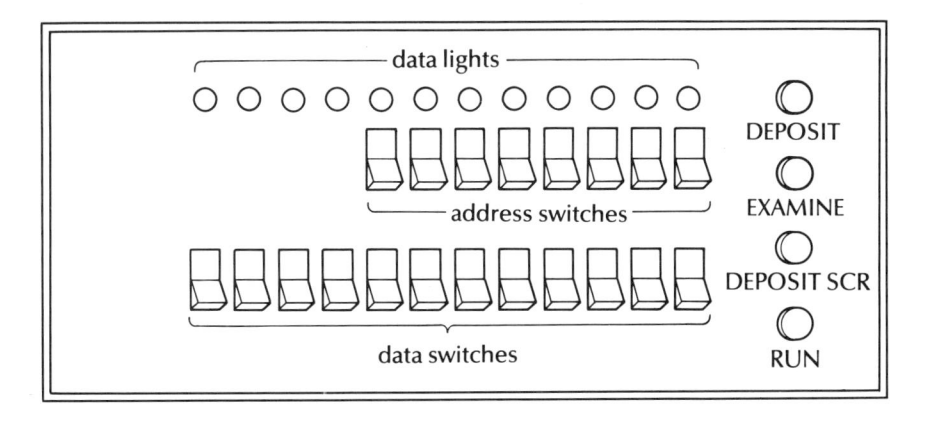

Figure 7.1 *The front panel of a small computer: the switches are all shown in the UP or '0' position; a switch DOWN would represent a '1'. The data lights would represent '0' if OFF and '1' if ON.*

You will see that there are several rows of switches, some buttons and some lights. The switches are divided into two groups, labelled *address* and *data*. Using the address group, and setting the switches to 0 and 1, we can set up the binary pattern corresponding to the address of one of the store locations in main store. At the same time, we set up the binary pattern corresponding to the data we want stored in that location, and when we are certain that both patterns are correct, we press the DEPOSIT button, and the data-pattern is loaded into the correct store location automatically. This process has loaded one piece of data (which at this stage is probably an instruction) into one store location. To load a complete program, we have to alter the address switches to the next address, change the data-pattern and press DEPOSIT again – and so on through the whole program.

This can be a very boring (and error-prone) process. Only a short program is ever loaded this way in practice!

Having loaded a whole program this way, it is wise to check it! Another button helps us in this. Whenever EXAMINE is pressed, the lights show (in binary) the pattern that is held in the location whose address is set up on the address switches at that moment. To inspect the whole program, we need to set the address switches to the first location loaded, and then press EXAMINE. Change the address switches, press EXAMINE again – and so on, through the program. The data switches are ignored when we press EXAMINE, whatever is on them.

Sometimes this is made easier, as the EXAMINE button, as well as displaying the contents of store, steps on to the next store location, as if we'd changed the address switches. To examine a 30-step program, we set up the first address, and press EXAMINE thirty times, watching the changing pattern of lights as we do it. It's still a boring process!

With our program in the computer, we still have to make it run. You know from Chapter 5 that this means setting the **sequence control register** (or **SCR**) to the correct starting address, and starting the computer running. This uses the other two buttons. DEPOSIT SCR puts the pattern on the address switches into the SCR, and RUN finally makes the computer begin its first fetch cycle (see page 73), which amounts to getting the instruction at the start of the program and executing it, and then moving on through the program.

This is a very tedious method of putting programs into the computer, and has the disadvantage that you have to work out your program in binary machine code first. Whenever this method was used, the first program, painfully loaded in this way, would be a very simple one, like the one in Figure 7.2. The next exercise shows you what the program in Figure 7.2 actually does.

EXERCISE to tackle before reading on

1 Imagine you are the computer, and the simple three-instruction program shown in Figure 7.2 has been loaded into store locations 1, 2 and 3. There is a data-tape with the program, already loaded into the paper tape reader. Work through the steps of the program until you run out of data on the tape, filling in the contents of store as they are loaded.

Main store

1	INPUT 2
2	STOP
3	GOTO 1
49	
50	
51	
52	
53	
54	
55	

Data on tape

INPUT	50
LOAD	13
INPUT	51
ADD	14
INPUT	52
STORE	15
INPUT	53
STOP	0

Figure 7.2 *An initial program loader. The instructions are shown in written form for simplicity: in reality they would be stored in binary. The* STOP *instruction in location 2 will never be executed!*

You will have seen, by working through the steps one at a time, that the program in Figure 7.2 performs a very useful job, in a rather laborious manner. The data on the tape really consisted of two types of data, interleaved. The first, third, fifth, and every other odd-numbered data item was an INPUT instruction. It was read in from the tape into store location number 2, while the computer was executing the instruction in location number 1. The effect of this was to cause the computer to execute the instruction that it had just read in (and the third instruction simply caused the process to happen over and over again!).

So every odd-numbered instruction was executed as soon as it had been read in. What about the even-numbered ones? Well, they weren't treated as instructions – not yet! Each *odd* instruction had the effect of taking the *even* instruction immediately following it on the tape and putting it into store. In our example, the even instructions were loaded into store locations 50 onwards. After the data-tape was out of values, and the program had come to a halt, we could set the SCR to 50, and press RUN, and the program that we have loaded would be executed.

In a way, what is happening is that the odd-numbered instructions are acting like we did in setting the switches on the front panel, and the even-numbered ones are those corresponding to the instructions we are loading into store.

EXERCISE to tackle before reading on

2 Can you see a way in which the data-tape could be organised so that the execution of the program in locations 50 onwards begins, without human intervention?

Since each odd-numbered instruction on the tape is executed as soon as it is read in, the last instruction (which is *odd*) could be GOTO 50.

The simple three-instruction program performs the task of loading a program (on a data-tape, in the even-numbered places). It is a simple **initial program loader**. It can be used with an absolutely empty computer.

BOOTSTRAPPING Even with the initial program loader, putting a program into the computer is laborious. We have to prepare a data-tape which is about twice as long as the program we're trying to get in. We're still not being very efficient! One way of being better organised is to pay some attention to the program on the data-tape. In this section, we look in some detail at an improved loader program; if you wish to skip this section, you will still have a good idea of how a program is loaded into a computer.

EXERCISE to tackle before reading on

3 Suppose that the program that has been loaded is the one shown in Figure 7.3. It occupies locations 47–57, but the first three locations hold data instead of instructions, which begin at location 50. There would be no way of telling this, simply by looking at the locations, because we should see only binary patterns, which could be data or instructions. However, as we wrote the program, we are entitled to know this!
What will happen when this program is executed, starting at the instruction in location 50?

98 Software

	Main store	
47	000000000001	← '1'
48	INPUT 0	
49		← holds a value from the tape
50	INPUT 49	
51	LOAD 49	
52	ADD 48	
53	STORE 54	⎫
54	STOP	⎬ this loop is repeated
55	LOAD 54	⎪
56	ADD 47	⎪
57	GOTO 53	⎭
58		

Data on tape:

100
1st instruction
2nd instruction
3rd instruction

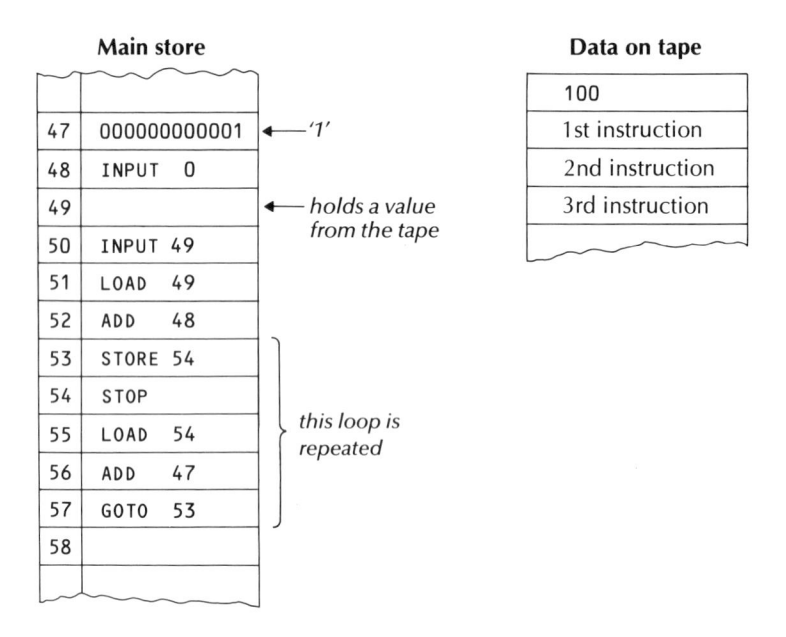

Figure 7.3 *A more sophisticated loader program: the program in main store begins with three locations holding data. When executing this program, we start at the* INPUT *instruction in location 50.*

Some very strange things happen when this program is executed, and we shall discuss them in rather more detail in a moment, but the overall effect of the program is to load another program (the one on tape, shown as '1st instruction', '2nd instruction' and so on) at a location specified by the first data item on the tape (100 in this case). The data-tape now need contain only the program and the start address for the loader.

How does the program work? It begins by reading in the first value from the tape (100) into store location 49, and having done this, it copies that same value, 100, into the accumulator (step 51). It now does something rather peculiar: it adds the contents of location 48 to the accumulator. This would not be strange, were it not for the fact that location 48 *appears* to contain an instruction – INPUT 0. The effect of this is to create a new instruction INPUT 100. To understand why it does this, look at Figure 7.4.

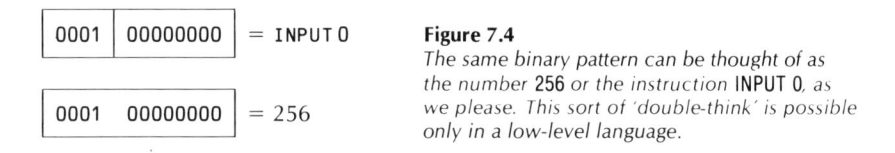

| 0001 | 00000000 | = INPUT 0 |
| 0001 | 00000000 | = 256 |

Figure 7.4
The same binary pattern can be thought of as the number **256** *or the instruction* **INPUT 0**, *as we please. This sort of 'double-think' is possible only in a low-level language.*

The binary pattern for INPUT 0 is shown: we carefully planned that it should be in location 48. But it is just a binary pattern – the way in which it is interpreted depends on how we use it. For the ADD instruction in location 52 we shall ignore the fact that it *could* be interpreted as an instruction, and just treat it as a number. Because the operation code for INPUT is 0001, it is the binary pattern for the number 256. Adding '100' to it simply makes it into the binary pattern for 356. Now the next stage is simply to store the result of this addition into location 54 (we put a STOP there to hold the place for us, but we shall overwrite the STOP when we store the '356' there). However, although we treated this pattern as a number in order to do arithmetic with it, we shall now treat it as an instruction again. It is, of course, the instruction INPUT 100 and so the effect of executing it is to read the first instruction from the data tape into location 100.

After our artificial instruction in step 54 has been executed, we need to alter the instruction, so that it refers to the next store, 101. We still have a copy of INPUT 100 in the accumulator, so we use the same trick again: forget that it is an instruction, treat it like a number, and add '1' to it (we had previously stored a '1' for just this purpose, in location 47. Now we loop back to instruction 53, where we store the new instruction INPUT 101 into location 54 and repeat the process.

This loader program is rather unfortunate, in that it never comes to a halt – it continues until the tape is out of instructions to be loaded. It would be a simple matter to make the loader program look out for a special signal on the tape, and stop when it is read. Or even, when the special signal is read, to set the SCR to 100 and begin executing the program loaded from tape.

EXERCISE for individual work

4 Describe how the program can be made to set the SCR, so that execution can begin – you will need to use the same sort of trick, but applied to a dummy GOTO 0 instruction.

EXERCISE practical

5 Write a loader program that will look out for the special signal 000000000000 on the tape, and use this as the instruction to start executing the loaded program from the start. You will need to use the BRANCHZ ('branch if zero') instruction.

This use of an initial program loader to load a program which is in turn a more sophisticated loader program is called **bootstrapping** (or sometimes **booting**). There is no reason to stop here, of course. The third program in this set, the one being read into locations 100 onwards, could well be an even *more* complicated loader program, perhaps reading something directly from disk storage.

The fanciful name comes from the idea of pulling yourself up by your bootstraps, and it's now become an accepted part of computer jargon. The basic idea is so useful that most computers have a simple initial program loader stored in firmware (page 94) and pressing the RUN button causes the loader to be executed. In this way, an 'empty' computer can be made ready to work at the press of a button.

TURNKEY SYSTEMS Although computers are reprogrammable, we may want unskilled people to use them with no knowledge of computer programming. The idea of bootstrapping can be carried even further, so that after the RUN button is pressed, one loader program after another is loaded until eventually a very powerful *applications* program (page 94) has been loaded. This means that the unskilled user can simply press RUN to make his applications program work. This is called a **turnkey** system, because it makes a program available just by 'turning a key'.

Programming language translators

Machine language programs are very difficult to write. It is easy to make mistakes, difficult to remember what it is you were doing yesterday when you last worked on the program, and not very helpful in explaining to other people what it is that you are doing. Very few programs are written in machine language.

Instead, a piece of systems software called a **translator** is used. To understand what a translator does, we need an example.

EXERCISE to tackle before reading on

6 Write a short machine-language program (using the machine-code of Figure 6.3 on page 74) that reads in two numbers and adds them together. You have done this sort of thing before, in Chapter 6, but this time pay particular attention to any *decisions* you make.

In solving the exercise, you did exactly what a translator program does. You took an 'easy' statement of what was required ('read in two numbers . . .') and turned it into machine code.

Translators don't understand English, as you do, so the rules for expressing what is required must be clearly specified. The complete set of rules governing what *you* are allowed to write, so that the translator can do its job, is the definition of a computer programming language.

The BASIC language for example, would let you express this program as:

```
100 INPUT X
110 INPUT Y
120 LET Z = X + Y
```

EXERCISE to tackle before reading on

7 Make a list of the jobs you had to do in translating the 'program' in Exercise 6.

There are more jobs than you might expect! The first statement is an `INPUT` statement – the translator 'knows' that this has to be turned into a `LOAD` instruction, but needs to know where to `LOAD` the data into. The programmer wants to call it X, and he doesn't need to know where X is stored, provided that the translator remembers, so that he can get at it again. So the translator has to check to see if X has been mentioned before (in which case we have already reserved a store location for it, and must take care to use the same location again), and if not, to find an 'empty' location and remember that that holds X. And it has to do the same job for Y. And the third BASIC instruction has to be turned into several machine-code instructions, to get the value of X, add it to the value of Y and store the answer somewhere else, called Z.

So any translator at all must handle problems of store allocation – which piece of data is to be stored where – and of conversion into instructions that the computer will recognise.

LOW-LEVEL AND HIGH-LEVEL LANGUAGES

The other jobs to be performed by a translator will depend to a large extent what they are translating *from*. The translation is always from a computer programming language of some sort, and it is usually a direct translation into machine code that will actually be executed on the computer we are using. Computer programming languages can be grouped very roughly into two types.

Low-level languages

Languages which are very close to machine code are called **low-level languages**, or **machine-orientated languages**. Usually it is possible to use words like `STOP`, `ADD`, `LOAD` and so on instead of the binary equivalents of these codes, and it is also possible to use names such as `COUNT`, `TIME`, `X`, `Y`, `Z` for locations where data will be stored. It is also common to be allowed to use a symbolic name to refer to a location where an instruction is stored, so that it is possible to write `JUMP BEGIN` instead of being forced to give the number of the store location.

A language with these facilities is usually called an **assembly language**. The language is simply the grammatical rules that tell you what it is possible to write. The program written out in assembly language will be translated into machine code by a piece of systems software called an **assembler**. A typical assembler program will carry out the following tasks:

a substitute the binary machine-code equivalent for operation-code names like `ADD`, `LOAD`, and so on;

b keep a record of which names the programmer has used for data locations, and substitute the binary addresses whenever one of these is referred to;

c select an unused location for any data that is given a name for the first time;

d allow the user to label locations in his program, and subsequently use these labels in statements such as `JUMP BEGIN`.

None of these tasks does anything that the programmer could not have done himself with care, but the provision of an assembler program reduces the possibility of error. Perhaps more usefully, if an assembly-language program has to be modified, perhaps by the insertion of some extra instructions, it will usually be possible to make the alterations to the original copy of the program and allow the assembler to create a new version of the machine-code program. It is very much easier for an assembler to shift all the instructions after the inserted ones (taking care of any JUMP instructions that have to be altered) than it would be for a programmer to carry out the whole process by hand.

More sophisticated assemblers also allow the programmer to write 'natural' instructions such as: LET X=Y+Z*C, which are turned into a sequence of machine-code instructions, rather than insisting on the 'correct' sequence of

```
LOAD C
MULT Z
ADD Y
STORE X
```

One final feature of assemblers is that they allow the user to insert comments (which are then ignored by the assembler program, but which will be present on any listing of the program) in order to document his work. Even with the ability to use sensible and descriptive names for his data locations, the programmer may find an assembly language program difficult to understand when he returns to it after some months working on some other program.

The actual choice of name – assembler – is a little confusing. It comes about because this piece of software *assembles* each instruction as it eventually is constructed, by copying bit patterns (addresses, instruction codes) from tables that it keeps. The simplest assemblers do no 'thinking' for themselves, but simply copy binary patterns that the programmer has chosen to represent as words.

Machine-code programs and assembly-language programs are examples of low-level, or machine-orientated, programs. To write a sensible program in machine language or assembly language, it is necessary to know a considerable amount about how the computer in use is constructed: for example, whether it has more than one accumulator, which output peripherals are in use, and so on. But many programs can be written without this detailed knowledge.

High-level languages

Knowledge of such matters is not required by the programmer if he makes use of **high-level languages** (also known as **problem-orientated languages**). They permit the use of quite general statements such as PRINT SQRT(X) which the computer can turn into a (quite long) sequence of instructions to compute the square root of the number X, and then to print out this value. In doing this printing, it will be necessary to convert from the binary code used internally in the machine to the characters that must be sent to the printer or VDU screen.

The important thing about the use of a high-level language is that it allows the programmer to write his program in a way which ignores the difficulties of such conversions and of similar problems. If, in solving the problem he has in mind, the programmer wishes to print out some value, or some message, he says this in his (high-level) program, and allows the language translator to solve the problems of knowing which instructions must be used.

Why not use high-level languages all the time?

High-level languages are very much easier to write programs in than, say, assembly language. The same high-level program can be sent to a friend, or to a different computer installation, where another translator can take the same high-level program and turn it into a new machine code version. In this way, a program written once can be made to run on many different computers. An assembly-language program will generally only run on the computer it was designed for. This ability to transfer programs is called **portability**, and is reckoned to be a great advantage of high-level languages.

But because high-level language programs are written without any specific knowledge of a particular machine, they cannot do all the jobs that are required of a computer program. For example, they cannot be used to write language translators! A language translator must 'know' quite a bit about the machine it is to run on – for example, what its machine code is, so that the user's program can be correctly translated into machine code! Any piece of systems software is generally written in a low-level language, such as an assembly language, because only in this way can the programmer have the control over the features of the machine that he wishes to use.

But it is also generally true that applications program (see page 94) are written in high-level languages, and it is high-level language that a user generally thinks of when he talks about a computer programming language.

TRANSLATORS FOR HIGH-LEVEL LANGUAGES

An assembler can be quite a simple program: it only has to identify the word used by the programmer and decide what its binary equivalent is. But a translator for a high-level language must be much more complicated, and hence is usually a very much bigger program, occupying more store locations. There are more jobs to be done, in addition to all those carried out by an assembler. For example, it will be necessary to check that the storage location in which a programmer has placed some text is not subsequently used as if it were a number. In an assembly language, the user would probably be allowed to do this, because it would be assumed that he was trying some very clever short-cut.

Also, it is possible to write nonsense in a high-level language, and the translator must check for, and report back, this nonsense. For example:

    LET 13 = Z

is fairly meaningless, and the programmer should probably be told that he should have written

    LET Z = 13

Nonsense is less possible in a low-level language. It may not be what you wanted to write, but it still usually makes sense! If location 100 is used for Z and location 101 stores the binary equivalent of '13', then both

```
LOAD  100              LOAD  101
STORE 101     and      STORE 100
```

are 'sensible' programs, and no assembler could tell which was the one that you truly required, and which didn't make sense.

Object code and source code

It is useful to have general names for the starting and finishing points of any translation. It is customary to call the version of the program as written by the programmer the **source code** and the translated version of this the **object code**. Object code is usually machine code, while the source code is usually in a high-level language such as BASIC, FORTRAN or Algol, although the source code for an assembler program is in the low-level assembly language. There are two different ways of producing object code from high-level source code.

Compilers and interpreters

A **compiler** is a translator that takes a program in source code and produces the equivalent program in object code. That is, it takes statements in a language such as FORTRAN and converts each to the machine-code instructions corresponding to that statement. After all the statements have been translated, we have a new program – one that a skilled machine-code programmer might have produced, in tackling the same programming task as the high-level language programmer.

This object code program is a completely self-contained program. Once the translation is complete, the compiler and the source code may be removed from main storage, making the space they occupied available for data. A compiled program, then, can be very economical on space. It can also be economical on time of execution. Once the program has been translated, the object code can be stored and used in future without any further translation.

However, there are problems in using a compiler to translate programs. If an error is detected when the object code program is executed, it will be difficult to tell the programmer where the error has been spotted. Any identifying labels, such as line-numbers, or suggestive variable names such as TIME, COST and so on will have been translated into addresses in machine code and will mean little to the programmer, who will have no idea where to look in his source code to make changes. This problem may be overcome, but at a price. It will be necessary for a table giving the addresses corresponding to variables (sometimes called a **name table**) to be kept in main store for use in providing helpful error messages when the program is executing. The compiler usually produces such a table as part of the translation, but by keeping it in store, the space it occupies cannot be freed for data.

Another problem occurs when the programmer wishes to change the program, possibly to correct an error. He must make his alterations to the source code, which must then be completely re-compiled. Even the smallest alteration will result in a complete retranslation. Nevertheless, programs which have been thoroughly tested, which will be used many times over (such as commercial programs) or for which speed of execution is important (such as large scientific programs) are usually compiled.

An **interpreter** works in a completely different way. The source code always remains in store, together with the interpreter. Translation and execution happen together. The interpreter takes a statement from the source code, translates that statement into object code and the object code produced is then executed. The interpreter then takes the next statement which is translated and executed in turn. If the source code contains a jump back to an earlier statement, that statement is re-translated. If the program contains a loop, the statements forming the loop will be re-translated every time around the loop. No complete object code program is ever formed, merely the fragments of code corresponding to the latest statement translated.

Because an interpreter does not produce a self-contained program in object code, neither the source code nor the interpreter itself may be removed from main store, and the space available for data is limited. Of course, the space occupied by a compiled object program is not required, but this is usually small compared to the size of an interpreter. The biggest disadvantage of an interpreter is the time that is taken in translation. Every statement will be re-translated each time it is executed, and there is no opportunity to store a completely translated program for future use.

However, interpreters do have considerable advantages, particularly when used for developing programs. Because the source code is always present, it is a simple matter to indicate to the programmer the location of an error using his own variable names or line numbers. When an error is to be corrected, this can be done by altering the source code and continuing with the translation. When the corrected statement is again due for translation, the altered version will be used and there will have been no unnecessary re-translation of unaffected statements. In this way, it is sometimes possible to correct a program while it is executing, without losing the results of calculations performed by other, correct parts of the program.

Because the advantages of an interpreter are most noticeable when a program is being developed and when the programmer is using an interactive terminal, it is usually those languages designed for interactive use (such as BASIC) that are interpreted, while languages used for large-scale commercial or scientific programs are compiled.

EXERCISE for research

8 Which languages are available on the computer systems you use? For each one, say whether it is a high-level or a low-level language, and (if possible) whether it is translated by a compiler or an interpreter.

○ EXERCISE for discussion

9 What reasons can you give for writing programs in low-level languages? You may be able to find more reasons than those given in this section.

WHY SO MANY LANGUAGES?

Every machine, even the simplest, has at least one language – machine language. Almost every machine has its own assembly language. And the bigger the machine, the more high-level languages for which it will provide translators.

Why are there so many languages, particularly high-level ones? As new features are seen to be desirable, computer manufacturers tend to invent new languages. This is preferable to altering an existing language, because there may have been many translators already written for the existing language, each one for a different computer. We cannot use the same translator, because it has to translate into a different machine code, even though it is always translating from the same high-level language. In addition, the users of the language will have expended a lot of time and money writing programs in the existing language, and they won't want to find that their translator now has new features. So once languages are defined, they tend to stay fixed, and new features are put into new languages. (This isn't strictly true, as languages *do* change somewhat with time, but not in a major way.) Finally, a new feature may directly contradict the way something is done in an existing language, and it may not be possible to change the language without making all existing programs useless!

Some of the popular high-level languages, and the features for which they are known are:

FORTRAN A language designed for scientific use, and particularly good at handling numbers, allowing the user to write complicated mathematical expressions, which the translator can then turn into quite lengthy machine-code. Because it is a good language for numerical work, it is relatively poor for non-numerical work, with data that consists of names, or with files.

COBOL A business-orientated language, where the work of defining the structure of the data is made easy for the programmer. We have seen some COBOL-like programs and data definitions on page 48. COBOL is unlike most other high-level languages, in that a COBOL program is arranged in four sections (called `DIVISIONS`) of which only the last contains instructions to be translated into machine code. The other divisions are used to record information about the way that the data is held on file, about which peripheral devices are being used, and identifying information about the programmer, computer and system in use. This information is usually held in a programmer's head when writing programs in, say, BASIC; but COBOL is designed to be used in a business environment, where a formal, efficient system of working has been shown by experience to be most productive. COBOL reads rather more like plain English than does a language such as FORTRAN.

ALGOL Originally, Algol-60 (invented in 1960) was an attempt to provide a general-purpose language for business and science. Although originally intended simply as a means whereby humans could communicate programs with each other, a compiler was soon written for it and it grew in importance as a programming language. It was superseded by Algol-68, an improved language with some very sophisticated features, mostly designed to assist in making programs better written, and capable of handling a wide variety of data. Both of the Algols are intended to assist in problem-solving of a general kind, rather than simply to provide fast calculating facilities, as some people claim for FORTRAN.

BASIC A language that is particularly good for starting programming, because it is very easy to learn. It is rather like the easier bits of FORTRAN. BASIC is a poor language for writing long or complicated programs, but many users are so comfortable at using BASIC that they carry on beyond the point where it would be well worth their while to learn another language.

PASCAL A language designed when it was recognised that, as programs got more adventurous and complicated, an enormous amount of money was being spent on programmers to write and maintain programs. Pascal attempts to make it easy to write good programs that will not have many costly mistakes, and that will be easy for another programmer to alter at a later date.

EXERCISE for research

10 Make a list of all the computer programming languages you can find, saying for each whether it is high-level or low-level.

EXERCISE for discussion

11 For the languages in your list, answer the following questions:
   a Who uses them (what sort of programmer)?
   b What features do they have that make them useful?

Operating systems

Language translators and loaders are not the only systems software programs to be found in a computer system. A number of other programs are usually lumped together as an **operating system** (or some name such as **supervisor**, **executive**, **monitor** and so on, that suggests that it is in control of what is happening to the system).

An operating system performs many tasks, and several of them can be seen in just one session at a computer terminal. Similar tasks will be carried out when the computer is used in the 'batch' mode, by sending off decks of cards, or coding forms, but the functions of an operating system show up quite clearly when we consider an interactive system.

It is the operating system which is the program that is running whenever the computer seems to be 'idling', waiting for someone to do something. There may be any number of terminals linked to the computer and at some of them people will be typing, while at others nothing will be happening. One job of the operating system, then, is **polling** the terminals – looking at each one in turn to see if the user has typed anything, and remembering what was typed, until the user has completed a statement, or a line of input. The operating system is also responsible for echoing back the characters which have been typed (see page 79).

When the user has completed a line of input (usually the operating system knows that the line is complete, because the user finishes it with the RETURN or ACCEPT key), the **command interpreter** (another part of the operating system) must be used to decide if what has been typed is a valid command or not. If it is, then some appropriate action will be taken. Some examples are shown in the table (Figure 7.5).

line typed in is . . .	action taken is . . .
a logging-in command	call on the **security** and **accounting** parts of the operating system, to check the user's identity, and record that he is using the system
a request to get a stored program from backing storage	call on the **file management** part of the operating system to discover where the program is stored, and to copy it into the computer
a request to save a program	call on the **file management** part of the operating system
a request to translate a program (there may be a choice of translator)	call on the appropriate language translator to perform the translation

Figure 7.5

There are many other functions of the operating system, but these are among the commonest encountered in interactive use of a computer. Often, a single command will cause several of these actions to be taken in sequence. It may be possible to type `RUN HISTORY` and have the computer find a program called 'HISTORY' on backing store, load it into the computer, use a language translator to turn it into a machine-code program, and then to run that machine-code program.

TIMESHARING Big, fast computer systems can often be idle while the user is typing in a command or simply thinking what to do next. But because one user is not actively making use of the system, this does not prevent the computer from dealing with other users. Such sharing of a computer is called **timesharing**. If nothing is happening in the system, the operating system will be polling the terminals. When a user has completed a command, the operating system will begin to execute that command. Some commands, such as those to transfer programs from backing storage can be started and then left to continue on their own, so that the operating system can continue polling, so that no other user is ignored. If the command is to run a program, then the program cannot be allowed to run until it has finished, because this could take so long that some other user's input is missed. So the operating system will allow the program to run for a very short space of time (usually called a **time slice**) after which the operating system polls all the terminals again.

If more than one program needs to be run, then the operating system will allow the first to run for a time slice, then poll the terminals, then allow the next to run, then poll the terminals again, and so on. In this way, programs execute a little at a time. But the computer is so fast that the user will hardly notice that other programs are being run at the same time, and indeed most users will contentedly think that they have the whole computer to themselves.

Interrupts

Often, a program will not need all of a time slice. A program that is printing something out on a terminal will send a character to that terminal and will then have to wait for the printing to finish before the next character can be sent. At this point, the operating system can switch back to polling terminals and running other programs, without waiting for the time slice to be used up. We have seen (on page 79) how a signal called an **interrupt** will tell the computer when the operation has been completed, and the program run again.

Using backing store

Because the user can think that he has the whole computer system to himself, he may want to make use of all of the available main store. This would seem to prevent any other users having programs running in the other time slices, but a clever operating system can get around this. The program actually running at the moment has to be in main store, and if there is no room for another program, it will be kept on some special backing storage device, such as a very fast disk (usually called a **swapping disk**). When the time comes for another program to have a time slice, it is swapped into the computer's main store, while the program currently in main store is written out on to the swapping disk. A clever operating system will arrange its work so that swapping is kept to a minimum, but even so, the user will probably not notice the time delays involved.

VIRTUAL STORAGE Because an operating system can swap different programs between main store and backing store, it is possible for users to 'pretend' that they have computers with even bigger main store than actually exists, and for the operating system to swap parts of a single program in and out, so that the instructions being executed at any moment are always in main store, while other parts of the same program are on the swapping disk. In this way, really large programs can be run on very small computers. The user is making use of **virtual storage** – main storage that isn't really there at all!

SHARING PERIPHERALS If programs are being executed, one time slice at a time, there are problems with using peripheral devices such as line printers. We cannot allow one program to print its first line on the printer, and then have the next program print its own first line during the next time slice. The output would be quite incomprehensible! What usually happens is that, instead of going to the line printer directly, output is directed to a temporary file on backing storage. When the file is complete, it is listed on the printer by another systems software program (called a **spooler**) which runs like a user program in the time slices allocated by the operating system. The spooler lists one complete output file at a time (after which the file is erased, and the space used again) so that the user's output does not get mixed up with that from other users.

Other systems software programs

Although there are many functions performed by an operating system, there is still a need for other pieces of systems software, especially in large computer systems. An important class of these programs is known collectively as **utilities**. These are programs that perform everyday tasks (such as arranging output in a suitable format for printing out, for printing identifying headings and so on, or sorting a file of data, adding line numbers to programs for editing and so on) which are often provided as part of the systems software, rather than forcing each user to write his own. One important utility program is a **text editor**, which is often used (sometimes without the user's knowledge) in preparing the original copy of a high-level language program. The editor program will handle the formatting of the text in lines, and will arrange for corrections to be carried out, lines inserted or deleted, and so on, if the user changes his mind. Often the editor is built into the language translator, so that the user is unaware of the job that is being done. For example, the BASIC language usually has a built-in text editor, so that writing and correcting a program can be done without asking the operating system to load a text editor and then a language translator. In BASIC, the text editor is there to start with and the translator is used when RUN is typed.

Finally, many computer systems have a **library** of useful **subroutines** (which are rather like very small utility programs). When a translator program needs to perform the task in question (calculating a mathematical function, for example, or printing the date), instead of writing the machine code that will cause these things to happen, use is made of the subroutine library.

Summary

Program *source code* may be written either in a *low-level (machine-orientated) language* or in a *high-level (problem-orientated) language*. Low-level languages are better able to take advantage of the computer in use, so are used for *systems programs*: *machine code* for them is generated by *assemblers*. High-level languages are easier to read and more portable, so are used for most *applications programs*: machine code for them is generated by an *interpreter* or a *compiler*.

We have looked at systems software such as *loaders, translators, operating systems* and *utilities*. These are probably stored in machine-code versions and need not be translated for each use.

EXERCISE for individual work

12 Say briefly what each of the following pieces of systems software does:
   a An initial program loader
   b A compiler
   c An interpreter

EXERCISE for discussion

13 In this chapter, you have seen that an operating system performs many tasks. How would you describe the overall job carried out by an operating system?

EXERCISE for individual work

14 Say briefly what each of the following parts of a typical operating system does:
   a A routine for polling
   b A command interpreter
   c Security and accounting routines
   d A file manager

EXERCISE for research and discussion

15 For a computer system that you have access to, make a list of all the jobs performed by the operating system. Even a very small computer, such as a microcomputer without timesharing and backing storage, will have an operating system.

EXERCISE for research

16 For a computer system that you use, make a list of all the pieces of systems software that you can find. Say briefly for each one what its purpose is, and whether the computer would be able to run at all without it.

EXERCISE for discussion

17 What features of a machine would a systems software program need to make use of that would require the program to be written in a low-level language?

FILMED
23/4/79
FILMED
23/4/79
FILMED
23/4/79
FILMED
10/5/79
FILMED
23/11/79

8 Preparing a job for a computer
SYSTEMS ANALYSIS and DESIGN

In the next chapter, you will see how a computer program comes to be written. This chapter is about how the user decides what programs to write, what they should do, and what sort of computer he needs, and indeed whether a computer is necessary at all.

You have already done some of this activity yourself, in Exercise 7 on page 91. Deciding which computer peripheral devices are needed is an important part of designing a computer system.

The whole process is known as **systems analysis and design**.

Phases of system development

Only the very rich (or the very foolish) buy a computer without deciding first what it is to be used for. Most often, the computer will take over some job that is already being carried out, probably by human beings. It is important to analyse exactly what jobs are already being done (this is not always obvious) and to decide which are best suited to a computer, and which should still be done by humans. The introduction of a computer may well cause new jobs to be required, and it is not uncommon for a new computer system to create more jobs than it replaces.

So the design of a computer system (that is, the hardware *and* the software) falls into several phases, and we shall look at some of these in more detail. The phases – obvious, but vital to success – are as follows:

Analysing the system Analysing the present system to decide what it *actually* does (not what people think it does!) and how it works.

Stating objectives Most well-designed systems have clearly-stated objectives: statements of what the system is intended to do. In fact, unless you know what the system is trying to achieve, you cannot afterwards decide whether it succeeds in achieving this satisfactorily. Sometimes, the stated objectives include **performance criteria**: statements that the system should be capable of doing such and such a task in a given time (or better), dealing with a given maximum number of people, and so on.
Humans are so good at adapting – unlike computer systems – that a purely human system, when analysed closely, often proves to have many more jobs in it than the users suspect. And often, it is achieving objectives different from those that managers would give you if you asked.

Designing the system If a new system is to be installed (and it could well be that systems analysis suggests that it shouldn't be), it must be *designed* – it shouldn't be developed piece by piece, as so many poor computer programs are. This includes choosing the tasks that are to be performed by computer, designing human procedures to fit around the computer tasks, designing forms to collect and summarise data, choosing the correct pieces of hardware, designing tests and fault-finding routines and so on.

Designing the programs Having designed the *system*, the need will be apparent for a number of programs – it is quite likely that a large system will have several different programs, to be run at different stages. These programs will themselves have to be designed. This design stage is similar to what many people call 'programming', but does not include the production of actual program statements in a specific programming language, which is the next stage.

Coding the programs 'Coding' is used to emphasise that there is almost no design work in this task – it is just turning designs into statements in a suitable language. The statements produced are often referred to as **code** rather than as a 'program', because any one programmer, if part of a team, may produce only fragments of the complete program.

Testing This means firstly the testing of the computer programs to iron out any 'bugs' that may be present, but secondly trying the system on real data as well, to make sure that it produces the same results (and if we're lucky, the *correct* results) as the existing system. This is often done by **parallel running** – running the business using the new computer system, but simultaneously continuing to use the tried and tested original system with the same data.

Documenting the system Providing operating manuals to explain the system to its users, and information that will enable changes to be made at a later date.

Going live This is what is was all in aid of – the new system takes over from the old.

Notice that there are many steps in the production of a commercially useful computer system which are treated very skimpily when you write a program for yourself. Many people are very inefficient at programming. They sit down at an interactive terminal, and start writing their program from the first statement. Bitter experience has shown professionals in computing that this is a ridiculous way to use a computer. It is more efficient to design carefully what is required, and implement it according to the recipe given above. Now let us look in more detail at the steps in designing and implementing a computer system.

Analysing the system

For systems analysis to be worthwhile, the 'system' need not be a computer system; it need not even be one where a decision is being taken as to whether or not to computerise: the principles of systems analysis are applicable to human systems (and indeed physical or chemical systems) just as much as to computer ones.

Systems analysis is a profession that requires considerable experience – it isn't always easy to see what you do next. As an illustration, let us take a simple example of a system – a library.

The first thing that the systems analyst does is to decide what the **boundaries** of the system are – that is, exactly what activities are part of the system. A *public* library might have meeting rooms for local clubs or societies, a *school* library might be part of a hall or classroom used for other activities. The analyst must first decide exactly which of these activities are part of the library system, and which are not.

Once we are sure about what we mean by 'library', the next task is to look at the **activities** carried out by people in the system. To find out about these, the analyst will visit, talk to, and observe librarians at work. He will be particularly interested in any forms or pieces of paper that are filled in, or that pass between people, and any telephone calls or verbal messages that pass between librarians or other library staff.

Most probably, when new facts come to light later on, the analyst will return and visit again people he has already observed. In order to get it right, it is important to keep going back to the people who will actually have to *use* the system. People are notoriously bad at understanding what it is that they do: quite naturally, they see their jobs as being centred around themselves, and do not always understand how their actions affect other people in the same system. In examining activities, the analyst may wish to go back and redefine the boundaries of the system.

It may be convenient (in the case of a library, it probably would be) to see the system as being composed of a number of **subsystems**. Cataloguing, for instance, is an example of a subsystem, separate from handling loans and from sending reminders of overdue books. It may be that the final decision is to computerise one subsystem but not another.

The analyst has now split his study of the system into a series of subsystems, and each one will be analysed in the same way. He has a list of the activities performed by people in the system – such as issuing a book to a borrower, sending an overdue reminder, and so on – and has broken down the whole operation of the library into a series of people carrying out activities. Each activity may in turn cause other activities to happen. So the analyst looks at the **flow of information** around the system. Some information comes from outside the system (an *external* flow): a book arrives from a publisher, a request for an inter-library loan. What 'outside' means will depend on where the analyst has drawn his system boundaries. Some information flowing is *internal* – forms filled in by a librarian to reserve a book, the placing of a catalogue card in a card-index and so on.

Now that the analyst knows how the system works at present, he can make suggestions about a new system.

Stating objectives

The first step on the way to designing a new system is to state quite clearly what the system is to achieve. General statements like *'keep track of all books borrowed'* are not very helpful. It's necessary to be very specific: *'maintain a file of accession numbers of all books and borrowers who have taken out books via the "loans" procedure'*, is probably more useful. It is easy to get the objectives wrong. For example, books leave libraries in many ways besides being borrowed by someone who walks in: they may be

> lent to another library
> damaged and destroyed
> sent by post to a bedridden borrower
> stolen

And so on. If the library wanted to check its stock once a year or so, an objective of the system should be to allow this to happen.

This is not just a matter of doing things in a formal way for the sake of it. The library is very unlikely to have a librarian who is skilful enough at computing to be able to do all the analysis, design and programming for the whole library system: it could quite easily have a large number of librarians, all of whom knew nothing at all about computing! They would probably employ a systems analyst, and the crucial part of *his* job would be to get the objectives of any new computer system right.

Defining the objectives is a critical handover stage; the analyst is saying, *'This is what I reckon that the new system should do, based on what I've seen you doing already . . .'* And the librarians are responding with, *'Yes, that's about right, but what about . . .'* until finally they are agreed that *'Yes, that's the set of objectives that we want our computer system to achieve'*.

Designing the system

The next stage is to get the system and the software designed. The objectives are rather like a contract in this — the library is asking someone to design and implement a system that will do the things listed in the objectives. If it fails any of the objectives, then the library has justifiable cause for complaint. But if they've forgotten to agree an objective that's important to the running of a library (like that the system should somehow cope with a stock-check once a year) then they can have no cause for complaint if the system makes it impossible to check the stock ever!

People can adapt so readily to changes that it comes hard to us to realise how inflexible a system, particularly a large computer system, can be. An often-quoted example is that of the Driver and Vehicle Licensing Centre (DVLC) at Swansea. A number of design faults appeared in the system after it had been implemented, mostly to do with a serious underestimate of the number of enquiries that might be made of the system. The problem *now* is not to identify what is wrong (you can be sure that if *you* ever design a computer system, there will be many people around to tell you what's wrong with it!) but how to correct the faults. The truth about the DVLC is that it is such a large system that is inflexible in the areas where change needs to be made, that in practice there is nothing much that can be done. One change, to relieve some of the pressure on the DVLC computers, was to alter licences so that instead of running for three years, they ran until the holder was 70 years old.

The moral is — get your systems analysis right the first time!

CHOOSING THE HARDWARE With the analysis complete, and the objectives agreed, the process of system design begins. As we saw in the last two chapters, a computer system consists of both hardware and software and both have to be designed — though in the case of the hardware, it is not so much a matter of design, as of choosing from what is currently on the market.

The most important decisions to be made concern peripherals. How much secondary storage will be required? Should it be magnetic tapes, or magnetic disks? How fast should it be? (Speed costs money, roughly speaking, but the whole point of the application may be speed – as in an airline booking system, for example.) How much spare secondary storage should be provided in case the data grows? What input devices are required? The library may need bar-code readers for reading book numbers, but it may very well need at least one keyboard somewhere (probably the system will need to be told the date each day). What about output devices? Will a line printer be too expensive and have too much speed? Could the system work with some cheaper and slower teletypewriters?

You can see the sort of decisions that have to be made. Sometimes the required mixture of peripherals will not be available, because of problems of using one manufacturer's equipment with another's computer, and a compromise is required. And can all of this be realised at reasonable cost?

Sometimes, particularly in public bodies, such as libraries, local councils, educational establishments and so on, it is necessary to put the system **out to tender**. A systems specification is drawn up, and circulated to interested computer manufacturers, who quote a price (or 'tender') for the system, obviously using their own equipment. Sometimes, the organisation is compelled by law to accept the lowest tender, which sounds like a useful way of saving public money (or indeed, anyone's money!). However, cheapest is not always best in computing; so many organisations evade the rules for going out to tender by writing a specification that could only be filled by the manufacturer they have already decided on!

Designing the programs

The software, as well as the hardware, has to be designed. Rather than write out the programs in a computer programming language, the designer of the system will specify them in words or as flowcharts. This can be a lengthy process; but if the programs that will be written as a result are likely to be large, this sort of design is necessary, so that a large number of different programmers can contribute to the programs at the same time without working at cross-purposes. Many programs being written today require several hundreds or possible thousands of man-years of programmers' time, and it would be impossible to write them without this sort of organisation.

A typical program specification will include a list of the possible inputs to the program, including mistakes, and will state the actions to be taken in each case – again including the mistakes. Anything that is to be printed will be carefully designed, probably using squared paper (called **layout sheets**) to ensure that each page of printout contains information arranged in a convenient form, with figures neatly arranged in columns, with headings which are repeated when the output continues on to a second sheet of paper, and so on. If the pages are likely to be distributed among several users, it might be necessary to make sure that each page is suitably titled with a date, and some identification to show which computer program produced it.

If output is to be a VDU screen, care must be taken to ensure that two pieces of information likely to be required together are not split on separate screens.

If the information spreads over two screens, equal care must be taken that the computer does not rapidly pass on to the second screen before the user has read what was on the first – some sort of 'please turn over' facility under the user's control must be provided.

Also to be defined are the file layouts, as we've seen in Chapter 4 (page 47). This is especially important where there are many programmers working, as a common way of dividing up their tasks is to get each programmer to work on a single program or routine that processes files set up by other programmers, and in turn produces new files. The definition of the file layouts is thus crucial, to allow each programmer to know where to start from, and where he is heading for.

DESIGNING FORMS AND PROCEDURES

It is easy to forget that the system designer is not just designing a computer system – he must also pay attention to the place of the humans in the system: one place where this is particularly important is in the **design of forms**. In Chapter 2, we saw that forms were designed with a view to making mistakes less likely, and to ease the preparation of data for a computer system. Questions on forms should be designed so that the person filling them in (who need not be someone inside the system) can understand what is meant. If a borrower was reserving a book in the library, would a space for writing *'number'* cause him to put down his own borrowers' number? The subject classification code of the book? The ISBN (International Standard Book Number)? The accession number of the book? Which does the library want, and how do they make sure the borrower gives it?

Manual procedures also have to be designed, to ensure that the correct information is passed between stages in the process. The library provides us with another example of this. A decision may be made to computerise the borrowing system, but to keep the reservation system manual (because not many books are reserved, compared to the number borrowed, perhaps). There must then be provision in the computerised system to note those books reserved, so that when they are returned to the library, they can be handed over for the manual reservations system, rather than being put back on the shelf. Even in the manual system, care has to be taken that the process of reserving a book gathers all the information that the computerised system will need. So the manual system will need to be designed with the computerised system in mind.

And vice versa too. When the reserved book is returned, the computerised borrowing system may need some special action to be taken to indicate that the book is not still on loan (so that the borrower who has just returned it doesn't get sent overdue reminders), but isn't lent again (so that the borrower who has reserved it has time to collect it before his allotted borrowing period starts).

And one important piece of design is the way in which the system will function if the computer breaks down! This could be a temporary return to a completely manual system, or it could be the borrowing of a similar computer for which 'standby' arrangements have been negotiated. But it does need to be thought about.

Testing

TESTING THE PROGRAMS

Many people, writing simple computer programs, forget the testing. But every single computer program, no matter how simple, should be thoroughly tested.

This means making sure that the program works, not only with the sort of data that you expect to put through it, but also with wrong data, and unexpected data.

For example, consider a program that simply sorts numbers into ascending order. This program should be tested with, at least, the following data:

    a set of numbers similar to those you expect to have to sort in real use,
    a set that is already sorted,
    a set that is in reverse order,
    a set where all the numbers are the same,
    a set where there are no numbers at all, and
    a set with just one number.

Many otherwise excellent sorting programs fail if asked to sort one number (a fairly easy task).

Testing should not just test that the results are correct, but also that they are laid out correctly, as required. What does the computer do when asked to print out a negative number – does the presence of a minus sign ruin the carefully arranged columns? How about putting the correct number of spaces where there is nothing to print? And so on.

Sometimes, testing the programs start with a **dry run** – not using the computer, but checking the behaviour of the programs 'by hand', following the steps in the written version of the program, and detecting any coding errors. In the next chapter, you will see how a **trace table** can be used (rather laboriously) to check the behaviour of a small fragment of program.

An important stage in program testing is the use of **test data**, provided by the program designer and part of the systems specification. The test data consists of a series of inputs, and the expected outputs (including not just the expected output *values*, but also where and how they will be printed); it also includes wrong and unexpected data, as mentioned above.

TESTING THE SYSTEM

But it is not just the programs that have to be tested; the operation of the whole system must be tested as well. Sometimes, it is possible to dry run a complete system: in any event, test data will be passed through the system, checking that manual steps and procedures can be comfortably and speedily carried out, and that the instructions are clear and unambiguous. Most purchasers of a computer system will be sure to demand that they see the system in operation with real data – possibly the same data that has just passed through the manual system that is being replaced by computer. This can be done at the same time – **parallel running** – so that checks can be made as to whether the new system can function under real operational conditions.

This is usually the last stage before **going live** – the stage at which everyone is convinced that they can put their trust in the computer system, and will allow it to take over from the manual system it is replacing. If all the stages of systems analysis and design have been carefully carried out, going live can be a satisfying end to a challenging process. If not, it can be the first moment of a calamitous catastrophe!

FEASIBILITY STUDIES AND PILOT SCHEMES Sometimes, with all the care in the world, it is not possible to predict whether or not a system will work. It may involve new procedures that can only be tried over a period of time, or it may involve the public, and the designers cannot be sure how they will react.

In such cases, a **feasibility study** may be prepared – an analysis to see if the system *would* work. This may well be followed by a **pilot scheme**, possibly using only one branch of the firm, or some selected employees, or one of the branches of the library, rather than all of them. The behaviour of the pilot scheme can later be used as evidence in preparing a full-scale systems specification.

Documenting the system

One stage of designing and implementing a computer system that is often neglected (at great cost!) is **documenting** the system. This means preparing written manuals with information for future users of the system. There are usually many different types of user, and each requires different documentation. The librarians in our example will require **user documentation**: instructions as to how they should carry out their steps in the system, which forms they should fill in, and how. This documentation need not mention the details of the computer programs, but should very carefully describe what goes *into* the computer, and what comes *out*. Computer programs, no matter how simple, require this sort of documentation, and you should produce it yourself as a matter of course, whenever you write a computer program that could be used by someone other than yourself.

The library computer system will presumably involve computer operators who will need to know how to batch up any input, which tapes or disks to load, which programs to run, and when. Documentation for these is called **operational documentation** and should include clear instructions about how to run each of the programs in the system. Perhaps more importantly, it should contain instructions about what to do if an error is discovered – the actions to be taken in such cases are called **recovery procedures**. In producing simple programs yourself, you may not see the need for operational documentation, but you should at least make a note of where a copy of the program is kept (it may be in a library on a disk, for example, or there may be back-up copies on cards or tapes). In practice, operational documentation may involve recording passwords, or specially privileged access techniques, so that operational manuals may not be made available to the general user in the same way as user documentation – in any event, the user of the system will not need to know how the system operates, merely what he himself has to do!

A third sort of documentation is **maintenance documentation**. No computer system is ever the same for any length of time. Sometimes errors are discovered soon after the system 'goes live'. Such errors should have been detected in the testing stage, but it is quite likely that some will slip through even the most rigorous testing procedure. Many years into the future, a change in the operation of the library may cause the existing system to need amendment. Even if the original system designer is available, he will not be able to recall all the details of his first design without extensive notes, and it is these notes that form the major part of the maintenance documentation. Included will certainly be a complete copy of the program source code, together with extensive annotation explaining exactly what each step achieves. You should find that this sort of documentation is useful to you when writing programs, and for a short program, a convenient way of achieving this is to include COMMENT or REMARK statements in the program itself. Where this is not possible, handwritten notes on a copy of the program are usually acceptable.

Better high-level programming languages are **self-documenting**. This means that it is possible to use variable names such as TIME, DISTANCE, TOTAL and so on that describe what is to be held as data; also that it is possible to give each section of a program a name, which can also describe what is being done; and lastly that extensive comments (to be ignored during translation) can be included easily. Maintenance documentation does not just comprise program listings, of course. File layouts must be included, and also details of the manual procedures that are part of the system.

YOUR OWN DOCUMENTATION

If you are studying computing, you will probably write many programs. It is easy to become so enthusiastic about the programming that documentation is completely ignored. For very small programs, this is probably not a serious fault, but it is a very good habit to get into the way of producing simple documentation with *every* program you produce – in this way, it will come naturally when you embark on larger programs, where good documentation is essential.

If you are submitting your programs as project work for an examination, then it may be necessary to provide documentation for the examiner, in addition to the three types mentioned above: you will need to explain your method of solution of any problems, and you may even wish to explain why you did *not* do things in some other way, because some thought convinced you that it would not be profitable in the long run.

FLOWCHARTING

Much of the documentation of a computer system and its programs will be written, or will be annotated copies of output and program listings. But some stages of a computer system can be conveniently documented by means of **flowcharts**. Flowcharts can be used to document the overall behaviour of a system (in which case they are called **data flowcharts**, or **systems flowcharts**) or they can be used to describe the steps in a computer program (**program flowcharts**).

Data flowcharts show how the data flows through the system – including the manual steps, as well as computer programs. You will meet data flowcharting in Chapter 10 on data processing, where you will see symbols used to show where output is produced, which peripherals are used, what files are held and what computer programs operate on the data. You will *not* see data flowcharts used to describe what a program does, because that job is done by program flowcharts. In a data flowchart, a program is usually represented by a single box.

Program flowcharts record the steps taken in a program. They record the tests made, and the actions taken as a result of those tests. Many people (wrongly) assume that a program flowchart is simply a copy of the program in a high-level language, with boxes of varying shape drawn around the statements to identify exactly what they do. This type of flowchart is almost useless! In Chapter 9 on program design, you will see how program flowcharts can be used as a means of *developing* your solution, so that the actual coding becomes almost automatic. This is how program flowcharts should be used – as an aid to design!

Summary

In this chapter we have looked at how a computer system comes to be designed. We have seen the steps in systems analysis and the subsequent design of a system, and these are listed here for reference:

Systems analysis
Statement of objectives
System design
   Choice of hardware
Program design
   Design of forms and procedures
Coding
Testing
   Feasibility studies and pilot schemes
   Testing of programs
   Testing of the system
Documentation
   User documentation
   Operational documentation
   Maintenance documentation

There have been no exercises during this chapter, as the process of systems design is not one that can easily be split into separate fragments. In the following exercises (which can take a considerable time!) you will be invited to carry out some small-scale systems design for yourself.

EXERCISE practical

1 Make a list of some systems that you are familiar with – such as a library, a club which you belong to that issues membership cards, or collects subscriptions. Other examples could be a gas or electricity board that reads meters and produces bills, or a sports league that keeps up-to-date league tables. Try to describe for each one, in a paragraph or two, what the system does.

EXERCISE for discussion

2 Choose *one* of the systems you have investigated in Exercise 1. Before choosing, you may like to read through the remaining Exercises 3–6 and see what you will be asked to do with this system. Be careful to choose a system where you can easily get the information that you require, and be careful too not to choose a system that is too large and complicated for you to tackle sensibly. You may have to guess at some information, or ignore part of the system, and if you have to guess too often, or ignore too much, the exercises will become pointless.

EXERCISE for discussion

3 For the system that you have selected, describe the *boundaries* of the system. This can be done by listing the activities in the system. It is also useful to list some activities that are *not* part of the system. For example, playing football is not an activity in the system that keeps league tables!

EXERCISE for individual work

4 Write down the *objectives* of the system you have chosen. This should include some reference to what data comes into the system, and should describe (but not in detail) what output is expected. The objectives should include some description of what is to occur when data is not available (what happens to the league table if a match is postponed?).

EXERCISE for individual work

5 Suppose that the system is to be computerised. Make a list of the computer equipment that will be required. Remember to list *all* the peripheral devices that will be required, not just the most obvious ones. For each, write a brief note describing why it is needed in the system. Remember that there should be provision for amendments to the system (maintenance) and that you may need to provide special peripherals for this purpose alone. Make sure that your output peripherals are the ones you need: a system with only VDUs cannot produce printed listings, remember; a line printer might be a nice idea, but is it really needed, or will a simpler, slower printer do instead?

EXERCISE for individual work

6 Design your system, using data flowcharts. Do not give details of the steps in any computer program you include, but make a short statement of what the program does (you may need to read through Chapter 10 on data flowcharts, first).

EXERCISE practical

7 Look back at some programs that you have produced, and for each one produce some user documentation. After a first draft, give your documentation to someone else, and see if he or she can use your program. You may need to amend your documentation, and possibly include some operational documentation besides.

EXERCISE practical for poor programmers

8 Produce maintenance documentation for *all* programs you have written! Good programmers will have done this automatically!

```
EXECUTIVE 5S:50HD2L/360448 26.06.81
JOURNAL: ON
     8:
     8:DISP- HH
     8:DISP- SM01 LOADED OK [SM01
     8:DLTD-EB 5639W
    L5:DISP- D98/MTS INPUT REPLY  000
   RT23-RPT LEVEL 9
    L6:DISP-
  OE01 - REPLY 000003 ADDRESS 23002A
   RT23-RPT LEVEL 9
    L6:DISP-
  OE01 - REPLY 000003 ADDRESS 230032
    L4:DISP- \DUES - VIDEO230026STILL OPE
   RT24-RPT LEVEL 9




  E CLOSE
   ERROR D
```

9 Instructing the computer
PROGRAMMING

In Chapter 8 we talked about how computer systems are planned, and the work that is done before any programs are actually written. In the real world of commercial computing, the programmer is a long way along the line of development of a computing task. When he starts his job, the problem has been so completely specified that all he needs to do is turn it into the appropriate code of the chosen computer language. The development of a program on this scale is beyond the scope of a chapter of this book. Indeed if it were not you might rightly ask for what commercial programmers are so highly paid! However, we can learn some lessons from the way in which programs are written in the 'real' world.

The job of a programmer

One of the worst ways to write a program is to sit down at a terminal with the idea of a program in mind and develop it interactively from scratch. Not only is this wasteful of computer use, you will most likely end up with an unreadable program which is thoroughly botched and inefficient. The planning that goes into a computer job in 'real-world' computing ensures that every task to be performed by the computer is fully specified before it reaches the programmer. When *you* write a program all of this planning has to be done by *you*, but it still needs to be *done* if your program is to have any hope of being efficient. A very useful exercise is for a pair of you to write specifications for programs which the *other* person will then write. The programmer will not make any decisions about the structure of the program, but will simply turn it into code in an appropriate programming language. This means that the person doing the specification has to define clearly all steps to be taken as well as the data and data structures to be used. In this chapter we use a case study to illustrate the various stages in the development of a computer program.

Describing the problem

We should like to write a program to get the computer to play the game of 'Mastermind' with us. The computer is to be the code-setter and we are to be the code-breaker.

Rules of 'Mastermind'

The code-setter produces a secret code which is an arrangement of a number of items which are defined before the game begins. The code-breaker, with certain help from the code-setter, attempts to guess the code within a given number of steps. The game is played by choosing an arrangement of four colours from a given six, and the exact arrangement has to be reproduced by the code-breaker.

When the code-breaker has made a guess at the code, the code-setter must 'mark' his guess. This involves saying how many colours are correct *and* in the correct position in the arrangement, which is done by giving a number of *black* markers; and secondly, saying how many colours are correct but in the wrong position, this being indicated by *white* markers.

As an example, suppose the code-setter produces (in secret of course):

    BLUE   RED   YELLOW GREEN

and the code-breaker replies with:

    RED GREEN YELLOW BROWN

This guess would be marked as

    1 BLACK   (for the YELLOW in the correct place), and
    2 WHITE   (for RED and GREEN in the wrong places).

The code-breaker then goes on to make another guess, helped this time by the information which he has received from his first guess.

After several guesses and the information received from each one, it should be possible for the code-breaker to deduce the correct arrangement. His score is linked to the number of attempts which he has made. If he is not successful within an agreed number of attempts then the code-setter has defeated him.

Developing the solution

This is the time when it is most tempting to rush off to the terminal and generate a few lines of program, and it is an urge to resist. Decide first what broad sections the problem breaks down into, and if possible express this diagrammatically for emphasis.

In this problem we can see four broad sections:

a the computer must generate a CODE;
b the computer must accept a GUESS from the player;
c the computer must examine the guess and work out the MARKS;
d the computer must inform the player of the marks for his guess.

The program must then loop back to accept another guess, and so on. We shall call these four sections INITIALISE, INPUT, PROCESS and OUTPUT, and a diagram of this (although fairly trivial at this stage) is shown in Figure 9.1.

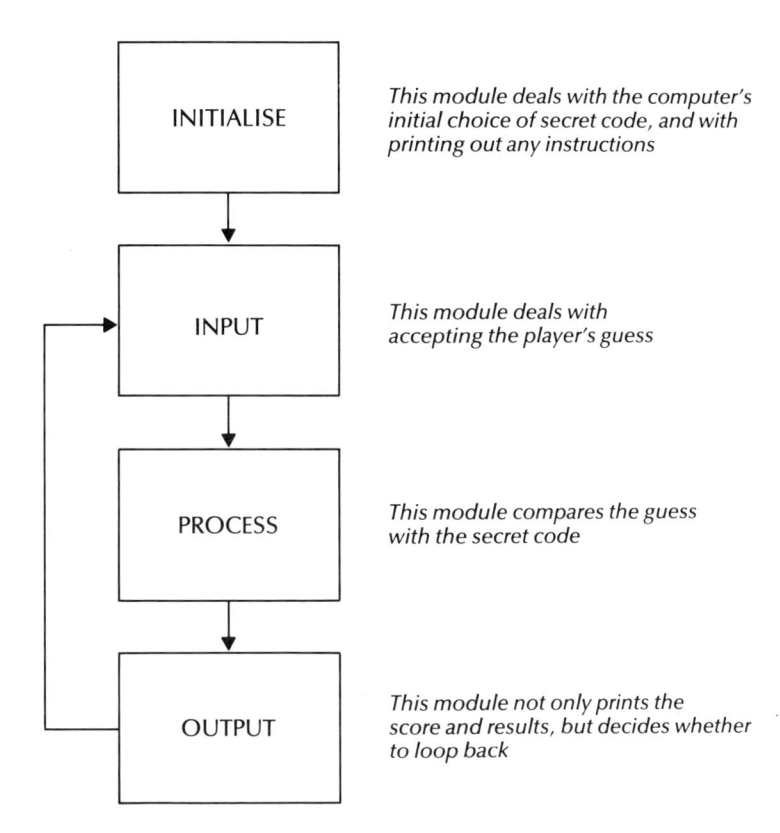

INITIALISE — *This module deals with the computer's initial choice of secret code, and with printing out any instructions*

INPUT — *This module deals with accepting the player's guess*

PROCESS — *This module compares the guess with the secret code*

OUTPUT — *This module not only prints the score and results, but decides whether to loop back*

Figure 9.1
A first flowchart for the program

Figure 9.1 illustrates very clearly the major parts of our program. We shall call them **modules.** The INITIALISE module will deal with the setting up of a code 'chosen' by the computer. The INPUT module will handle the input of a guess by the player. The PROCESS module will deal with the comparisons between CODE and GUESS, and the production of BLACK and WHITE scores. The OUTPUT module will deal with informing the player of his score after comparison.

Of course, unless the player is very lucky the first time, his guess will be wrong and he will want to guess again, so we need the possibility of returning to the input stage for another guess to be made. This is known as building a **loop** into the program. The looping process will depend on certain conditions being fulfilled, such as:

   Is the guess correct?
   Have all the guesses been used up?

and the answers to questions such as these will help to link the parts of the program together.

The four modules can, and should, be developed separately. When they are eventually linked together it should still be possible to see them as distinct parts of the program. This will make the program easier to read and understand, and also easier to alter at a later stage if this is required.

The rest of this chapter will concentrate on just one of the four modules, the PROCESS module. We shall show the various stages in its development until it is ready to be turned into the code of a programming language. The other modules will be left to you, and although you may think at this stage that we are leaving you the easier task, you may be surprised when you actually start to do it!

CHOOSING THE DATA STRUCTURES

Before we can start to plan the PROCESS module, a most important decision has to be made. What form is our data going to take within the computer for most convenient and efficient use?

To decide that, we have to be clear about what data is involved. The input data is to be a guess of four colours. Whether you decide to use names of colours, initial letters of colours, or even numbers to represent colours, is up to you later. The code chosen by the computer must be in the same form to allow comparison.

Whichever of the above possibilities you choose, there are several ways in which these four items of data can be represented in the computer:

a By separate variables; e.g. FIRST, SECOND, THIRD, FOURTH

   For example: FIRST = 'RED'
                 SECOND = 'BLUE'
                 THIRD = 'GREEN'
                 FOURTH = 'YELLOW'

b By one continuous string; e.g. GUESS

   For example: GUESS = 'REDBLUEGREENYELLOW'

c By an array or list; e.g. GUESS(X) (where X is the **subscript** of an item)

For example: GUESS(1) = 'RED'
GUESS(2) = 'BLUE'
GUESS(3) = 'GREEN'
GUESS(4) = 'YELLOW'

The first of these is *just* possible for a guess of four colours. However, if you wanted to amend your program later to cope with a guess of five (or more) colours, you would find it inconvenient. Whatever you had done for FIRST and SECOND and THIRD and FOURTH would now have to be altered to include FIFTH and possibly SIXTH. It would involve major alterations to your program, as well as becoming very complicated to organise.

The continuous string would not be suitable. A string is handled by the computer as a single item of data, and requires complicated processing to split it up into parts.

The list is in fact the most suitable structure. It is recognised by the computer as an ordered set of items which can be accessed individually whilst still remaining part of the whole. Thus it has *both* the advantages of the earlier possibilities. We therefore make the decision to store the input data in the form of a list.

The output data is much less complicated. We simply want to output a score, the number of 'black' points and the number of 'white' points. This can be done using simple variables, say BLACK and WHITE.

SPECIFYING THE PROCESS MODULE

We are now ready to start describing the steps of the PROCESS module in more detail than just 'process'. However, we won't plunge into fine detail too quickly. Let us first set up an outline of what the process will look like.

Here is a set of instructions:

1 Set both BLACK and WHITE counters to zero.
2 Get the first item of GUESS and check with CODE to see if it earns a black.
3 If it *does* earn a black, add 1 to the BLACK counter and erase the matching items from both GUESS and CODE.
4 If it does *not* earn a black, ignore step 3.
5 Repeat this process with subsequent items of GUESS and CODE, until all matching pairs are found and erased.
6 Get the first item of GUESS (if not erased) and compare with each item of CODE in turn until it earns a white, or the last item is reached.
7 If it *does* earn a white, add one to the WHITE counter and erase the matching item of CODE.
8 If it does not earn a white, ignore step 7.
9 Repeat from step 6 until all items of GUESS have been tested.

You can see an outline of the process emerging. One important feature of the set of instructions is that it splits up nicely into two parts. This means that we can have two separate modules within the PROCESS module, which will add to the clarity of our program.

This way of listing the steps which we want to take can very quickly become unwieldy and difficult to follow, so the steps in specifying a module of the program are often expressed in the form of a **program flowchart**. Figure 9.1 was a very simple flowchart. We start at the first box and 'flow' on to the second and third boxes following the arrows. In a more complicated flowchart it is useful to identify some of the steps as a particular type by the shape of the box, and it is customary to represent commands in a rectangular box, and questions for decision in a diamond-shaped box. See Figure 9.2.

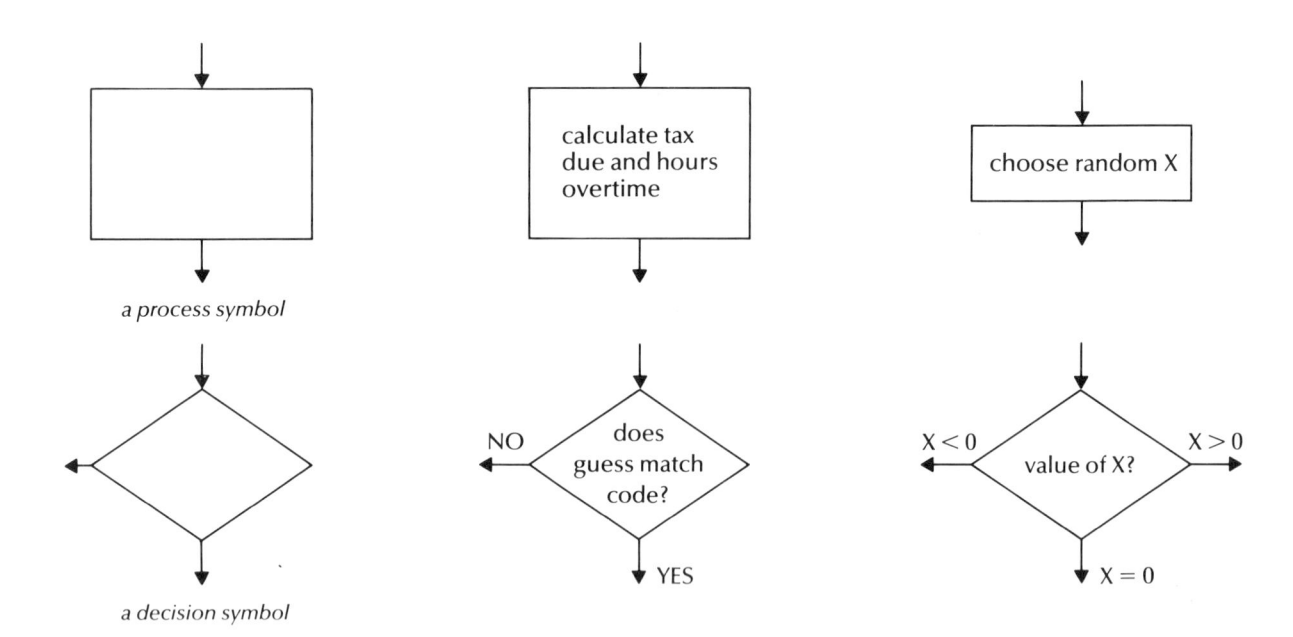

Figure 9.2 *Some flowchart symbols, and how they are used*

In Figure 9.3 we have drawn an **outline program flowchart** for the PROCESS module as we see it so far. We have included the nine steps which we have already mentioned with just a few refinements. Start at the first box and work through it following the arrows. Make sure that you see how it handles the various alternatives which may occur. Check it with a piece of real data. Does it work? Try a different piece of data and check again.

This process of checking your flowchart at each stage against real data is important. It is often easy to miss a vital step, and if you do not discover it until your program is written you could have a great deal of difficulty in finding where the program goes wrong and correcting it. The process is known as **dry running** or **tracing** your flowchart.

Developing the solution 133

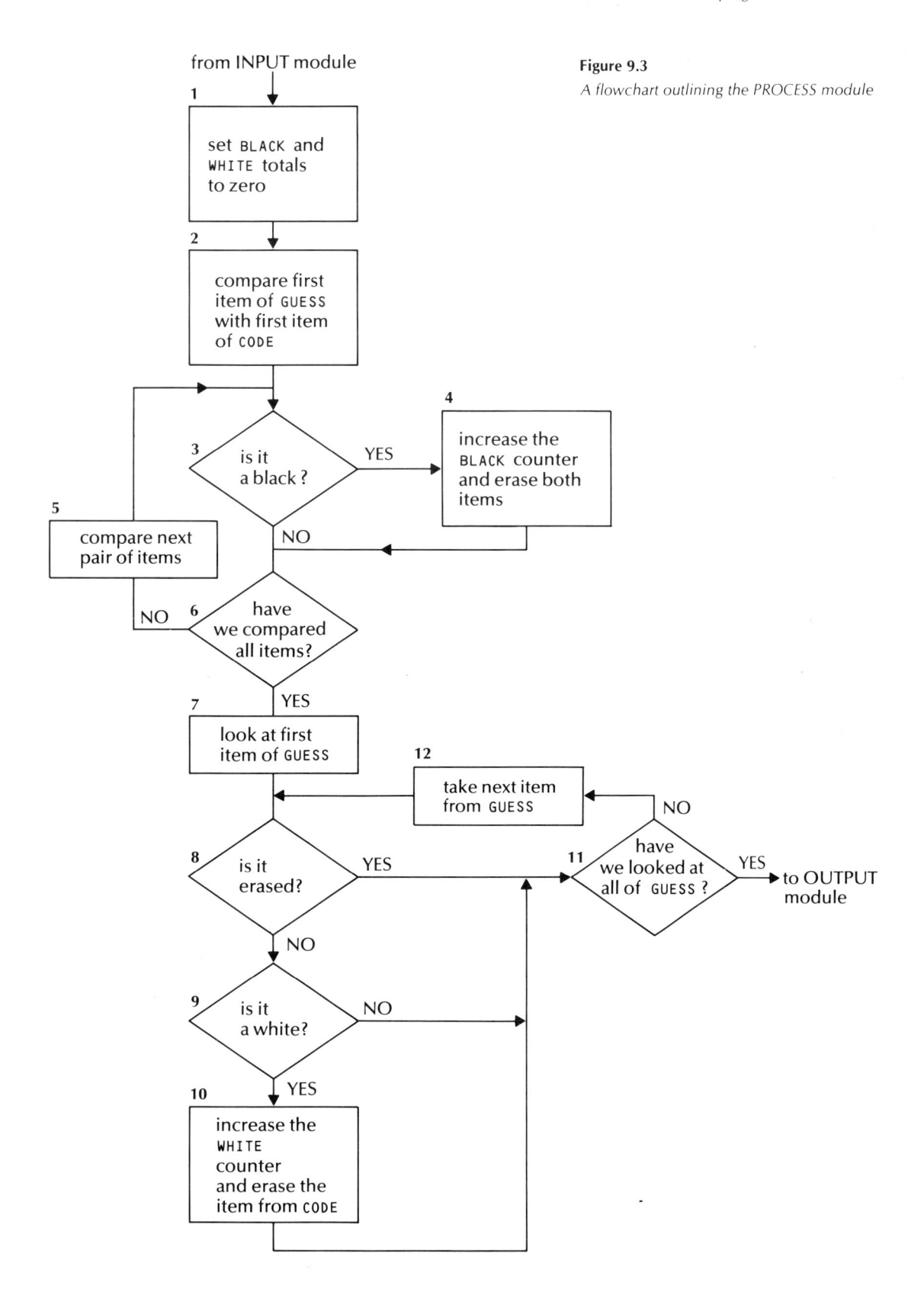

Figure 9.3
A flowchart outlining the PROCESS module

FURTHER REFINEMENTS

Having checked that the flowchart is correct so far, we can now be more specific about some of the steps in it. For example, 'is it a black?' is rather vague. We have to tell the computer precisely *how* to check for a black.

This is where our choice of data structure begins to be helpful. We can select any element of a list and use it as if it were a single variable, though it still remains part of the list. We start by comparing the first item of CODE with the first item of GUESS. If they are the same we want to add one to BLACK. A fragment of flowchart which represents this is shown in Figure 9.4.

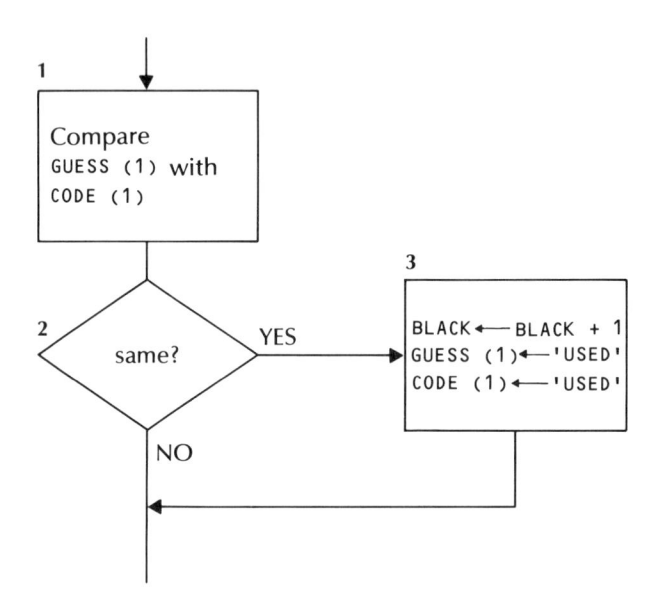

```
1
┌─────────────────┐
│ Compare         │
│ GUESS (1) with  │
│ CODE (1)        │
└─────────────────┘
         │
         ▼
2      ╱╲           YES      3  ┌──────────────────────────┐
      ╱  ╲ ─────────────────▶   │ BLACK ← BLACK + 1        │
      ╲same?╱                    │ GUESS (1) ← 'USED'       │
       ╲  ╱                      │ CODE  (1) ← 'USED'       │
        ╲╱                       └──────────────────────────┘
         │ NO                               │
         ◀─────────────────────────────────┘
         │
         ▼
```

Figure 9.4 *Making part of the flowchart more precise*

Notice that the decision box has two exits to take care of each possibility. Notice also the 'assignment' arrow in the first command box which assigns a value of 'BLACK + 1' to the variable BLACK. In other words it takes the original value of BLACK adds 1 to it, and puts the new value into BLACK. This is commonly known as **incrementing** BLACK.

When the answer to box 1 is 'yes' the matching items of both GUESS and CODE must be erased to avoid comparing them again and thus having a possibly false score. Erasure is done simply by assigning 'USED' to their variables as shown in box 3.

The process of checking for a white is similar, but slightly more complicated. Figure 9.3 has not taken into account that checking for a white involves comparing each item of GUESS with all the items of CODE. We could again erase *both* matching items but as it is not actually necessary to erase the item of GUESS we shall not waste time by doing so.

We now have the kernel of each of our two modules; what remains is to build the loop controls around them.

In the 'is it a black?' module we want to examine each item of the lists in turn, starting with item 1 and ending with item 4. A simple **count** will do this for us and we shall use the variable I for this purpose. See Figure 9.5.

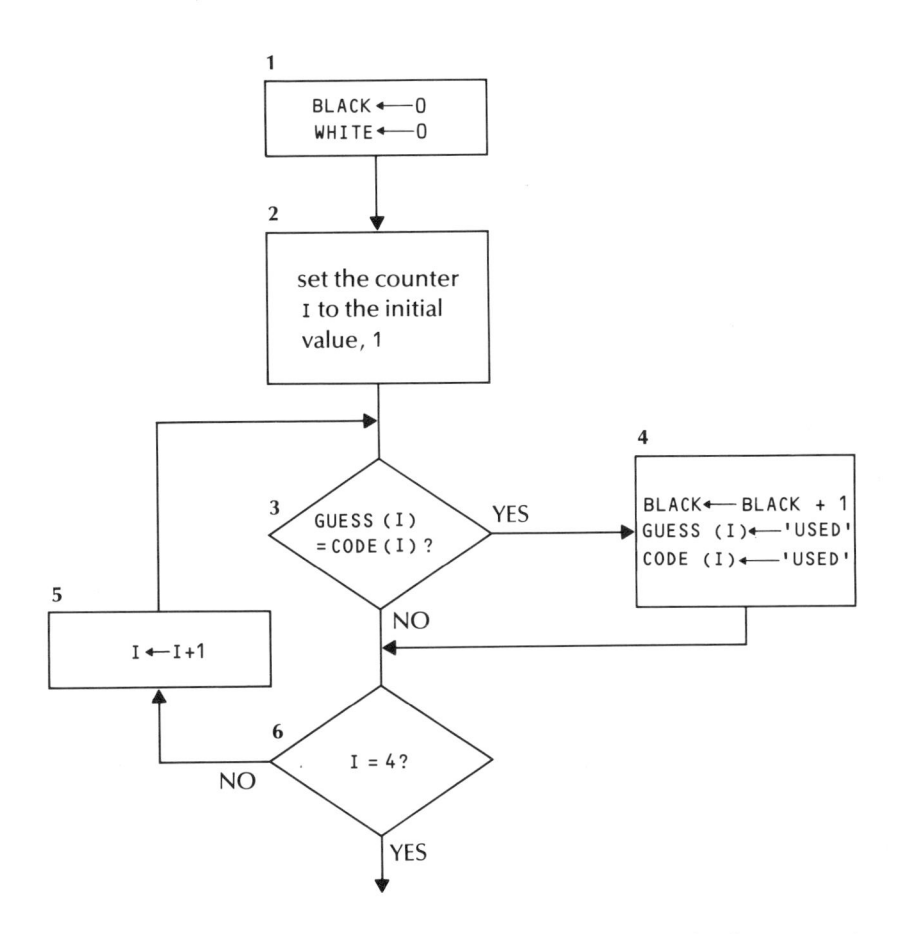

Figure 9.5 *A further refinement of Figure 9.4 to include looping: notice that the contents of the boxes are getting closer to programming language statements and further from English.*

Loop control in the 'is it a white?' module is a little more complicated. We want to take each non-erased item of GUESS and compare it with each item of CODE in turn. So in fact we need two counts, one to count through the items of CODE, and the other to count through the items of GUESS. To make sure that the item of GUESS has not been erased, we must first check that it is not 'USED' before starting to compare. This time we shall use the variables I and J for the two counts. We may use I again without worry as we have finished with the 'is it a black?' module where it appeared. We should of course have to be more careful with any variable which carries its value from one module to the next. Figure 9.6 shows the complete 'test for a white' module.

Our PROCESS module is completed now by fitting together the two modules which we have just developed.

Figure 9.6

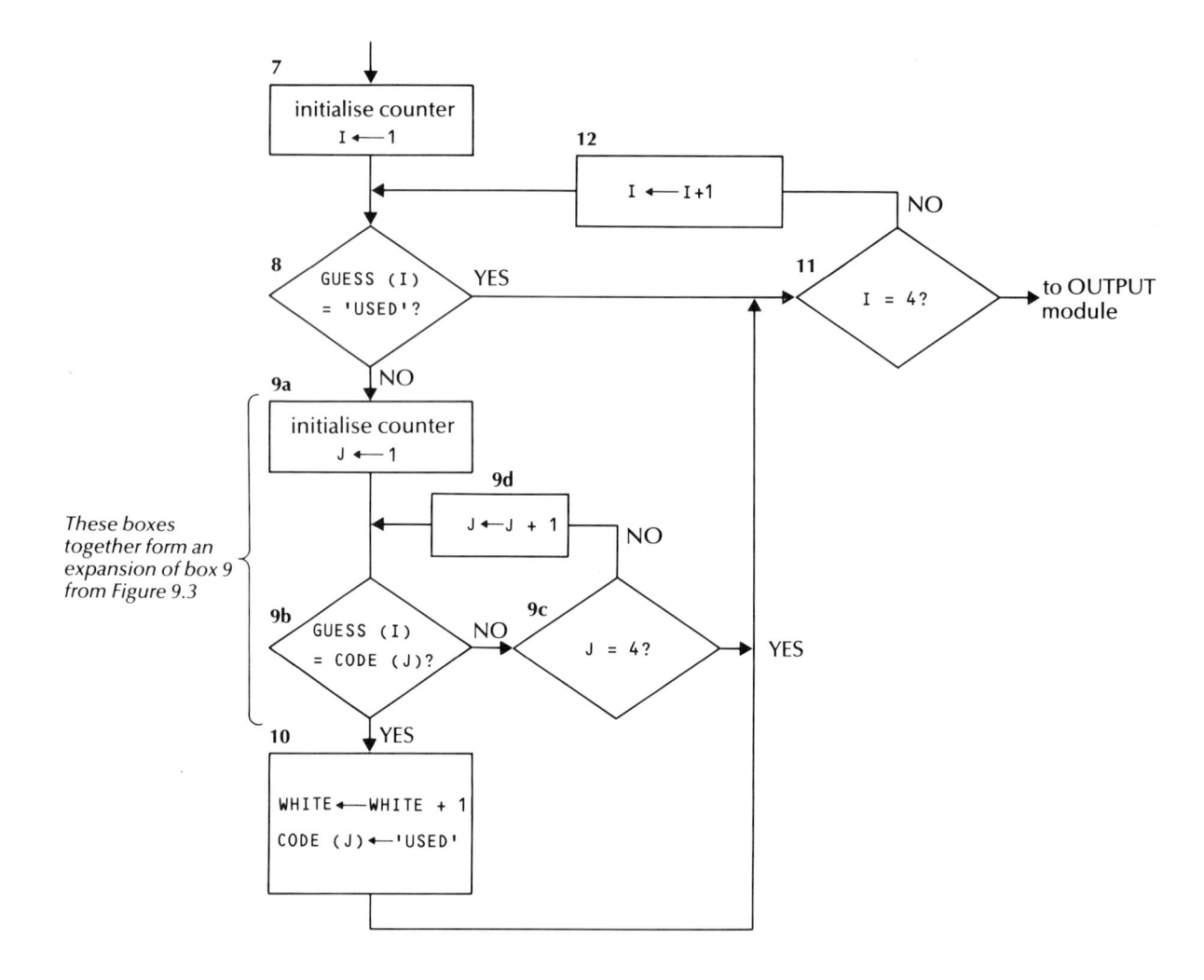

```
        7
        ↓
   ┌─────────────┐
   │ initialise  │              12
   │ counter     │         ┌──────────┐
   │ I ← 1       │←────────│ I ← I+1  │←──────NO
   └─────────────┘         └──────────┘         
        ↓                                       
    8   ◇                                  11   ◇
     GUESS (I)    YES                      I = 4?    ───→ to OUTPUT
     = 'USED'?   ─────────────────────────→                 module
        │
        │ NO
   9a   ↓
   ┌─────────────┐
   │ initialise  │
   │ counter     │
   │ J ← 1       │              9d
   └─────────────┘         ┌──────────┐
        ↓          ←───────│ J ← J+1  │←── NO
                           └──────────┘
   9b   ◇              9c   ◇
     GUESS (I)   NO       J = 4?    YES
     = CODE(J)? ────────→          ─────→
        │
   10   │ YES
   ┌─────────────────┐
   │ WHITE ← WHITE+1 │
   │ CODE(J) ← 'USED'│
   └─────────────────┘
```

These boxes together form an expansion of box 9 from Figure 9.3

Figure 9.6 *Refinement of 'is it a white?'*

TESTING THE FLOWCHART

We have already mentioned the process of dry-running or tracing a flowchart. It is impossible to overestimate the importance of this before you start to write a program, as many errors in your flowchart will carry through into your program. The way to dry-run a flowchart systematically is to write down all your variable names as headings, with any values with which they start underneath. Then work through the flowchart, box by box, obeying the instructions by altering your variables accordingly and taking the appropriate path at each point.

To make this clear we have drawn out a **trace table** in Figure 9.7 which rather laboriously examines each box of the flowchart and makes a note of the consequent action. In practice it is not necessary to be quite so detailed so long as you are sure that no step has been missed.

Developing the solution 137

For this trace we have chosen as data:

```
GUESS = RED      CODE = BLUE
        BLUE            RED
        YELLOW          YELLOW
        YELLOW          GREEN
```

Box number	I	GUESS (I)	CODE (I)	J	CODE (J)	BLACK	WHITE	Decision	Notes
1						0	0		
2	1	RED	BLUE			0	0		
3	1	RED	BLUE			0	0	NO	
6	1							NO	
5	2	BLUE	RED			0	0		
3	2	BLUE	RED			0	0	NO	
6	2							NO	
5	3	YELLOW	YELLOW			0	0		
3	3	YELLOW	YELLOW			0	0	YES	
4	3	USED	USED			1	0		GUESS (3), CODE (3) are 'USED'
6	3							NO	
5	4	YELLOW	GREEN			1	0		
3	4	YELLOW	GREEN			1	0	NO	
6	4							YES	all black checking done
7	1	RED				1	0		
8	1	RED						NO	GUESS (1) not 'USED' above
9a	1	RED		1	BLUE	1	0		
9b	1	RED		1	BLUE	1	0	NO	
9c				1				NO	
9d	1	RED		2	RED				
9b	1	RED		2	RED			YES	
10	1	RED		2	USED	1	1		CODE (2) 'USED'
11	1							NO	
12	2	BLUE		2	USED	1	1		N.B.: J not altered, yet
8	2	BLUE						NO	GUESS (2) not 'USED' above
9a	2	BLUE		1	BLUE	1	1		J set back to start
9b	2	BLUE		1	BLUE	1	1	YES	
10	2	BLUE		1	USED	1	2		CODE (1) 'USED'
11	2							NO	
12	3	USED		1	USED	1	2		
8	3	USED						YES	GUESS (3) 'USED' as a black
11	3							NO	
12	4	YELLOW		1	USED				
8	4	YELLOW						NO	GUESS (4) not 'USED' above
9a	4	YELLOW		1	USED				J reset unnecessarily!!

Figure 9.7 Trace table for Figures 9.5 and 9.6. This is incomplete: there are twelve more steps for you to add.

TEST DATA It has probably already occurred to you that the one test which we have done is probably not sufficient to establish beyond doubt that our flowchart is error-free. In fact to do this with certainty would mean testing with every possible combination of data which it is likely to encounter. In this particular problem that would require a lot of tests!

So, a compromise is needed. Try a code in which each item is the same, e.g. all RED; and a code in which three items are the same, and so on. Try varying the form of your guess accordingly. After a few such tests you will begin to have confidence in the flowchart, or find errors which need correction.

Judging when you have tested sufficiently is not always easy and it is very tempting to stop testing and start writing the program after just one or two successful tests. As you gain experience with programming your judgement should improve; especially if you start a few programs too early and then discover that they fail due to major faults in your flowchart!

Coding the program

Here is the big moment. We are now ready to write the program for our PROCESS module.

We may at this stage have to make a decision about which programming language we are going to use, but this is unlikely. In the real world of computing this decision will have been made very early in the development of the solution of the problem as the choice of language often influences the method of solution. There would, for example, be little point in choosing data structures which the language to be used could not handle.

We have developed this solution with the language BASIC in mind, as this is the language most commonly available in computer systems which are used by schools. However, it would be possible to write the program in some other language, e.g. FORTRAN, Algol or Pascal, if you happened to have one available. Make sure that the language has the possibility of handling lists and strings before you start.

One word of warning. The language BASIC has different **dialects** depending mostly on the machine which implements it. All dialects, however will require you to append a $ to any variable which contains a *string*, and most dialects will not allow you to use long variable names such as GUESS and CODE. Possible alternatives might be G$ and C$, and this would make no difference at all to the logic of the program.

We have not given the program that we developed for playing 'Mastermind'. To do so would have been confusing, as the details of one computer system differ from those of any other. And we would like you to experience the pleasure of developing your own program in your own way.

THE OTHER MODULES As we promised earlier, we are leaving you to develop and write the program for the INITIALISE, INPUT and OUTPUT modules. However, there are some important points which we feel that we ought to mention nevertheless.

The INITIALISE module

This module will handle the setting up of the computer CODE, for which you will need to use the random number generating facilities of your computer. One thing to remember is that the code generated will be partially erased whenever the player scores a point. For this reason it will be necessary to provide a copy of CODE for use in the process module, so that CODE itself is preserved for copying in subsequent guesses.

The INPUT module

In planning this module remember that the program should loop back to receive another guess as long as the previous guess is incorrect. You may decide to put a fixed limit on the number of guesses which you will allow, or perhaps allow the player to set his own limit. If you decide on the latter it is important to let him make the decision before he starts the game rather than interrupt his game repeatedly with the question. A means of allowing the player to exit from the program before he has used up all his guesses may also be a good idea. You could build that into your input statement.

When the player has presented his guess at the request of the computer, it will be very important to check that the input received by the computer is of the required form for processing. Otherwise the program could fail due to incorrect data being presented in the PROCESS module. If you are using BASIC, the system will check for you whether numeric or string data has been entered and give some error message if string data is entered for a numeric variable, but this often halts the program and you may prefer to make your own check. Other checks which are necessary are:

a that the data is in the form which you have specified
   e.g. that the player has not typed just B instead of BLUE

b that the data given is part of the set of valid data which you have allowed
   e.g. that the player has not typed GREY, when this is not an allowed colour.

This process of checking is known as **data vetting**, and is vital to the success of the program. We discuss this further in the next chapter.

In order that the player knows what is expected of him in the game, you will have to give him a set of instructions. However, nothing is more tedious than having to wait for a set of instructions to be presented every time you start to play a game if you know them already, so do give him the option of refusing the instructions if he has read them before.

The OUTPUT module

There are two points of output that we see from this program. The first is the output of the current score at the end of execution of the PROCESS module. This tells the player how he has fared in his most recent guess. The second is the message to the player at the end of the program which will be one of congratulation if his most recent guess was successful, possibly informing him at the same time how many guesses he used; or one of condolence in that he has run out of guesses without guessing the code exactly, and this should also of course tell him what the code was.

It will be necessary to deal with these two parts separately as some looping control will be necessary between them.

You may also wish to give the player a chance to play another game without exiting from the program and starting it up again.

Testing the program

Just as we tested the flowchart, it is vitally necessary to test the program before we release it to some poor unsuspecting player. However, unlike our laborious efforts in testing the flowchart, most of the hard labour is in this case done by the computer.

As with the flowchart we need to test every possible type and combination of data which the program may have to accept – as well as other data which though incorrect may well be presented. This will test your data-vetting routines! If at any stage you find that the program fails then it's 'back to the drawing board'.

The process of checking through a program to see why it has failed is called **debugging** it, the errors causing the failure being known as **bugs** in the program. You may approach this debugging by dry-running your program in much the same way that you did in your flowchart, using the data which caused it to fail. When you find the bug, you then correct the program and go back to the computer to try again. The bug may show up a piece of incorrect logic in the construction of the program, and this may necessitate your going back to your flowchart. Be warned!

Some computer systems have a built-in error detection facility known as a **trace program** which you can use. This does not actually point out your errors to you but helps you to spot them yourself. The trace program prints out the values of your variables at vital stages of your program such as after assignments or branching statements, in much the same way as you do when dry-running the program. In fact the trace program saves you much of the tedious work of dry-running.

If your computer system does not give you the trace facility, you can build a trace into your program using dummy statements which you can delete later. These statements should allow the value of a variable to be printed out every time it changes, and appropriate messages to be given whenever a branching statement is obeyed. You have to consider whether the work in doing this will be more than that involved in dry-running before you start.

Documenting the program

Any program that you have developed systematically in the way we have described will presumably not be trivial. You will not want just to throw it away once it is complete. You may wish to keep it in some library of your own programs, or you may wish it to be available for other people to use, or you may wish to develop it further at some future date. In any of these cases the program alone will not be sufficient. If you look back on a program which you developed six months ago, can you remember how you developed it? Can you see from reading the code exactly what the program does, and how?

When you first complete a program, you are so closely involved with it that the need to write down what you have done does not seem so great. How could you ever possibly forget what it is about? And if anyone else wants to use it, well you can explain it to them, can't you?

Unfortunately this familiarity with a program quickly wears off, and you *do* forget how you have developed it. If a program is to be useful it needs to be thoroughly documented. That is, you need to write down at every step the decisions that you have made, options which you have adopted – or not – and some assessment of the final product: its capabilities and limitations. We list some sections of which this documentation might be composed:

Introduction What is the program being designed to do? Do you see any limitations or possible extensions to this?

Information Details about the subject of the program which need to be known in order to appreciate the program.

Outline solution The bare bones only. Identify separate modules. Outline program flowchart possibly, or perhaps a data flowchart (see Chapter 10).

Data structures Explain which, and why. Make sure the language which you will eventually use can handle them.

Detailed solution May be split into several parts showing successive refinements. Program flowchart.

Coding The program. Don't forget to document the program itself, and annotate it suitably for clear understanding.

Testing Sample runs of the program with test data which should be as comprehensive as possible.

Results The proof of the pudding!

Conclusion A critical look back. Have you succeeded in what you set out to do in 'Introduction' above? What are the limitations of the program? How could it possibly be extended?

As a conclusion to this chapter, let us look critically at the program which we have developed. We shall assume now that you have done *your* bit and that the other modules are complete, that the entire program has been tested and results produced, and that we are satisfied with our efforts.

We set out to write a program to enable the computer to play 'Mastermind' with us by being the code-setter, to our code-breaker. The results will show that we have achieved this for the test data demonstrated. The game can only be played at the moment with a choice of four items (colours) from a possible six. However, the choice of data structures allows this to be altered without too much difficulty, to make the game tougher. No provision has been made in the program for a change of roles between computer and user – i.e. we have not considered the possibility of programming the computer to break a code which *we* set.

A note on languages

We developed the solution to the 'Mastermind' problem with the BASIC language in mind. We did this because it is probably the most well-known language, and the ideas we were talking about would have been familiar to many people. But before deciding to use it, we checked that it had several features that were important for the program we were developing.

a The correct *data types*: BASIC allows only two different types of data — numbers and strings of characters. As our program used very few data types — strings for colours, and numbers for counting round loops and for the score — BASIC is a satisfactory language.

b The correct *control structures*: BASIC allows you to alter the flow of your problem by means of tests like `'IF ... THEN ...'`. Some later, more modern versions of BASIC allow `'IF ...THEN ... ELSE ...'`, which is more flexible. Our program did not have very complicated logic, so these control structures were adequate. Programs do often need other types of conditional statement in order that they may be easily written: `'WHILE ... DO ...'`, for instance, or `'REPEAT ... UNTIL ...'`. Loops are also important: our program did not need to use them except where we handled the control of them ourselves, but BASIC does provide a sort of packaged looping facility in the `'FOR I = 1 TO 10 STEP 2'` structure.

SUBROUTINES One other important feature of a language is the way in which it can be 'segmented' into pieces, in order to make the program flow appear clearer, or for ease of writing. In the 'Mastermind' program, four clear modules appeared almost as soon as we began to think about the problem. In a professional computing organisation, these four modules could well have been developed separately by different teams of people.

But even in shorter programs, written by a single person, or within the modules mentioned above, subsections might become apparent. For example, there may be several points at which input is requested from the user, and at each of these the same checks must be made, for invalid data, for a request to quit the program or for help. Repeating the same program statements would be wasteful of program storage space, and if changes needed to be made, they would have to be made in several different places in the program. It is better to separate the input instructions and make a **subroutine** of them — an independent piece of program to perform just the task of checking the input. When the input checks are required, the subroutine may be called up from the main program. In BASIC this would be done as:

```
100 GOSUB 5000
```

indicating that a jump was to be made to a subroutine beginning at line 5000. At the end of the subroutine, say at line 5099, there would be a corresponding statement:

```
5099 RETURN
```

to send the program back to the line following 100.

If the subroutine was used only at statement 100, there might be little value in going to this trouble. But we would insert `GOSUB 5000` at several places in the program, and the `RETURN` statement would ensure that we went back to the correct place in the program after each use of the subroutine.

Versions of BASIC which allow *only* the `GOSUB` facility for subroutines are significantly inferior to other high-level languages which have a more sophisticated subroutine structure. One major advantage of a subroutine is that it may be written quite separately from the main program, even by a different programmer, and the main program can then **call** it when required. If this happens, it is important that variable names in program and subroutine should not 'clash' and so it is customary for the computer to recognise main program and subroutine as separate units whose variables are 'local' to these units. In this case, a subroutine would be called from the main program by use of a given name, together with the values of variables in the main program that are to be passed to variables in the subroutine. Such values are known as **parameters**.

For example, the main program might call a subroutine named `CHECK` requiring three values to be passed, by the statement:

```
CALL CHECK (X,Y,Z)
```

where `X`, `Y` and `Z` hold the values required by the subroutine. The subroutine may well assign these values to variables `A`, `B` and `C`, but the main program need not 'know' this. Indeed, the main program may use `A`, `B` and `C` for quite different purposes without any fear of a clash.

The `GOSUB` facility allows no such passing of parameters, and so the authors of program and subroutine must be careful that variables with the same name are not used for different data items. It is not possible for programmers to work on different subroutines in the same program (a common professional practice) unless they take considerable care to avoid clashes.

Summary

In this chapter we have developed a *computer program* to play the game of 'Mastermind'. The *coding* of the program into a *programming language* was a very late stage in this development, and when writing your own programs, you may be sure that a better finished product will emerge if you resist the temptation to rush off to the terminal at the start of the project!

One feature of our solution has been the way in which the problem was split into separate *modules* which were discussed independently of one another. Experience of programming has shown that this is one of the more efficient ways to prepare computer programs, whether they are being developed by one programmer or by a team.

○ EXERCISE practical
○
○ **1** Write a program to play 'Mastermind'.

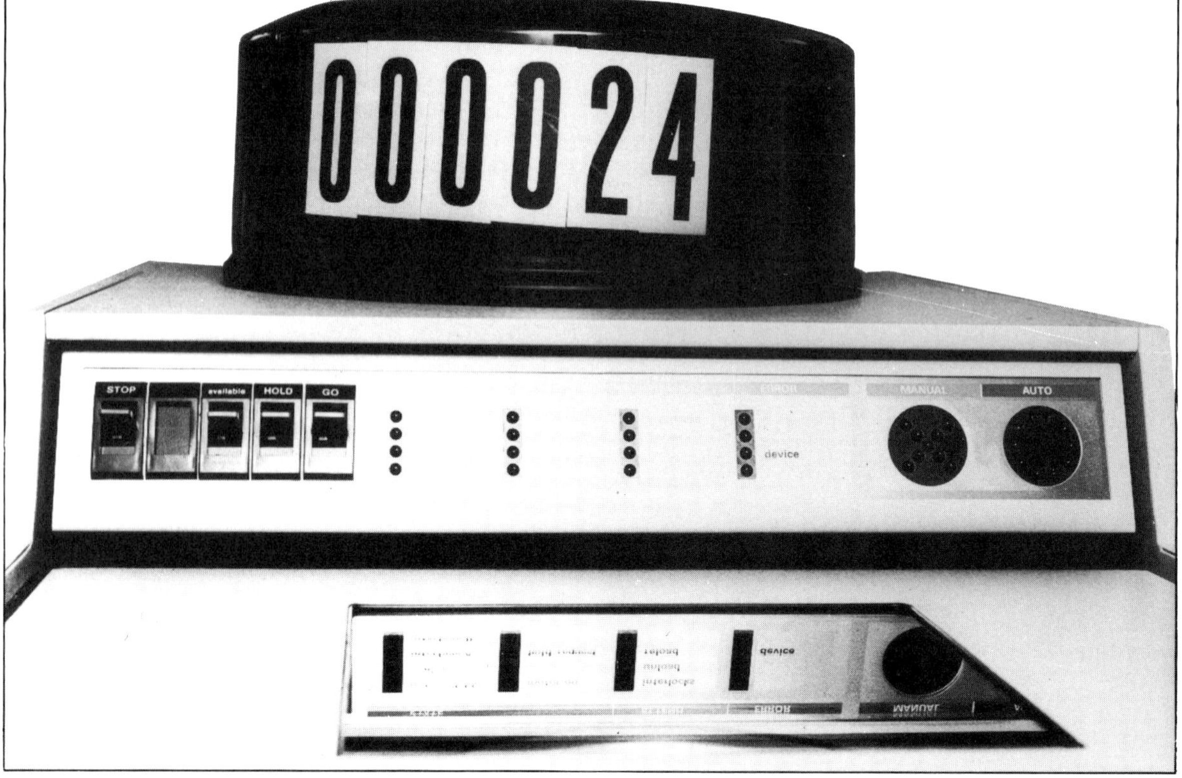
000024
STOP
available
HOLD
GO
MANUAL
AUTO
device

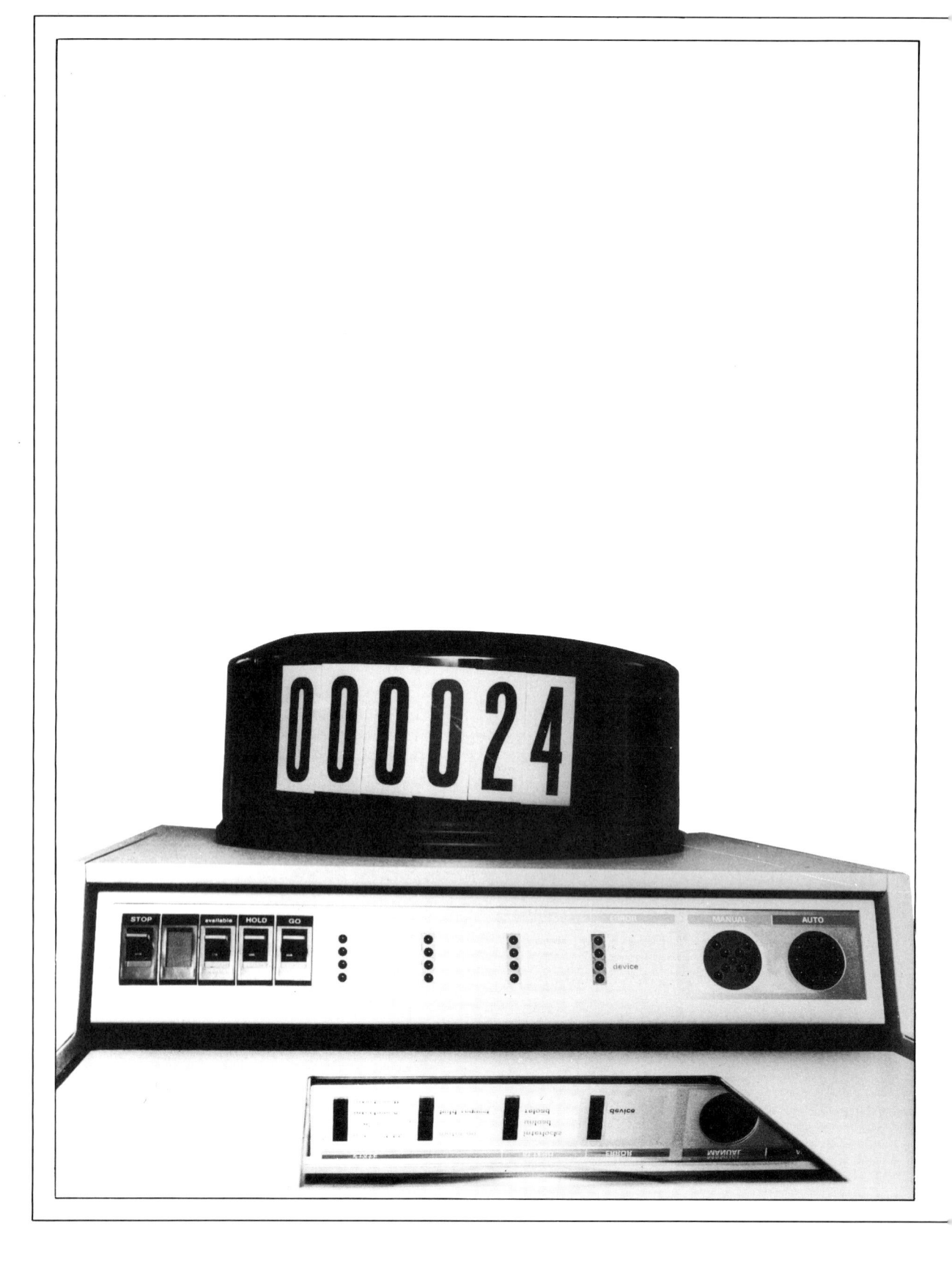

10 Computer applications
DATA PROCESSING

You may be curious about what you are going to find in this chapter. After all, most of this book so far has been concerned with how a computer processes data, and indeed part of our original definition of a computer on page 1 was that it is a data processor.

In this chapter we are going to talk about **commercial data processing**; that is the use of the computer by commercial or business firms, to do much of the work which would previously have been handled by clerks or book-keepers. This is usually referred to just as **data processing**, or even by its initials, **DP**.

It may not be immediately obvious why this processing of data by business firms requires a separate chapter to describe it. Is it not just the same as any computer processing, except perhaps on a larger scale? The clue to the answer to this question is in the words *'larger scale'*. It is the vast quantity of data which has to be handled which imposes particular requirements on the handling, and we hope to show you in this chapter what the particular requirements are.

Examples of commercial DP

Let us look briefly at some tasks which are involved in commercial DP.

Any company of size will have a number of employees working at different jobs, at different rates of pay, and under a variety of different conditions. They will all have one thing in common, however – they will expect to receive their pay regularly from the company. The working out of the amount each one should receive as well as the personal deductions such as income tax and social security contributions, and final production of a payslip, is an immense task. It is a task well suited to a computer, which does not get bored with repetitive tasks nor make errors in dealing with long lists of figures. The job of handling this process of payment to employees is known as the **payroll**.

The business of many companies involves the keeping of an enormous amount of stock, either as raw materials for products which the company manufactures, or as ready supply for distribution to customers. The administration of warehouses where this stock is held involves keeping records of all items, updating the number in stock as items are used, and re-ordering when the numbers of particular items get too low. This process is commonly known as **stock control** and is again well suited to computer handling.

A third process well suited to computer handling is that of processing orders and invoices. A mail-order company, for example, will receive orders from customers, dispatch goods as a result of the orders, and consequently generate invoices to prompt payment from the customer. The entire process – from identifying the goods required, through issuing a despatch note to the warehouse, to producing the relevant invoice – could be done automatically by the computer, and is known as **order-processing**.

Other DP applications include the public library, which uses the computer to keep track of loans and returns of books; the gas and electricity boards, which produce and process bills; and to some extent banking, in keeping customer accounts up to date.

All of the above examples have one important feature in common – they process vast amounts of data in a similar way by passing the data through a common program or **suite** of related programs. Of course, in producing payslips, the personal details of Mr Smith may be quite different from those of Mr Jones, but the basic procedures to be followed in producing a payslip for the two men are very similar. The kind of processing involved is known as **batch processing**, as the data is presented to the computer in 'batches' rather than individual transactions.

There are other applications which are not at all like the ones that have just been described, where batch processing would not be appropriate. Such an application might be an airline or theatre booking system where each transaction needs to be handled individually. The reason for this is that the state of the system must be known before each new transaction can be processed. If the last ticket of a particular flight is sold at 10.00 on a particular day, it is vital that the person trying to book a seat at 10.01 is not also given a ticket.

Applications which require immediate updating of the system in this way whenever a transaction takes place are called **real-time applications** and we shall be looking at these in more detail in Chapter 11. For the rest of this chapter we are going to concentrate on systems using batch processing.

Requirements of a DP program

We could have chosen any of the three examples mentioned above. We have chosen to look at payroll rather than stock control or invoicing as the details are fairly standard and not too dependent on the type of business done by a particular company. We suggest that an excellent follow-up to this chapter would be to organise a visit to a local firm which uses a computer for one or both of these other tasks: a mail-order firm would be very appropriate. You could then discover the areas in which the other applications are similar to, or differ from, the payroll example.

HANDLING OF LARGE AMOUNTS OF DATA

In a firm which has thousands of employees it would be inappropriate to hold their personal details in a large array in main store. The store just wouldn't be big enough! A file of records would need to be kept, where each record holds the personal details of one employee. The program must then be able to control such a file, and an appropriate piece of hardware must be available to hold the file. There would be little point in writing a program which depends on the use of magnetic tape files if the system has no magnetic tape reader.

ABSOLUTE RELIABILITY

However large or small the firm, each employee is an individual who depends on his salary arriving on time, whether it is a weekly pay packet or a monthly cheque to his bank. If the computer omits to pay him on a particular day, it could be a personal catastrophe in his life. He has to go on living and paying his bills whatever happens and there could be serious consequences for him if the money he expects is not there. So the greatest care must be taken to ensure reliability.

MINIMUM OF HUMAN INTERVENTION

The printing of thousands of payslips, even when the processing is done at computer speed, is a lengthy task. It could take a whole day, or more. To have the programmer standing by in case anything goes wrong during this time would be very expensive in programmer-hours. The program must be thoroughly tested so that it is free of errors. For example, if the line printer runs out of stationery – that is, the payslip forms – this must not cause a breakdown of the program. The only person present is likely to be a computer operator who knows nothing about the details of the program, but who *can* change the roll on the line printer and restart the program, provided that this is possible. Of course, under these circumstances the program must stop immediately the roll runs out and not print a few payslips in thin air, otherwise the firm would have a few worried and irate employees!

PRIVACY AND SECURITY

Any data about people is likely to be *private* data. People quite reasonably expect that their employer, while knowing a considerable amount about their family situation, about their salary, and about their past history, will keep this knowledge confidential. So a commercial computer program will take many steps to ensure that the data it uses will not be made freely available. This may be achieved by means of elaborate security procedures, by the use of **passwords**, or even by using some code or cipher to disguise the contents of the data files.

Also the system should be *secure* against accidental or intentional attempts to alter either the programs or the data. Again this may involve passwords and security procedures. Frequent checks will be made on the number of records in files to ensure that extra records have not been inserted, and that none have been erased.

The firm must honour its obligations to its employees by paying them the correct amounts and at the right date. Any failure in this due to the payroll program having been corrupted or lost in some way will not be an excuse that the employees would readily accept. If your pay is wrong, or does not arrive on time, being told to blame the computer doesn't improve anything, let alone your temper!

GOOD DOCUMENTATION

Whenever there are any changes to be made in a payroll, such as a general pay rise, or changes in the tax rules, the payroll program will need to be updated. This will require the programmer to alter some parts of the program. However, it could well be that the programmer who originally developed those particular parts has moved on to another job, and his successor has the problem of altering a program which someone else wrote.

In order to be able to do this successfully he must be privy to the thoughts of the original programmer when the program was designed. This is only possible if these have been written down in some detail. This detail is known as documentation, and we talked about it at some length in Chapter 9.

CHANGES: TO THE DATA, NOT THE PROGRAM

Despite what we said in the last paragraph, changing the program is a costly business. As well as the programmers' time, a lengthy recompilation will also be necessary. (See Chapter 7.) If the program is well designed it should only rarely be necessary to alter it. For example, changes in tax codes could be taken care of by inputting the tax code as *data* rather than building it into the program. Thus a change would require alteration of the data, but not the program. Thus the data for the program might alter week by week or month by month for use with a program which remains, as far as possible, fixed.

RECORD OF OUTPUT

As well as printing a payslip for George Smith, the program should somewhere make a record of the details of this payment for the firm's records. This is necessary for the accounts department in two ways. Firstly, should George Smith have any reason to query his pay, the department need to be able to look up his records to answer his query, and they would appear rather silly if they had to ask *him* what he had been paid. Secondly the accounts department have to make their books balance and this is checked regularly by auditors who want evidence of all transactions, including payments to employees.

VETTING AND VALIDATION OF DATA

However good the program is, if the data is faulty then mistakes are bound to occur. Did George Smith *really* work 169 hours last week? Although there are only 168 hours in a week, this figure may be a result of overtime which is reckoned at double rate. Was Sarah Jones *really* born in 1878? This may *seem* unlikely, but an employee who is over a hundred has as much right to her pay as everyone else.

Mistakes in data can easily creep in however carefully the data is handled, and so a good program must have built-in checks to ensure that as many errors as possible are trapped before they can cause harm.

IMPROVEMENT ON EQUIVALENT MANUAL SYSTEM

A computerised payroll usually supersedes some manual system, and it is by no means automatically a fact that the computerised system will be better. The original design should have been well planned to ensure that the computer system does not use more staff or take more time than the manual system. Also the design of the program should have taken care to include all features of the manual system. A computer system which cannot handle promotion of employees, for example, is less efficient than the manual system which can. A computer system will inevitably be less personalised than a manual system so it must be correspondingly more efficient to counteract this.

The word 'better' can cover a multitude of features such as cost, speed, reliability, demands on personnel, and so on; and all of these must be carefully considered before the computer system is adopted. We looked at this in Chapter 8.

Data flowcharts

In order to talk about data processing, it is useful to introduce another kind of flowchart at this stage. This is known as a **data flowchart** rather than a programming flowchart (which we saw in Chapter 8). The reason for this is that a programming flowchart is necessarily detailed enough to make clear all the steps which are required for a program to be written. Such a detailed flowchart for an entire system would be much too complicated for the features of the system to be clear. It would be a case of not seeing the wood for the trees.

A data flowchart, as the words suggest, shows the flow of the data through the system; where and in what form it is received by the system, how it is organised and vetted for errors, how it is input to the computer, what storage media are used to hold it, and so on.

Figure 10.1
Data flowchart for a payroll program

```
          ┌──────────┐
          │  clock   │─────────── **Data collection**
          │  cards   │            Getting the data,
          └────┬─────┘            possibly from a
               ▼                  variety of sources
        ┌───────────┐
        │ punch and │──────────── **Data input**
        │verify data│             Key punching
        └─────┬─────┘
              ▼
          ╭───────╮
          │ input │─────────────── *this is just one*
          │ file  │                *of the many*
          │       │                *intermediate*
          ╰───┬───╯                *files*
              ▼
        ┌──────────┐        ┌────────┐
        │   data   │───────▶│ error  │  **Data validation**
        │validation│        │ report │  Checking if the
        └─────┬────┘        └────────┘  data is correct
              ▼                         (as far as possible)
          ╭───────╮                     and only allowing
          │ valid │                     valid items through
          │ input │
          │ file  │
          ╰───┬───╯
              ▼
         ┌────────┐
         │  sort  │─────────────── *this is the sort*
         └────┬───┘                *that puts the*
              ▼                    *input file into*
          ╭────────╮               *order : we need*
          │ sorted │               *to say which*
          │ valid  │               *order : e.g.*
          │ input  │               *employee number*
          │ file   │
          ╰────┬───╯
   ╭──────╮    │
   │ B/F  │    │
   │(brought)  │
   │master │──▶│
   │ file  │   ▼
   ╰──────╯ ┌──────────┐       ┌────────┐
            │process data│────▶│ error  │  **Processing**
            │and update │      │ report │  This is where the
            │master-file│      └────────┘  actual calculation of
   ╭──────╮ └─────┬─────┘                  wages takes place –
   │ C/F  │       │                        errors are possible
   │(carried)     │                        here too
   │master │      ▼
   │ file  │  ╭───────╮
   ╰──────╯  │ valid │──────────── *Sometimes this file*
             │output │             *needs to be sorted*
             │ file  │             *too : into factory*
             ╰───┬───╯             *locations for*
                 ▼                 *example, rather than*
            ┌──────────┐           *employee number*
            │payslips and│         *order*
            │ cheques  │
            └──────────┘────────── **Output**
                                   This is the final step :
                                   the output of the
                                   data, including any
                                   totals, reports and
                                   summaries that are
                                   required
```

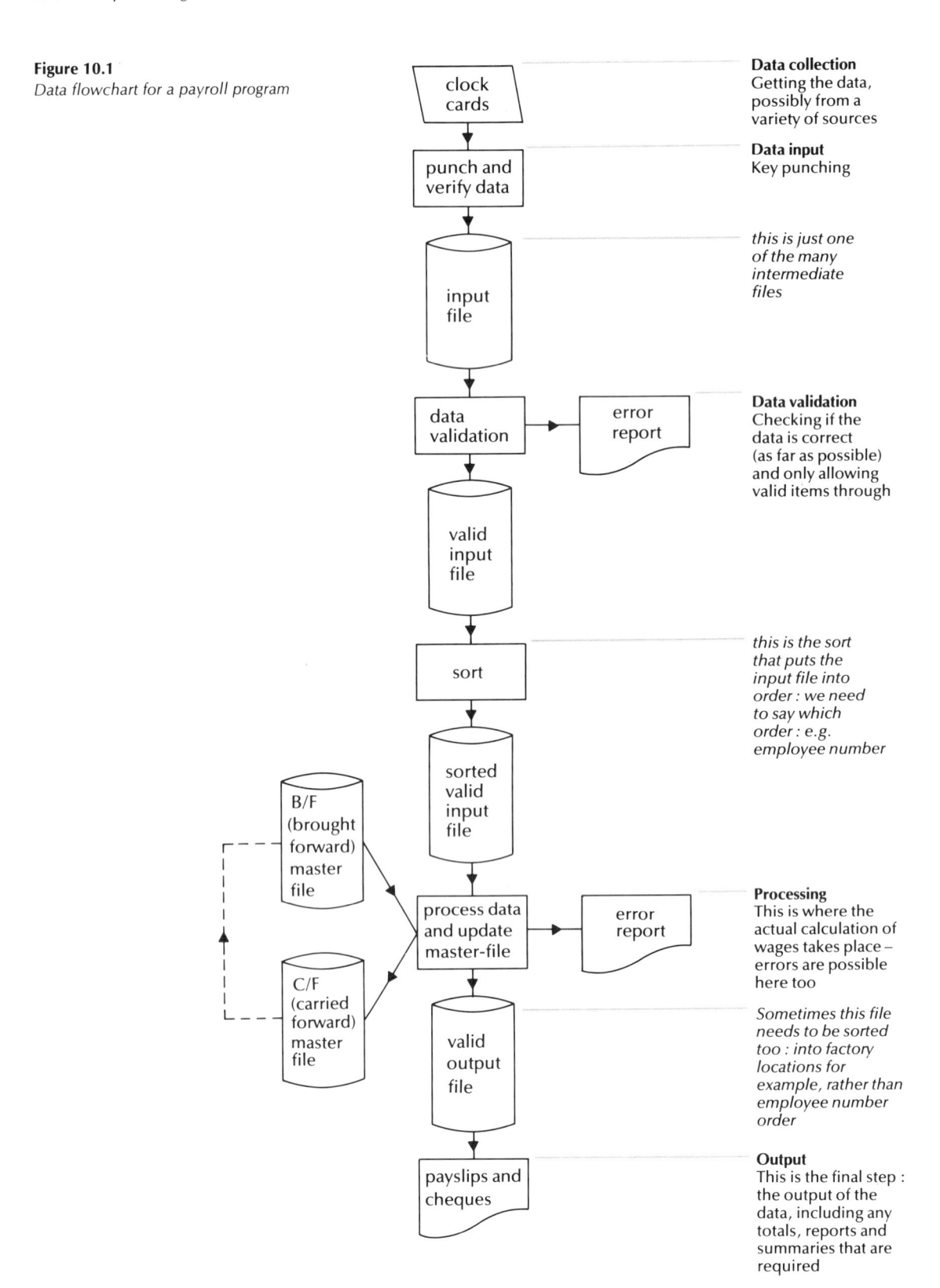

Data flowcharts 151

You will notice that we are now talking about the system rather than just a program. Indeed, while we were discussing the payroll 'program', many of our points referred to the system as a whole rather than just the program. Control of the line printer for example, and operator intervention in reloading it when empty, are vital parts of the system although not of the program. The program flowcharts will certainly be written, but the data flowcharts will come first. Another common name for data flowcharts is **system flowcharts**.

Because data flowcharts need to be simple to make the important aspects of the system clear, they sometimes look rather silly and unnecessary. Figures 10.1 and 10.2 are examples of data flowcharts. In Figure 10.1 we see a flowchart suitable for the payroll program which we have discussed. You can see that it gives no details about how calculations are done in working out the pay of an employee, but instead it traces the data about one employee through the system from his clock card to his eventual payslip. Figure 10.2 on the other hand is the data flowchart for a mathematical program which has the task of finding all the prime numbers which are smaller than a given number. This involves a complicated program, but its data flowchart is extremely simple. Once it is drawn, however, its very simplicity serves as an assurance that the system is indeed no more complicated than it appears.

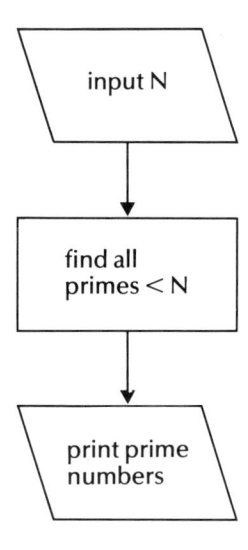

Figure 10.2 *A very simple data flowchart*

In looking at these flowcharts you will see boxes of different shape to those which we described in Chapter 9. Figure 10.3 points out the use of these new shapes, with a few others which we have not used in the payroll example.

152 *Data processing*

CLOCK CARDS	general input or output symbol – independent of how input or output is achieved
INPUT FILE	input by punched cards – the double symbol indicates a batch of cards
ERROR REPORT	document output – the double symbol is used for large-scale output
PAYSLIPS	
MASTER FILE B/F	a magnetic disk file
MASTER FILE C/F	a magnetic tape file
VALID TRANSACTIONS FILE	a general symbol for any on-line file
DATA VALIDATION	a symbol to indicate processing of data
PROCESS ROUTINE	indicates the use of a subroutine

Figure 10.3

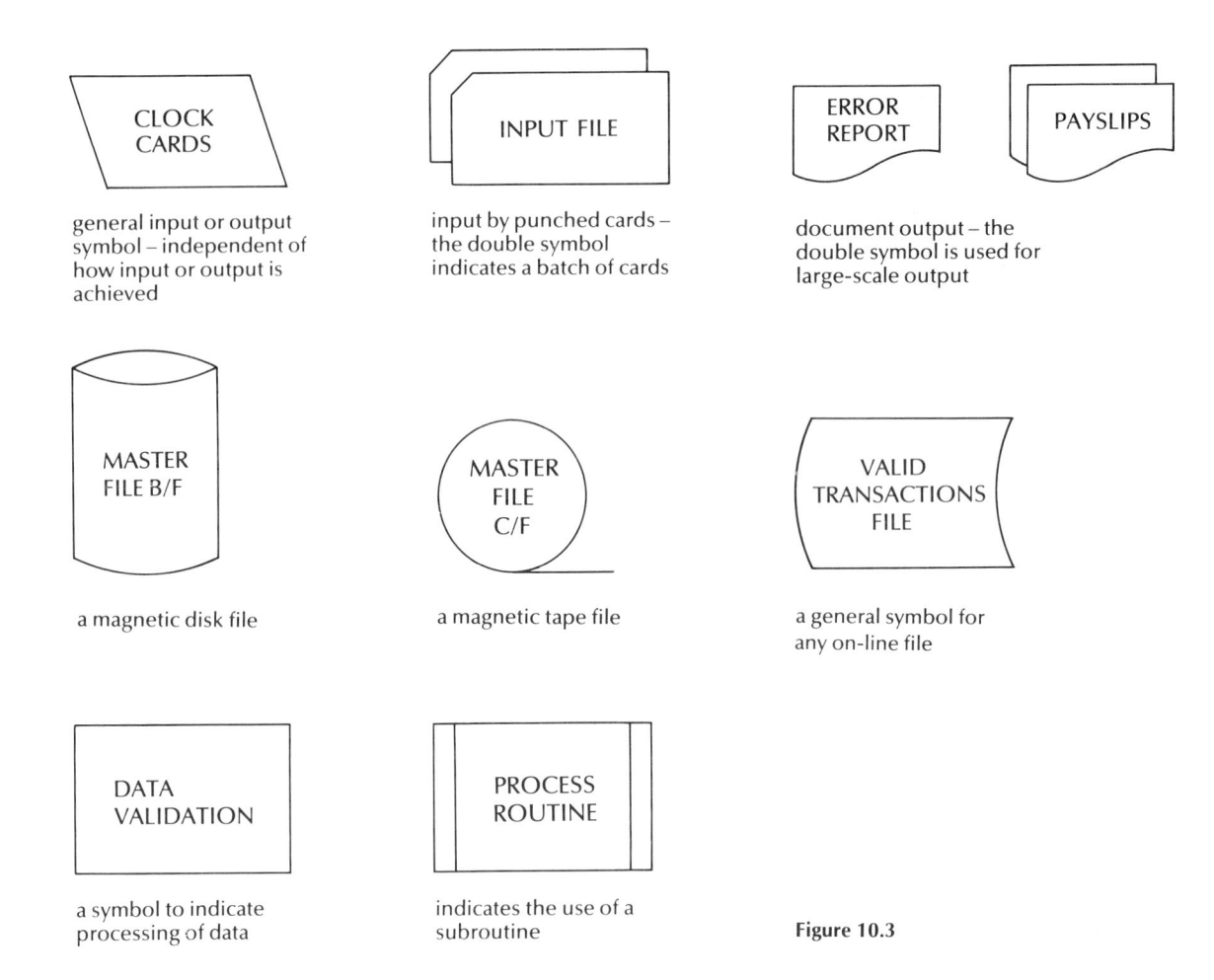

The data processing cycle

From Figure 10.1 we can see that the data flow falls into six parts:

1 the collection of data
2 the preparation of data, including its verification
3 the input of data, including its vetting, or validation
4 the sorting of data
5 the processing of data
6 the output and reporting of data, including the errors

One important thing to notice is that the computer is only actually involved in the final four stages, and that processing only takes place at stage 5. Yet stages 1 and 2 are vital to the system and therefore of equal importance in the cycle. In fact many of these stages will overlap; data for the next payroll may be being collected while the present payroll is being processed, for example.

This is the reason for calling the process a *cycle*. The six steps are performed over and over again, changing the data each time, although not the program.

A word of warning here: the computer world uses a lot of jargon and some of the words for similar processes will vary from one group of users to another – for example, 'systems flowcharts' rather than 'data flowcharts'. If you read other books on this subject do not worry about different terminology or presentation – if for example they have seven stages to the cycle rather than six. The important thing is to understand the processes involved and how they fit together, rather than what they are called.

COLLECTION OF DATA At the start of the data processing cycle, the data which is required must be collected together, and this is not as obvious a process as the words suggest. For the payroll program, the data will originally be in several different places. Some of it, the less changeable or 'fixed' data, as it is often called, will be already in the system. This will include details such as an employee's name and address, works number, basic pay and tax code, items which change only infrequently. To avoid repeatedly entering them to the system with the consequent chance of errors creeping in, they are kept permanently on a file which can be updated separately if necessary.

The changeable data includes such details as the number of hours worked and whether these are at normal or overtime rates, whether bonuses or piecework rates are applicable. These details could be found on clock cards or supervisors' daily record cards. They might be handwritten, punched, or marked for mark sensing. Whichever is the case, the details for all employees must be collected together and organised for input to the computer (if they are already in machine-readable form) or for preparation into machine-readable form.

Part of the original system design should have ensured that all documents on which data is to be recorded are designed suitably, so that when the data is collected together it is in the form and order most convenient for the next stage of the processing.

For example, handwritten details written by supervisors regarding piecework of employees would be impossibly slow to interpret if it were left to the individual supervisors as to how they organised them. A predesigned document is obviously necessary so that details are recorded in corresponding positions, regardless of who makes the entries. It is then a relatively simple matter to read these details from the documents.

The documents containing the original data will be collected together to form a batch for processing simultaneously. At this stage certain totals will be calculated for later checking to ensure that no documents are lost in subsequent handling and that data on them is transferred to the computer correctly. Some special documents will be included which contain details of the batch, with batch and other control totals. We discuss the necessity for, and the checking of, these totals later in the chapter. The collection of data and its preparation for input to the computer has always been one of the slower parts of the DP cycle, chiefly due to there being a considerable manual effort involved. People work more slowly than the computer. In order to reduce the amount of time involved at this stage of the process, various devices have been invented which reduce the manual involvement and aim to speed up the process.

Amongst these devices are **Kimball tags**, small tags punched with holes, which can be attached to an item of merchandise, and torn off when the item is sold. The tag is then sent to the computer department where it is used for direct entry of information for stock update to the computer. Special electronic tills at points of sale in a store, where the assistant may key in a code number attached to an item and have details of the item recorded on magnetic disk or tape for sending to the computer department – the till may at the same time produce the price of the item in response to the code number; bar codes or magnetic price tags may also be used in connection with the tills just described – in this case, instead of keying in a code, the assistant uses a light pen or magnetic code reader which is passed over the tag on the item, allowing the code number to be recorded automatically and cutting out errors by the assistant. Mark sense coding allows forms to be prepared by placing marks made by a suitable pencil on predefined areas of the form. The form can then be read directly into the computer. These devices were described in more detail in Chapter 6. When such devices are used to collect data at the place where it is generated in this way they are known as **point-of-sale devices**.

PREPARATION OF DATA When the data which is collected is not already in machine-readable form, the next job in the cycle is to convert it. The information contained on the employees' clock cards must be translated into some form which the computer can accept – it must be punched on to cards or paper tape, or keyed on to magnetic tape or disk. The most common method for many years has been punched cards, and although quicker and more efficient methods are now available, punched cards are still being used.

Punching cards, or indeed tape, is one of the most boring jobs in a computer department and it is easy for the person doing the punching to make mistakes. However, an error at punching stage, if not corrected, would lead to corrupt data entering the system and so this must be prevented. Normally, all punching is checked for errors by a process known as **verification**. In the case of cards this involves a batch of newly punched cards being 'repunched' by a different person at a **verifier**. When the second person types the same characters as are already punched the machine accepts the character and advances the card; but when a character is different the machine stops, allowing the typist to check for an error. If the error was in the original, this will be rejected and a new card typed, which will in turn be verified.

When a batch of cards have been punched and verified they form what is usually called the **input file**. This is the file composed of records which are to be input to the computer to provide data for the payroll program. In this case it consists physically of a set of cards; but it could equally be on a roll of paper tape, a magnetic tape or a magnetic disk.

Many modern systems have abandoned punched card as an inefficient and wasteful means of data preparation. After all, a sizeable card can usually hold only 80 characters and this is expensive of both paper and preparation time. Keying directly to magnetic tape or disk has become more common. This means that characters are typed at a keyboard and transferred directly on to magnetic cassette, tape or disk. This causes problems of verification in the same way as punching cards, and is handled similarly by switching the machine into verification mode and retyping. The machine is designed to help this process by displaying characters, fields and records as they are typed on a VDU screen. In verification mode, fields will be aligned and spaces printed automatically to speed the process. If the typist keys a character different from that originally typed, the keyboard locks and sounds a bleeper. The typist may then check the original record and if necessary edit or retype it.

Implications of batch processing

We have emphasised the need for uncorrupted data, and verification was one means of detecting and eliminating errors. However, there are errors other than those introduced by a typist in preparing data for input. Data may have been incorrectly recorded at the collection stage – an employee's works number may have an incorrect digit; where 'M' for 'male' is required, the whole word 'MALE' might have been written; where an entry should be numeric, an alphabetic character may have crept in; or an entire document may be lost by slipping unnoticed from a batch on to the floor. The person typing the data at the keyboard is unlikely to know what the data is supposed to mean or what conditions are imposed on it. He or she will only ensure that an accurate copy of what is there is typed into the machine.

In batch processing a batch of records are presented to the computer for processing as a single job. The necessary program will be started at the beginning of the batch and stopped at the end by appropriate records at the beginning and end of the input file. No corrections to data may be made during this time and it would be disastrous if the program were to fail due to errors in the data or, maybe even worse, produce false results such as incorrect payslips.

So, precautions are taken to check every possible source of error, so that if the program receives incorrect data this will first of all be recognised, and secondly reported as output with some suitable error message without stopping the program which will proceed with subsequent records.

INPUT, VETTING AND VALIDATION OF DATA

When the data input file has been produced the computer can be brought into the process, but before the payroll data records can be used with the payroll program, procedures of data vetting and validation must take place. Thus the input file first of all goes to a **validation program** which has the purpose of checking records for the kinds of error we mentioned above, and producing a **valid input file**.

Data **vetting** and **validation** are terms which are very close in meaning and are thus easy to confuse. *Vetting* means the checking of input data to make sure that it is in the correct form: for example the data vetting routine will reject a record if it finds alphabetic characters when numeric characters are expected; or if a field should be limited to twenty characters and actually contains thirty.

Validation follows vetting, and checks that the data presented is *valid* data. For example, if the item of data represents a date of birth then data vetting will have checked that it is numeric and possibly that it is 6 characters long. The validation routine will then check that it is a valid date of birth: that is, that the digits representing the month lie between 1 and 12; and that the day digits lie between 1 and 28, 30 or 31 depending on the month. Possibly the routine will check the year to see if February 29th is allowed.

In fact the entire program is often referred to as the validation program, so if you find it hard to appreciate the difference between the two processes referring to it all as validation is acceptable.

Checks on totals

Not all errors are simple matters of a data-item being incorrect. A DP program may well produce incorrect results, even where each individual record is correct, simply because one or more records have been omitted or lost during some transfer.

To avoid this problem as far as possible, it is usual to attach a **control total** to any batch of data at the time it is gathered together. This total depends in some way on all the records in the batch, so that if any are subsequently lost, the total calculated afresh will not agree with that attached to the batch. Some examples of control totals are:

Batch total A simple count of the number of records in the batch as a check that no records have been lost.

Hash (or nonsense) total A total of all numeric items in corresponding fields of individual records. It is in itself meaningless, but if it checks as correct then it is likely that the individual records are all present. Hash totalling may also be used to check on the correctness of one single record. For example, if employee number 45327, aged 35 years, has worked for 38 hours in a particular week a hash total might be the sum of these three numbers: 45327 + 35 + 38 = 45400. 45400 would first be worked out and written down at the data collection stage, punched at the data preparation stage and then input and checked by the validation program. If 45400 is the total at this stage then it is likely that the other numbers have all been input correctly.

Check digits

These consist of extra digits which are added to a number to act as a check that the number is entered correctly. A very good example of their use is in International Standard Book Numbers (ISBNs). All books have these – the one for this book is 0–17–438126–3 and you can see it on the cover. The very last digit is called a **check digit** and is worked out from the preceding digits in the following way:

Multiply the 1st digit by 10,
the 2nd digit by 9,
the 3rd digit by 8,
the 4th digit by 7,
the 5th digit by 6,
the 6th digit by 5,
the 7th digit by 4,
the 8th digit by 3,
the 9th digit by 2,
the 10th digit by 1.

(In England the first digit is always 0.) After working out the above products we add them together and divide by 11. If the remainder is zero then the number is valid.

The check digit is part of the number and is chosen to make this arithmetic work out correctly. In the case of this book, the publisher started with the code number: 0–17–438126. He worked out the total, as above:

$(0 \times 10) + (1 \times 9) + (7 \times 8) + (4 \times 7) + (3 \times 6) + (8 \times 5) + (1 \times 4) + (2 \times 3) + (6 \times 2)$

which comes to 173. The next higher multiple of 11 is 176, so he added on the check digit 3 and quoted the book number as 0–17–438126–3. If a check digit of 10 were required, the Roman X would be used instead.

If a number with a check digit is entered to the computer, part of the validation program will work out what the check digit should be. If this does not match the number input then the record will be rejected.

Field checks and range checks

Where fixed length records are concerned, the number and type of characters allowed in a field will be specified for each field. A field check would make sure that the number of characters does not exceed the maximum allowed and that the type of data (i.e. alphabetic, numeric, etc.) is correct. Range checks are checks on numeric data in a field to ensure that it lies within a given range – for example, that the height of an adult male lies between 100 cm and 250 cm, or that the days worked in a week lies between 0 and 7.

Garbage in = garbage out

When computers first began to have an effect on people's lives there was a saying 'garbage in = garbage out'. In other words, if you put nonsense into a computer you should not be surprised to get nonsense out.

However, we hope that you will have realised by now that to get nonsense out of a computer is not acceptable. If you write a program you must make sure that anyone trying to put in data which is nonsense will get some message – maybe a rude one! – saying that the data *is* nonsense. He should not be left to discover this by receiving nonsensical output.

SORTING OF DATA

After all the checks described, the data in the input file should now be correct, as any records with errors have been rejected. However, the valid records will be in the file in whatever order they have been presented to the computer. In the actual processing of the data, the records of this input file will need to be compared with records of a master file and will need to be in the same order as the records of the master file. The records of the input file must therefore be sorted into the same order before processing can take place.

There are many methods of sorting. When a relatively small number of data items has to be sorted, this can be done with all the items held in main store. However, in large DP applications, the number of records to be sorted is often too large for all to be held in main store at the same time. In this case different methods have to be employed. As sorting is an exercise that has to be done in very many computer applications, it is likely that the sorting programs used will have been provided by the computer manufacturer as part of the systems software.

The valid input file is used as input to the sort program and the output from this is a **sorted valid input file**. This contains exactly the same records as before, but they are now in the order required for processing.

PROCESSING OF DATA

All the preparation has now been done and the 'real' part of producing the payroll begins.

The payroll program requires data from two sources: the input file whose progress we have followed, and the file containing the 'fixed' data which we mentioned earlier. This file is commonly known as the **master file**. It will contain employee details which do not change from week to week, as well as running totals which need updating on each run. It will be stored with records in a particular order according to some key field, e.g. works number. If any of the fixed details need to be changed in a particular week, the items for change may be indicated in the corresponding employee record in the input file so that an update of the master file can take place at the same time as the payslips are being produced; or alternatively, changes to the master file may be made using an entirely separate program for this purpose alone.

The input file is sometimes known as the **transaction file**, **change file** or **update file**, since it very often contains information which causes changes or updates to be made to the master file.

In order to produce a payslip, one record is read from the master file and one from the input file, into main store. The program extracts the information that it requires in order to calculate the pay of the employee and outputs the relevant information to the line printer where a payslip is produced. If any of the 'fixed' data is to be changed or running totals updated, the record for the master file is altered accordingly and the correct master record is output to the updated version of the master file. This process is repeated until all the payslips have been produced.

The updated version of the master file will then be kept for use as the master file for the next run of the payroll program.

If this latest version of the master file were damaged in any way this could be disastrous for the next payroll run. For this reason there is a special security procedure with regard to master files, called the **Grandfather–Father–Son procedure**. When a new version of a master file is produced the previous version is not immediately destroyed: at any time, the last two versions of this file are kept as well as the most recent one. These three versions are commonly known as Grandfather, Father and Son, the Son being the most recent. The three files – and probably copies of them as well – are kept under lock and key in fireproof containers. If the computer system fails in any way while the Son is being used, it is still possible to revert to the Father or even the Grandfather if necessary and regenerate the newer versions. For this reason the transaction files for the last two generations must also be kept.

The payroll program is a special example of this processing stage of the DP cycle as it is likely that *all* records of the master file will be processed. In other applications, stock control for example, at a particular update there may be records which are not required for processing. Thus there may be stock items for which the number in stock has not changed, so that no re-ordering need be done and no change made to the record in the master file. In this case the record would be read into main store, compared with the current record of the transaction file, and since it requires no amendment it would be written out to the new file unchanged. Figure 10.4 (page 160) shows a flowchart which outlines this process.

Reconciliation errors

Sometimes an apparently valid input record passes all of the tests applied during vetting and validation, but no corresponding record can be found in the master file during the processing stage. This may be due to an error in the master file itself (an employee's record has been removed from the file by mistake, perhaps) or to an error in the input. In either case, the error, a **reconciliation error**, must be included in the error report for manual action.

OUTPUT AND REPORTING OF DATA

As a result of the processing there will be several forms of output. One of these, which we have already described, is the updated version of the master file. Also of course, and most important, is the output of data to be printed on the payslips and possibly on to bank cheques (for payment by cheque rather than cash). Other data output is a copy of all the payslip details for the firm's accounts department, and a report of all the errors which have been encountered during the run of the program.

The payslips are most likely to be printed on preprinted stationery by a high speed printer. The data will have been organised by the program so that each item is printed at the correct position on the slip which will already contain sections and headings to make the data understandable to the person reading it. The printer concerned will be fully occupied by this task while the payroll job is in progress and so will be unavailable for any other job during this time.

Consequently, the other forms of output will need to take place at other printers. The error report will have two purposes: first to inform the accounts department that payslips have not been produced for certain employees, so that these can be produced manually in time for payday; and second to alert the computer department to errors that have been detected at various stages of the computer process. Each error will be reported with information as to its source, and this might occasion the computer manager to warn his data preparation department to be more careful of errors at the data punching stage, or maybe, more seriously, indicate as yet undetected bugs in the program and create for the programmers a few headaches in correcting them.

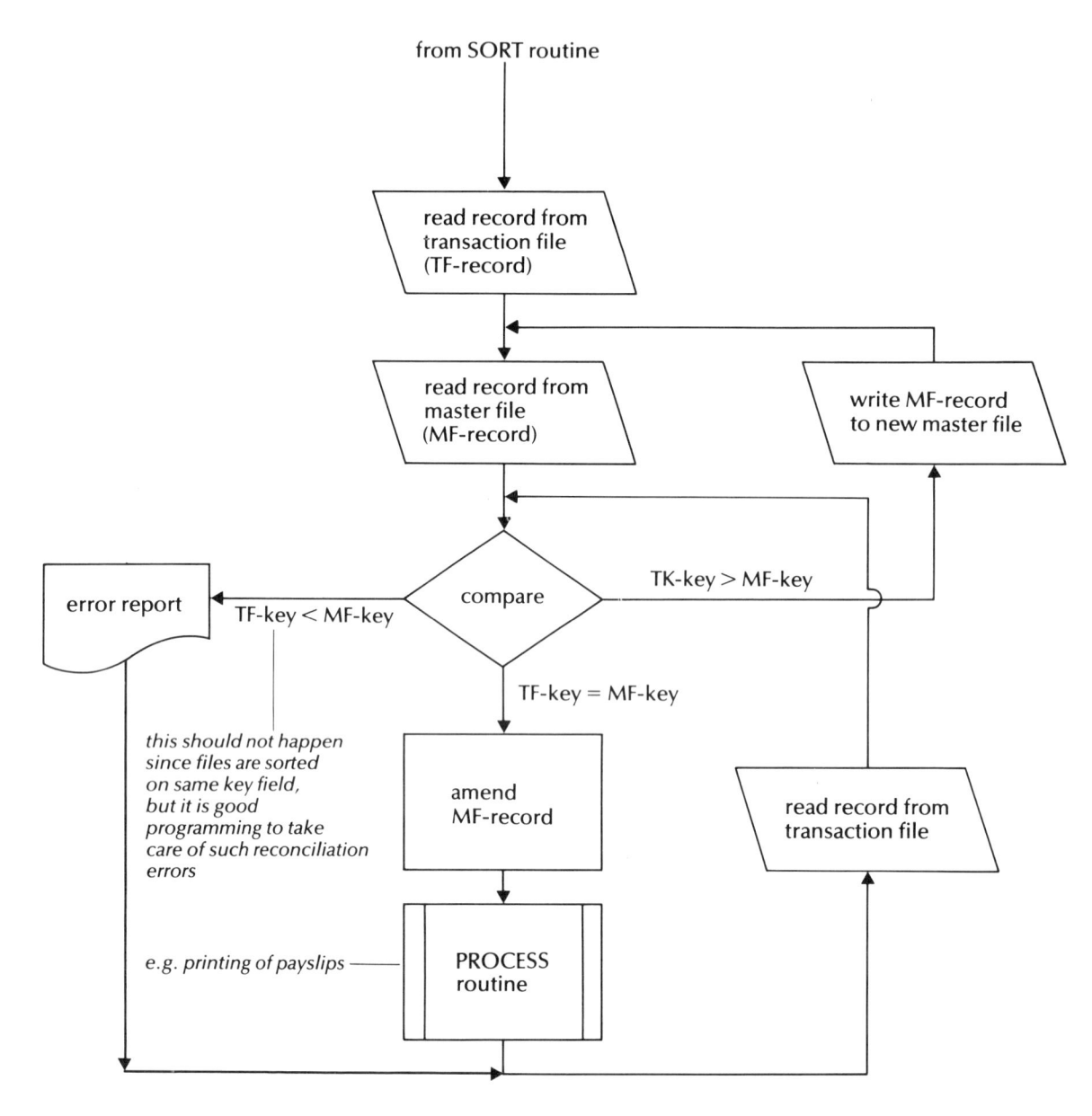

Figure 10.4 *Updating the master file. This flowchart is incomplete: it does not account for what happens when the end of records in a file is reached (see Exercise 6).*

Reports to the accounts department will be printed at yet another printing device, the data this time being formatted in the most convenient way for reading by book-keepers, accountants and auditors.

When every payslip has been printed and the reports are complete, the various files will be put into a close security store. It is quite likely that preparation will have already started for the next payroll run and the entire cycle will be in the process of repeating itself.

Computer personnel

In studying data processing, we have seen that there are several jobs that need to be done. While it is probably true that no two data-processing departments are alike, it is possible to pick out from our typical example a number of people whose counterparts will appear in almost any establishment of any size that uses a computer.

Firstly, because the computer department is usually an important part of any business, it will be organised with its own manager, who is responsible for the overall running of the department, for suggesting new equipment to buy, for appointing new staff and so on. He is usually called the **data-processing manager.** Sometimes, a department is large enough for this job to be divided into an **operations manager** who handles the running of the whole system, and a DP manager, who has administrative responsibility over the operations manager. Sometimes, just to be confusing, these titles are swapped around!

Under the manager of the department, there are likely to be three main areas of activity. There are those staff concerned with preparing the data and responsible for its flow through the system; those concerned with the actual running of the hardware; and those responsible for maintaining the computer software.

The staff who deal with preparation of data are usually known as the **data-preparation staff**. Their head is called something like a **data-preparation manager**, or supervisor, or sometimes a data-controller. The people in the department are usually known as data-preparation clerks, or, if appropriate, key-punch operators.

Running the computer is the job of the **operators**, organised into teams of chief operator (or shift leader) and junior operators. They are responsible for loading tapes, taking any remedial action that is necessary, and generally interacting with the operating system to control the system.

The last group is not so directly concerned with the DP cycle. These are the **programming staff**, who are responsible for writing new programs, amending existing ones to take account of changes in the business, and coping with 'bugs' discovered in existing software. It is common to divide programmers into **applications programmers**, and **system programmers** (see page 94). Where the department is large, teams of programmers may work together under a **chief programmer**. If the department is really large, and the company

162 *Data processing*

expect to continue to expand their computer department, there may also be **systems analysts** on the staff, led by a chief systems analyst. It is quite common, however, to hire such staff as systems analysts when the department is planning a major development.

There may also be other staff, such as tape librarians (responsible for keeping tape files in order) control clerks, documentation assistants and so on. In a really large installation, there will be a resident engineer, perhaps supplied by the computer manufacturer, so that there is skilled help always on call.

The main jobs are arranged in Figure 10.5, which shows the interrelation of jobs in a large DP department.

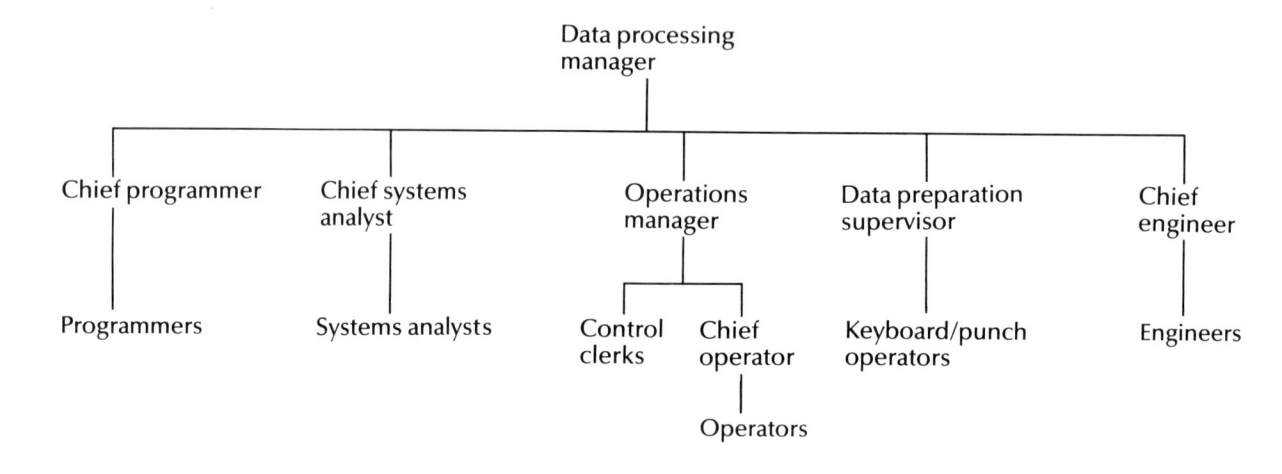

```
                        Data processing
                           manager
   ┌───────────┬──────────────┼──────────────┬──────────────┐
Chief        Chief systems  Operations    Data preparation  Chief
programmer   analyst        manager       supervisor        engineer
   │           │          ┌────┴────┐        │                │
Programmers  Systems     Control  Chief   Keyboard/punch   Engineers
             analysts    clerks   operator operators
                                   │
                                Operators
```

Figure 10.5 *Computer personnel*

Summary

This chapter has been about *commercial data processing (DP)*. It has looked at the particular problems and requirements of data handling on a large scale, by means of *batch* processing.

Three typical examples, *payroll, stock control* and *order processing* were considered. The particular requirements of the payroll application were examined and the *data processing cycle* was described with reference to these requirements. This included the *collection, preparation* and *verification* of data; its *input* with *vetting* and *validation* procedures; the *processing* of the data and its *output* together with *reports,* including *error reports. Data* or *system flowcharts* were introduced as a means of representing the processes involved.

The chapter ended with a description of the *personnel* working in a computer department and the jobs which they do.

EXERCISE for individual work

1 The words *verification* and *validation* are easy to confuse. Explain briefly what is meant by data verification and data validation to show that you understand the difference between them.

EXERCISE for individual work

2 500 questionnaires are processed as a batch. As part of the processing, the *total number of questionnaires* processed is calculated and also the total of all *ages* (age is a piece of information required in the questionnaire) recorded. The first of these is known as the *batch* total, and the second as a *hash* total. Explain the reason for calculating these totals.

EXERCISE for individual work

3 A mail-order firm identifies its agents by nine-digit numbers. As a check on the correct recording of these numbers, a 10th digit is put at the end which is calculated in the way described for book numbers on page 156. Explain why such a check digit is necessary and calculate the digit which would be fixed to the number 123456789.

EXERCISE for individual work

4 Explain what is meant by the three generations of a file known as *Grandfather*, *Father* and *Son*, and why these are necessary.

EXERCISE for individual work

5 An important output of the payroll program is the error reports. Describe *three* different types of error which would need to be reported.

EXERCISE for individual work

6 Redraw the flowchart in Figure 10.4 to allow for the correct behaviour when an attempt to read a record from a file shows that there are no more records in that file. If this occurs with the master file *before* it occurs in the transaction file, this must be an error, because there will be some records left in the transaction file. But it would be perfectly possible for the transaction file to run out of records before the master file, in which case you must take steps to ensure that the remaining records of the master file are copied to the new master file.

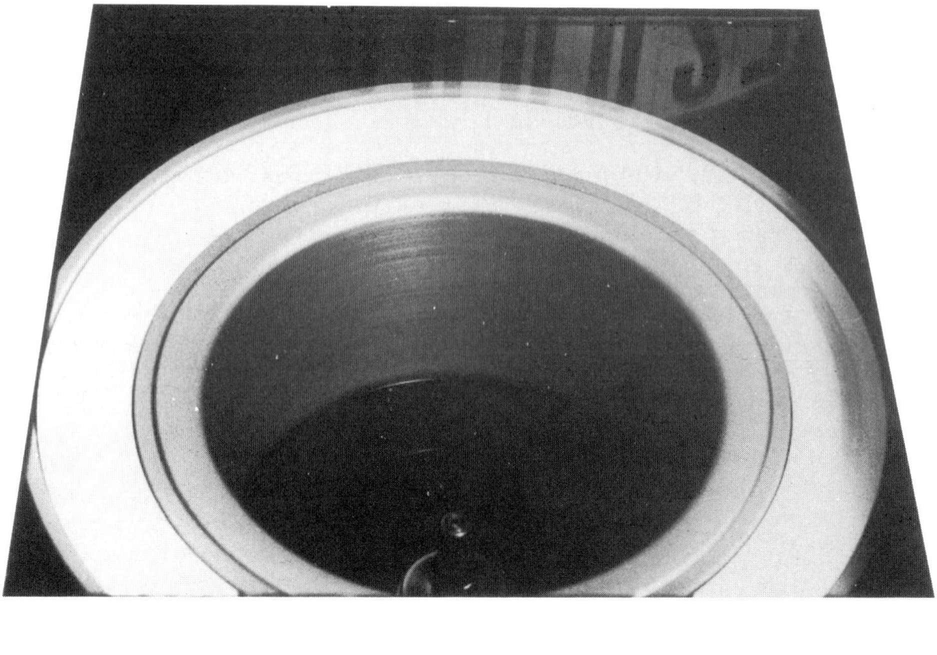

11 Computer applications
REAL-TIME SYSTEMS

In this final chapter of the book, we first take a look at some uses of the computer where the amount of processing that is done seems to be very small indeed. We shall look at systems where the computer is used simply to store data so that it may easily be retrieved.

This may seem to be wasting the power of the computer: we have seen in other chapters how the computer can be used to perform mathematical calculations at breathtaking speed; we have seen how the computer can be programmed to follow the rules of games like 'Mastermind'.

But we have also seen that the important uses of computers – certainly the most frequently encountered ones – are the less glamorous ones: the payroll, library systems, order processing, stock control and so on. In these applications of computers, what processing is done tends to be simple and straightforward, at the level of totalling columns of figures.

Information retrieval

Using a computer as a means of accessing a large quantity of stored data is called **information retrieval**. Like 'data processing', it is a peculiar choice of name, as almost any serious use of the computer involves retrieving some data from storage – and hence retrieving information that the data represents. But the term commonly means using a computer to ask questions about a large quantity of data stored in the computer. We shall look first at a system where the user does not change the data, but merely asks questions about it, and then at a system where the use of the computer is to keep the data fully up to date, so that the user makes changes as well as asking questions.

The first system is the Police National Computer Unit (PNCU): it has been the subject of many arguments between people who think that it is an intrusion into people's privacy and others who believe that it enables the police to do a better job.

The second is an airline reservation system, such as that used by British Airways. There are many such systems, used not only by airlines but also by theatre-ticket agencies, credit card companies and so on.

Real-time working

Even a little thought should convince you that the requirements of systems such as these are very different to those of a payroll system, say. While it is crucially important that the payroll is produced, the time it takes is of secondary importance. In the two systems that we shall look at, the time taken for the computer to respond is possibly the most important objective.

Systems that work rapidly enough to provide results before they are out-of-date, or too late to be useful, are called **real-time systems**, because their scale of working is the scale of everyday life. An enquiry from a policeman on the beat can be answered while the policeman waits; a question about flights to San Francisco can be dealt with while the customer is standing at the airline ticket desk, or the travel agent's counter.

THE POLICE COMPUTER The idea behind the police using a computer seems a good one. Police forces keep records of people convicted of crimes, and also (because their job is preventing crime) records of people that they *suspect* of crimes. Many crimes involve motor cars, and part of the store of data to which the police have access is a complete record of all vehicle registration details: the details that can be seen on the registration document – the colour, make, owner's name, registration letters and so on.

This enables the policeman (on the beat or on patrol in a car) to call up the central police station on his radio, and ask the computer operator sitting at an interactive terminal on-line to the computer to request a print-out of the details of any car he wishes. A policeman, spot-checking late at night outside an unattended car park where there have been a lot of thefts, can stop a driver and ask him to identify himself: if he cannot give the name and address that the computer has on record, or if he has put false number plates on the car and the details no longer match, the computer may have enabled the police to catch a criminal. Very few people would complain that this is anything but a worthwhile use of computers.

Computers can also be used to simplify the equally worthwhile task of identifying fingerprints. There are many fingerprints of convicted people on record, and the task of matching prints found at the scene of a crime to those on record is a skilled (and probably boring) task. Fingerprints are now being added to the data held by the police computer. The major problem has been in turning a fingerprint into digital data in a way that makes it easy to pick out a match, particularly where the print taken from the scene of the crime is incomplete, or smudged. But this task has been solved, with some ingenuity.

If information about a *person* is required, then this too is available on computer: police data is structured so that it is as easy to find out about a person from one of his aliases as from his real name; and if details of his known associates in crime are required, the files will contain cross-references that enable the details of these people to be retrieved as well.

Arguments for . . .

The motor vehicle example given above is part of the evidence that the computer does a good job for the police. When the police are questioned about their system (as they are frequently, because the system has many opponents), they usually reply that the computer is only making easier the jobs that the police have always been doing and that record keeping, even about suspects rather than known criminals, has always been a part of good police work. The arguments against the police use of computers are rather more subtle.

. . . and against

Many people (and not necessarily just the guilty ones) have an instinctive aversion to records being kept about them: it seems in some way to be an invasion of their right to keep themselves to themselves as long as they harm no one. The police claim that they are keeping no records that they didn't keep before, but publicity about police use of computers has awakened alarm in people that perhaps they should have felt before.

A much more serious worry that is voiced is the increase in power that is given to the police when two collections of data are merged, or where a perfectly proper collection is handed over from its proper keepers to another group of people.

For example, details of all motor vehicles are collected by the Driver and Vehicle Licensing Centre (DVLC) at Swansea; they collect this data because it is their function to record all legal drivers and vehicles. But this data, collected for one purpose, has already been made available to the police for another — it seems, with good effect. Opponents of this point out that there are other collections of computerised data that would be much more useful to the police, but which it would be much more worrying for them to be allowed to have: people's tax or National Insurance records, for instance, which give details of the jobs people hold and where they live. There is no requirement to register your address with the police but if the police had access to these records, this is what would, in practice, be happening.

It is also argued that because it is now so easy to store and retrieve data about people in the police computer, the police will be less careful about the data they do record, checking less fully to see that it is fact and not suspicion or supposition. It is impossible to argue for or against this without knowing what details the police do have on file, and for obvious reasons they are unlikely to publish this! This very secrecy is another argument against that is often put forward: if the police have nothing to hide, why do they hide it so effectively?

But perhaps the biggest fear that people have, with ample reason, is that computerised data can more easily be abused: the checks on who can use it, and what they do with it, are likely to be less effective than with manual systems. In part, this last reason is because people are taking a little while to adjust to the effects of computers on their everyday lives. Just before this book was written, a court case was brought in which the operators of a casino were accused of using a contact in the police force to obtain names and addresses from the police computer of car owners who had been seen leaving rival casinos. Such a misuse of public records is clearly deplorable, but the important question is — how much is the computer to blame?

SYSTEMS DESIGN FOR THE POLICE COMPUTER

With a system such as the police computer, where real-time operation and the ability to respond to enquiries within seconds is particularly important, the system has to be designed in a particular way. For example, no form of serial access (see pages 66–7), where other records have to be read through before coming upon the correct one, is likely to be of any use. Random or direct access devices, such as disk drives, are likely to be the most visible feature of a real-time system.

In going directly to the desired record, use must be made of the *record key*. But an information retrieval system such as that of the police will need to allow the user to search for records without knowing their primary key values. For example, if a suspect is described as 'blonde, blue-eyed' then a search must be made for all records of people that contain this description. It seems at first as if this implies a search through every record (several million of them!) rejecting those that do not meet this test. But the use of indexes can help (see page 54). A feature of a retrieval system such as the police one is that it keeps several indexes to the features of a record that may be needed, such as descriptions. A quick scan through the index will provide the locations (on disk) of all the records that must be printed, and a clever operating system can rearrange these records into a convenient order, so that they may be accessed at the time that they are most conveniently available on the disk.

Updating

Clearly, data is also put into the police computer system, not just retrieved. This causes some problems, which we shall see better in looking at a second real-time system, where the user not only retrieves data, but also enters it from his terminal.

AIRLINE RESERVATION SYSTEMS

Booking seats on an ordinary scheduled aircraft (that is, where you buy the ticket alone, and not as part of some holiday package, booked long in advance) is an enormous problem for airlines. For a start, many people only decide to travel at short notice. It is not sufficient to say that if a seat is empty, it can be sold: a passenger may be joining the flight at an intermediate stop and intending to occupy that seat. Worse still, the information about which passengers wish to fly from where to where is not available at some convenient central point, but rather is spread over several airports in different countries, often thousands of miles apart. So it was natural that airlines should use the computer.

With a computerised system, data about the capacity of a flight – how many first-class seats, how many economy and so on – is held (usually on disk) by a central computer. This computer is connected to terminals (usually VDUs) in airports, travel agents and airline offices around the world.

When a booking is to be made, the airline employee at the desk will use the VDU to call up details of the flight in question. If the traveller is not particularly concerned about exactly when he or she flies, it may be possible to ask about available flights before selecting one to make a booking on. As the booking is made, the clerk enters the details of the passenger into the system, and the data on the disk is altered to note these details, and also to reduce the number of available seats for future bookings.

Problems begin to arise when the flight in question is almost fully booked. It takes perhaps three minutes from the time that the clerk first calls up details of the flight until the passenger's confirmed booking is made, and his details entered. During these three minutes, another clerk, possibly somewhere on the other side of the world, must not be allowed to sell the last seat on the flight. Access to the record with details of this flight must be **locked** against further access until the first clerk relinquishes it.

But this sort of protection is not necessary when the flight is still relatively under-booked. So from experience, the airline's computer system will be 'tuned' to make educated guesses – allowing two airport desks to have access to the same flight record while the flight is lightly-loaded, but taking stricter precautions when the flight gets closer to take-off and presumably is more fully-booked.

It is interesting to try to list the objectives of such a system. For example, does the airline feel prepared to risk over-booking because passengers usually drop out close to departure? Is a fast response better than an accurate one? If a disk drive containing details of a particular flight becomes unavailable because of a breakdown, should *any* booking be allowed? (This is a subtle question: the answer is far from obvious, if there *is* an answer.) Back-up copies could be kept of all transactions, just as in the payroll system, but this will slow the system down, and cost more – is it worth it? Is the inconvenience of a few passengers worth less than a fast, but not totally secure system?

SYSTEMS DESIGN FOR THE RESERVATION SYSTEM

An airline reservation system can theoretically be accessed by any of thousands of terminals at once. Does this mean that the system should be an enormously large and expensive version of a time sharing system used to develop programs on? Probably not. First, each terminal will request data only infrequently, so the load on the system may not be as great as might at first seem. Secondly, all the terminals in one airport may be linked through some 'concentrator', arranging their requests in order. So the software in the central computer could imagine it was talking to a network of concentrators, rather than a much larger network of terminals.

As you might expect, a reservation system would use direct access hardware, as in the police system. There would also be indexes, although probably fewer of them as only the flight number and route are likely to be important. Another question of interest is whether passenger names are worth holding.

Mixed batch and real-time systems

Not all the jobs to be carried out by an airline system need speedy response. The same data is used for printing out documents such as passenger lists, load factors, for analysing ticket sales and so on. These tasks can comfortably be handled as batch jobs which run in the gaps between the system being fully occupied in dealing with user requests. Such a mixed system is sometimes called a **foreground/background system**, as some jobs are being processed in real-time (the 'foreground') while other batch jobs are run in-between (in the 'background'). It need not only be batch jobs that run in the background: the development and testing of new programs could be a task carried out by programmers using on-line terminals that have a lower priority than the terminals servicing booking requests.

Databases

We have already mentioned that the airline system will have programs that produce reports and analyses, in the background, while the main system is running. With systems that use serial devices, such as magnetic tape, it is convenient to organise the data in files specially designed for the use they are to be put to. The file needed for passenger lists, for example, would be a copy of the main booking files with some data omitted, and perhaps sorted into a different order. As soon as two separate files exist, with the same data copied into more than one place, a problem emerges. If an alteration is made to one file, that alters a piece of the common data, the second file cannot be similarly updated at once, and possibly never will be. So serial access systems, based on files, run the risk of some programs working on out-of-date data.

With direct access devices, such as magnetic disks, it is possible to avoid this, by keeping each piece of data only once — imagining the whole collection of data as one enormous file, rather than several separate ones. Such a collection is called a **database**. Some people use the word to mean simply any very large collection of data, but it has a more precise technical meaning, implying that attempts have been made to avoid duplicating data (and other more subtle design features that we shall not discuss here). With any database, such as an airline database, goes a piece of software called a **database management system (DBMS)**. This has the job of making sure that the user does not have to face the problem of threading his way around extra pieces of data that he does not wish to know about (in a tape-file system, these items would have been left out when the file was prepared, for economy). The job of the DBMS is basically to keep the programmer thinking that he is still using a tape-file based system.

QUERY LANGUAGES

Of course, it is necessary for the user of an information retrieval or a database system to be able to specify quickly and easily what information it is that he wishes to have retrieved. In order to do this sensibly, he must have some idea of what information is in the database. More correctly, he must have some idea as to how it is structured: knowing that hair-colouring is referred to as `HAIR` and not as `COLOUR` and so on.

The way in which the user tells the system what information he wants can vary in complexity and ease of use. Quite often the user is allowed to phrase his queries in a language rather like a programming language (usually called a **query language**, as it is used for posing queries).

Figure 11.1 (page 172) shows some examples of the sort of dialogue that might result from a user interrogating a database. At the top are some examples of queries being posed on a system where the data held is about the chemical elements; below is the same system being used on a database that contains details of the nutritional make-up of various foods. At the bottom, a commercial database is shown being accessed for information about orders placed for part number 8082.

In each case, you can see that queries can be built up by using a mixture of special words — `LIST`, `WHERE`, and so on in the bottom example — together with names of data-items — `VALENCY`, `DENSITY`, and so on — and values used for testing and selecting from the whole collection of data.

```
:QUE VALENCY = 4 AND DENSITY < 10
:PRI ELEMENT SYMBOL NUMBER
:GO
Searching file: PTABLE
For: VALENCY = AND DENSITY < 10
ELEMENT          SYMBOL NUMBER
=======          ====== ======
CARBON           C      6
SILICON          SI     14
TITANIUM         TI     22
GERMANIUM        GE     32
SELENIUM         SE     34
ZIRCONIUM        ZR     40
TIN              SN     50
TELLURIUM        TE     52
       8 records matched



Searching file: FOOD
For: NAME SUB "CREAM"

NAME                         FAT  ENGY
====                         ===  ====
CREAM HORN                   41.6 519
CREAM SLICE                  28.9 402
DOUGHNUT - JAM AND CREAM     12.4 328
CREAM - DOUBLE               48.3 448
CREAM - SINGLE               22.2 222
CHEESE - CREAM               37.7 381
POTATOES - CREAMED            5.3 120
ICE CREAM                     9.2 180
ICE CREAM - DAIRY            12.7 219
WAFERS - FOR ICE CREAM       12.4 427


      10 records matched



LIST SUPPLIER-NUMBER, ORDER-NUMBER, PART-NUMBER,
    QUANTITY WHERE PART-NUMBER = '8082'

SUPPLIER-NUMBER   ORDER-NUMBER   PART-NUMBER   QUANTITY
       887           10573A         8082          200
       887           10573B         8082          100
       905           14316J         8082          500
       982           27961F         8082          300
```

Figure 11.1

Computer networks

We saw, in discussing the airline reservation system, that while the data was held centrally, it could be convenient to use concentrators spread around the world to help make the computer's task easier. This idea can be extended. As soon as we are doing *any* computing outside of the main computer, it becomes possible to do a *lot* of it outside. Instead of just concentrating requests from terminals into an orderly stream that is presented to the computer one request at a time, why shouldn't the concentrator be a fully-fledged computer system in its own right, using its own data storage to keep records of flights departing from the airport where the concentrator is sited? Thus, in New York, the New York concentrator holds details of all the flights out of New York. In London, the computer holds only flights out of London.

Now, whenever New York clerks need to make an outward booking, they can simply use their own local computer without bothering about the transatlantic link. Of course, this benefit is exactly balanced by the London clerks needing to link up with the New York computer every time they want to make the return half of a booking!

But even so, this system could make savings, because most bookings (not all, but most) out of New York are made from New York itself. In any case, the idea we have seen here is an important one, with other applications besides reservation systems. We have designed a computer **network**. That is, a set of computers, usually spread around a country, or even the world, and linked by land-lines or satellites. Each user makes use of his own 'home' computer until he requires a program, or data or computing power that is only available on another computer. He then uses special commands to link in to another computer on the network. Possibly, the operating systems of the computers in the network co-operate, sending work from one heavily loaded computer to one with more spare capacity, and sending the results back – possibly without the user knowing!

Of course, this causes some problems: the computers in the network may well be different makes, and some standard of communication between them is required. Rather than have a link from each computer in the network to every other, they will probably be arranged in something like a telephone network, with the route between any two particular computers being partly over links shared with other computers in the network. When data, or requests for action are sent around the system, this is usually done by splitting the messages up into 'packets' of fixed size, adding an 'address' of the destination computer to the front of the packet and sending it off to find its way through the system – this is known as **packet switching**. (This is the opposite of what normally happens when you use the telephone: dialling the number sets up a circuit between your phone and the phone you are calling, which is used exclusively by you until your call is completed. This is called **circuit switching**.)

Not all real-time systems are simply information retrieval ones, of course.

Other real-time systems

Real-time uses of a computer tend to be the more glamorous, and as computing hardware becomes cheaper, we should expect to see more and more of them. Before you read on, you may like to discuss the following exercise.

EXERCISE for discussion

1 What real-time uses of a computer do you know of?

You may know that if you make a telephone query to the gas board, or the electricity board, or even the telephone accounts office, the query is probably dealt with by someone sitting in front of a VDU screen, able to call up the details of your account, and answer questions about it. In order for this to happen fast enough, the system must be a real-time system. Probably it is designed like a database, without duplicate copies of the data, so that one clerk is not preparing an overdue reminder at the same time as someone else is recording that you have just paid your bill! Quite possibly, the system is running enquiries in the foreground, while a batch program to print bills, reminders and so on is operating in the background.

CONTROL SYSTEMS Another important use of real-time computing is in the control of (for example) manufacturing processes. Many car assembly lines are now so automated that a computer is necessary to control the operation – welding, spraying with paint, and so on. Because manufacturing processes are not naturally digital, and because digital computers are usually preferred (because they are easier to reprogram) an important piece of equipment in a real-time control system is an **analog-to-digital converter**. This is a piece of hardware that receives readings (say of temperature) and converts them into a digital form. In this way, the computer is receiving digital data. In order to affect the process, corresponding **digital-to-analog converters** are used: on receipt of the correct digital signal, such a device might turn up the heat under a chemical vat, for example. Such converters are necessary, because the real control mechanisms are usually instructed by analog signals (a higher voltage means more heat, for instance) and a digital computer can only process digital data – it can only receive digital data as input, and it can only produce digital data as output.

It is necessary to understand the process being controlled very well indeed, in order to make sensible use of a computer for control. Suppose that the purpose of a small part of such a control system is to keep the temperature of a bath of fluid (photographic developer, perhaps) in the allowable range of 18°C–21°C. What happens if the computer reads that the temperature has risen to 22°C? Clearly, the heater must be turned down. But the heater will take some while to respond and if the computer looks at the temperature again too soon, it will still detect a high temperature, and may turn the heater down even further. It could be that this happens so often that the heater is turned right off, and the fluid now becomes too cold. Such see-sawing backwards and forwards should be avoided, or the fluid may never stay at the correct temperature for long enough to develop a photograph.

A control program must also test that the device which it is controlling has responded correctly. If the heater is malfunctioning, and signals to turn it down are being ignored, the computer probably needs to ring an alarm bell, or shut down the whole process.

Timing is important, too. A program to measure shutter speeds on a camera (which could be as short as 1/1000 second or as long as several seconds) must ensure that the timing routine cannot be interrupted (perhaps by some background processing that uses the computer while it is apparently idle) until the shutter closes, or else the timing will be out.

THE PROBLEM OF SECURITY

Because a real-time system has to respond quickly, it may not always be possible to carry out all the checks necessary on the data. Consider the uses of a computer in a bank. Many of the uses are simple, straightforward batch account with withdrawals, standing orders, and so on. But where the computer is also used to control a cash dispenser, the possibility arises of the wrong person attempting to draw money. In the regular passage of a cheque through a bank, a human being compares a specimen signature against that on the cheque. With present-day cash dispensers, signing is not possible. Usually, the person drawing money is given a card, which has coded into it, on a magnetic strip, a secret number – a sort of password – which the user has to key into the dispenser at the same time: this takes the place of the signature, although it is far less secure. Usually there is an upper limit to the amount of money that can be drawn from such a cash dispenser. This is the amount that the bank is prepared to lose (rather unwillingly) in exchange for the convenience of providing dispensers. Hopefully, there will be no fraud, but if there is, the amount is limited to this maximum sum.

There are other security problems, too. It must be remembered that the computer operators often see the data that a computer holds – it is often necessary for them to see this, in order to do their jobs properly. Steps must be taken to ensure that illegal use cannot be made of this information. Usually, only those people who need to visit the computer to do their job effectively are allowed into the computer room. Programmers, for instance, are usually *not* allowed in! In this way, they cannot amend their programs when they are in the machine to increase their own salaries, for example. Alterations made outside the computer will be documented, and usually seen by several employees, which should prevent any such fraud.

RECOVERY PROCEDURES

You have seen in the chapter on data-processing, that care is taken to ensure that a commercial program is reliable and secure. But with the best care in the world, accidents will happen – a piece of hardware breaks down, or a program is discovered to have a fault that was not revealed by testing. In such cases, it is necessary to have well-documented **recovery procedures**. These are programs that can be run to correct mistakes. Such programs might take a fresh copy of the data from a back-up copy of a disk (back-up copies are often taken at the end of each day). Then the recovery procedure must amend this data with all the changes that have been made since the last back-up copy was taken. For this reason, it is usual to keep a copy of every single input to the computer (since the last back-up) in a file called a **journal file** (this just means 'daily record'). The process of making new back-up copies and freeing the previous copies is often called **archiving**. Special care must be taken, in case an error occurs during archiving. It is possible that some such error corrupts the file that is being read from. It is for exactly this reason that the **Grandfather-Father-Son** method of master file archiving described on page 159 is used. If an error occurs while the 'Son' file is being created, it could be that the 'Father' file is corrupted. But the 'Grandfather' file, which is not part of this process, will still be available as a safety back-up.

Word processing

We have left one computer application until last, because it is a rather special one – a rather personal one if you are writing a book.

In producing this book, the people involved – authors, publishers and printers – were working all the time with the same set of words. We, the authors, wrote out a first draft and then changed our minds and corrected the spelling mistakes, rewrote some sections and generally mangled the manuscript so much that some sections of it vanished under a sea of red pencil!

After we were happy with the manuscript, some sections were so untidy that they had to be re-typed, before they could go to the publisher. After the publishers' editor had made his corrections to the manuscript, it was handed over to the typesetter who worried (for the first time) about making the left-hand margins straight, positioning the headings correctly, leaving space for diagrams and so on.

There were many other stages as well, but at every one of the stages mentioned, people were processing text. That is, they were processing digital data. It seems like an excellent opportunity for a computer to be involved, and indeed it is! The application is known as **word processing**, and is most usually found in offices, rather than at printers. Instead of typing a letter directly on to a typewriter, the typist will prepare a first draft using a VDU screen, with a small computer storing the text on backing store as it is typed. There is an opportunity for the author of the letter to look over a draft of the letter and make any corrections necessary. The typist then goes back to the VDU and calls up the text of the letter from backing store, making the corrections then and there. This process of correction and drafting can happen as many times as required, until a perfect copy is arrived at. As at each stage, only errors are being corrected, we can be sure that no new mistakes are being introduced as previously correct pages are re-typed.

When the final draft is agreed, a copy may be made on a high-quality typewriter-like device. If required, headings may be centred, margins aligned and so on.

But this is only the beginning. There are many documents that are very similar to one another – legal contracts, advertising letters, subscription renewal reminders and so on. Sophisticated word processors allow the typist to call up from backing store complete chunks of a letter, and to arrange these together with a few 'personal' paragraphs to make what appears to be an individual letter. Perhaps even the complete text of a letter is stored, together with 'holes' into which names, addresses and so on are to be inserted. The word processor can then be instructed to spend hours typing out the same letter, but taking the 'personal details' from a file, also held in the word processor.

The printers' job can also be made easier with the aid of a computer. Instead of selecting pieces of type (either by hand or by a typesetting keyboard), the task can be handled by computer – again coping with positioning, spacing, margins and so forth. Proofs can be run off and corrections made to the backing storage copy of the text, possibly before it is committed to an expensive form ready for printing. If a second edition is required, but perhaps with some changes, the complete text of the first edition can be held in store and retrieved for appropriate insertions.

Text editors are actually an important part of almost all computing practice. Although we naturally think of commercially-slanted word processors, it is worth remembering that when you first type a program into an interactive computer system, it is just text – until a translator is used, the characters have no meaning to the computer: and any mistakes that you make in typing are corrected by the use of a text editor, even if you do not have to announce that you wish to use one.

Perhaps the only important question is – if word processors make life so easy, why didn't we use one?

○ EXERCISE for discussion ○
○ ○
○ 2 Why didn't we? ○

Summary

This chapter has looked at applications of computers that fall outside the general description of 'data processing'. Of course, all these applications process data – because that is a fundamental part of our definition of a computer – but the ones in this chapter are those which make use of the *real-time* capabilities of a computer.

We have not provided you with extensive case studies of the use of a computer in different organisations – partly because we do not wish to deny you the real pleasure of investigating yourselves, and partly because computing is so changeable that such descriptions would rapidly take on a rather antique air. What *is* important is that you should be able to take an open mind to the study of any computer application, and be able to apply the principles that you have read about in this book.

EXERCISE for discussion

3 Is the Police National Computer Unit a good or bad thing? The answer will not simply be 'yes' or 'no'.

EXERCISE for research

4 What information retrieval systems do you know of? For each one, describe briefly how queries are posed to the system — if possible, giving an example.

Appendix 1
SOLUTIONS TO EXERCISES

This is *not* a fully comprehensive set of answers to the exercises in this book.

Where exercises are contained in the text, the answers are often supplied in the text immediately following the exercise. Where this does not happen, there are three possibilities:

a A precise answer is possible and this will be found below.

b The question may be answered in a number of ways for which we outline a possible solution, or give hints towards one.

c No answer is supplied.

In the third case we feel that there are questions for which our solution would be of little help and you are advised here to discuss your 'answer' with your teacher or tutor.

SOLUTIONS TO CHAPTER 1

1 a Not reprogrammable.

b This would seem to satisfy all of our requirements – the fact that many people think that such a calculator is *not* a computer is possibly due to the significant difference of scale in such matters as speed of operation and size of store, and to the inability of such a calculator to work with any data other than that representing numbers: such features are not fundamental to our definition.

c This processes washing, not data – certainly not digital data, also not reprogrammable.

d Not reprogrammable.

e Not reprogrammable.

f Not reprogrammable.

g Although a certain amount of reprogramming is probably possible in such devices (to cope with new customers, new coinage and so on), it seems likely that this is accomplished by altering the data, and hence this device is not reprogrammable.

h Not automatic, nor reprogrammable.

Note that these solutions do suggest that there are many devices capable of acting in a computer-like manner, except that they are dedicated to a single task, and cannot be reprogrammed to carry out any other task.

2 a Temperature is not naturally digital, but we usually write it down as a number, and we have thus converted it into digits; such a conversion implicitly causes some loss of precision, because we are representing a continuously varying quantity as a discrete quantity.

b Yes, these are digital, the digits being the letters of the alphabet, possibly enhanced by some special linguistic signs.

Solutions to exercises 181

- **c** This is rather subtle! The *words* are digital, in the sense of **b** above; if we meant the *sounds* uttered by a speaker, the answer is less clear. Phonetic alphabets attempt to provide a set of digits that can be used to express spoken words as digital data, but these are not fine enough to distinguish between, say, a male and a female speaker. At the time of writing, there is some evidence that speech analysers and synthesisers are moving towards the successful representation of the spoken word as digital data.
- **d** Nothing changes by moving from English to French, so the answer is the same as for **c**.
- **e** Digital.
- **f, g** These are both similar to temperature, see **a**.
- **h** As a recipe is expressed in words, it clearly can be expressed as digital data.
- **i** The Roman numerals are as much digits as the familiar Arabic numbers 0, 1, 2, 3 . . .
- **j** As with **c**, it rather depends on what we mean! If we are trying to represent *positions* on a map, then these can be dealt with as we have done with similar numerical type data in **a, f** and **g**; the commonest method (at least for maps of the UK) is the National Grid reference. A map seen as a *picture* is not really digital, except that we could consider that a map consists of a series of grid references, together with information about what is found at that reference; in this case, a suitable digital representation is probably possible (indeed, many cartographers do use digital computer techniques).
- **k** A knitting pattern is as much a recipe as that given in **h**; indeed, there are many similarities between knitting patterns and computer programming languages – both have some sort of repetitive looping structure, for example.
- **l** This is very much a case of 'What do you mean by people?' If you merely require to give each person some unique identifier, simply numbering them will suffice – attaching an obviously digital representation to each person. Incorporating more information about each person doesn't alter the nature of the solution, as age, occupation, address, phone number and so on are capable of digital representation. It is likely, however, that something more subtle is intended, in which case a digital coding in anything but a coarse way is likely to be impossible.
- **m** Surprisingly, there are two different ways of arriving at the same answer here. First, programs are as much recipes as knitting patterns or cooking recipes – they can be expressed in words and symbols, and so are clearly digital. A second argument runs: as we *know* that computer programs are processed by digital computers, they must be digital! This second argument is underlined by the fact that computer programs occupy the same store as the data they operate on.

SOLUTIONS TO CHAPTER 2 No exercises require solutions.

SOLUTIONS TO CHAPTER 3

2 4 bits allow 16 patterns (2^4)
8 bits allow 256 patterns (2^8)
Patterns available with 4 bits are:
```
0000  0001  0010  0011
0100  0101  0110  0111
1000  1001  1010  1011
1100  1101  1110  1111
```
In general, for a location of 'n' bits there will be 2^n patterns available.

3 **a** 26   **b** 76   **c** 139   **d** 228

5 is represented by **00000101**
38 is represented by **00100110**
152 is represented by **10011000**

4 **a** 15 The 16 possible patterns represent numbers from 0 to 15.
   b 255 The 256 possible patterns represent numbers from 0 to 255.

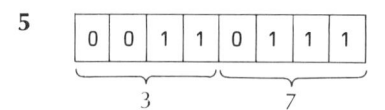

5

| 0 | 0 | 1 | 1 | 0 | 1 | 1 | 1 |

  ⎵⎵⎵ ⎵⎵⎵
    3   7

1 location required to store '37'

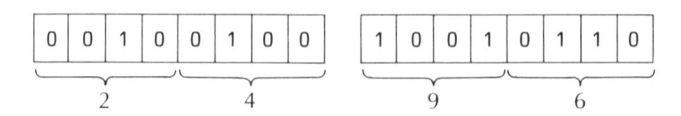

| 0 | 0 | 1 | 0 | 0 | 1 | 0 | 0 | | 1 | 0 | 0 | 1 | 0 | 1 | 1 | 0 |

  ⎵⎵⎵ ⎵⎵⎵   ⎵⎵⎵ ⎵⎵⎵
    2   4   9   6

2 locations required to store '2496'

'37' could be stored in an 8-bit location in pure binary:

| 0 | 0 | 1 | 0 | 0 | 1 | 0 | 1 |

To represent '2496' in pure binary would need 12 bits.

Solutions to exercises 183

6 Sign-and-magnitude   One's complement   Two's complement
-5 = 1101 -5 = 1010 -5 = 1011

```
  1101  (−5)        1010  (−5)        1011  (−5)
 +0101  (+5)       +0101  (+5)       +0101  (+5)
 ─────              ─────             ─────
 10010 ≠ 0         1111 ≠ 0          10000 = 0
                                       ↑
                                     'lost'
```

7 -10 = 11110110
-52 = 11001100
-115 = 10001101

8   10001100
change digits   01110011
          add 1   01110100 = +116
           thus   10001100 = −116
     Similarly,   11011011 = −37

9
1234.5   = 1234.5 × 10^0 mantissa = 1234.5,   exponent = 0
123.45 × 10   = 123.45 × 10^1 mantissa = 123.45,   exponent = 1
12.345 × 100   = 12.345 × 10^2 mantissa = 12.345,   exponent = 2
1.2345 × 1000   = 1.2345 × 10^3 mantissa = 1.2345,   exponent = 3
12345 ÷ 10   = 12345 × 10^{-1} mantissa = 12345,   exponent = -1
123450 ÷ 100   = 123450 × 10^{-2} mantissa = 123450,   exponent = -2

10 a 42.57   = 0.4257 × 100   = 0.4527 × 10^2
                                    mantissa = 0.4257,   exponent = 2

b 5097   = 0.5097 × 10000 = 0.5097 × 10^4
                                    mantissa = 0.5097,   exponent = 4

c 0.00265 = 0.265 ÷ 100   = 0.265 × 10^{-2}
                                    mantissa = 0.265,   exponent = -2

d 0.852   = 0.852 × 1   = 0.852 × 10^0
                                    mantissa = 0.852,   exponent = 0

184 Solutions to exercises

11 a 01100000 represents +0.11 in binary
which is +0.75 in denary
00000010 represents +10 in binary
which is + 2 in denary
The number stored is therefore $0.75 \times 10^2 = 75$
b Similarly $0.6875 \times 10^{10} = 6\,875\,000\,000$
c Similarly $0.875 \times 10^{-14} = 0.000\,000\,000\,000\,008\,75$
If the base used were 2, as is often the case, the answers would
be: **a** 3 **b** 704 **c** $7 \times 2^{-17} \simeq 0.000\,053\,4$

12 The details will vary from language to language (even between different versions of BASIC). It will certainly be necessary to identify each line by a suitable variable. It may be necessary for you to declare how much storage space is required for each line, or for the address as a whole. Alternatively this may be handled by the language, allowing the computer to recognise string lengths and reserve space accordingly.

15 See pages 23–4.

129 in pure binary in eight bits is:

| 1 | 0 | 0 | 0 | 0 | 0 | 0 | 1 |

129 in BCD allowing eight bits for each digit is:

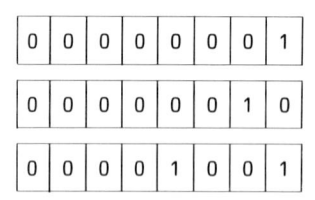

| 0 | 0 | 0 | 0 | 0 | 0 | 0 | 1 |

| 0 | 0 | 0 | 0 | 0 | 0 | 1 | 0 |

| 0 | 0 | 0 | 0 | 1 | 0 | 0 | 1 |

16 Numeric data – see pages 23–31.
Alphanumeric data – see pages 31–2.
A, b, d, f and **g** are likely to be alphanumeric, while **c** and **e** are likely to be numeric.

17 You should mention here the problems of fixed-point storage for non-integer numbers, particularly limitations on range and accuracy of numbers stored in this form. This leads to the advantages of storing non-integer numbers in floating-point form and thus the need for a greater amount of storage space.

18 See pages 25–7 for parts **a**, **b** and **c**.

Discussion of the advantages of two's complement representation should include its allowing only one pattern to represent 'zero' (rather than two patterns) and that it facilitates 'ordinary' arithmetic.

One disadvantage of the two's complement representation is that it is not obvious what the representation of a given negative number is, without going through the steps of conversion shown on page 27.

19 a i) +53   ii) −67   iii) −118   iv) −128
   b i) 00110101   ii) 10010000   iii) 11111101

20 a +80 and −7
   b 0.625×10^{-7}
   c Instruction code 5, address 249.
   Using the machine code instructions of Chapter 6, this is
   SUBTRACT 249

SOLUTIONS TO CHAPTER 4

9 This only works where there is just one key. In that case, when you retrieve the actual book record, you must be doing so as a result of looking up the key in the index, so all the information which you require will be together. But if there is more than one key, say ISBN and title, we might use the ISBN index to find the record and hence not be able to find out the title, which is in another index. So it is necessary to repeat all the key fields in the record as well as in the index.

SOLUTIONS TO CHAPTER 5

1 A long tape is cheaper than several smaller ones, as a way of buying the same amount of tape. But if a long tape is used for saving copies of several programs, it may be necessary to wait for the computer to read over unwanted programs while searching for one towards the end of the tape. Even by careful use of the fast-forward and rewind keys, together with a note of counter numbers, some time will be wasted. It will almost always be simpler, although more costly, to use shorter cassettes.

2 Direct access is the ability to go directly to any record without reading through other records first. Serial access is the retrieval method which involves reading through all preceding records in order to locate the required one. In order to make use of direct access methods, it is necessary to have the file stored on some medium that allows access to any part of the file. This will necessarily involve using some form of addressing, such as sector addresses on a magnetic disk, as each record will have to occupy a position on the medium that can be noted down independently of the positions of other records. In using serial access files, only the position of a record in the file is relevant. For this reason, magnetic tapes are quite suitable for serial files.

3 Fixed-length records are convenient, in that the address of a record in the middle of a file can be calculated simply. However, the length of the record must be carefully chosen before the file is set up, as it may waste a considerable amount of space if the length is too long. In any event, the length must allow for the longest possible record, and it will not be possible to store any longer records (which may be presented after the file has been set up). Variable-length records allow each record to occupy exactly the space required, but it is now more difficult to access the record. If serial access methods are used, variable-length records will suffice, but if direct access methods are used, an index to each record will be required.

4 One possible solution is shown below.

FILEA: SECTOR	1	LINK: 4:12:6
START: 4:12:5	2	LINK: 0:0:0
FILEB: SECTOR	1	LINK: 3:9:8
START: 4:12:7	2	LINK: 3:8:5
	3	LINK: 3:7:1
	4	LINK: 0:0:0
FILEC: SECTOR	1	LINK: 2:11:5
START: 3:7:2	2	LINK: 2:11:6
	3	LINK: 2:8:4
	4	LINK: 2:8:5
	5	LINK: 2:4:1
	6	LINK: 0:0:0

SOLUTIONS TO CHAPTER 6

3
50	INPUT 59	– Get the next number
51	LOAD 59	– put it in the accumulator
52	ADD 60	– add in the total so far . . .
53	STORE 60	– . . . and store the new total away
54	LOAD 61	– get the COUNT from store . . .
55	SUBTRACT 62	– . . . and take 1 away
56	BRANCHZ 63	– if we've done, go to the STOP . . .
57	STORE 61	– . . . if not, store the new COUNT . . .
58	GOTO 50	– . . . and go back for more.
59	000000000000	– A temporary store used to hold the number on input
60	000000000000	– The TOTAL is accumulated here
61	000000001010	– The COUNT, set initially to 10, and decreased
62	000000000001	– A binary '1' used by the instruction at 55
63	STOP	

4 a
50	INPUT 59	– Get the number N
51	LOAD 59	– put it in the accumulator
52	ADD 60	– add in the total so far . . .
53	STORE 60	– . . . and store the new total away
54	LOAD 59	– take N again . . .
55	SUBTRACT 61	– . . . and take 1 away
56	BRANCHZ 62	– if we've done, go to STOP . . .
57	STORE 59	– . . . if not, store the new N . . .
58	GOTO 52	– . . . and go back to add it in.
59	000000000000	– A store used for the changing value of N
60	000000000000	– The TOTAL is accumulated here
61	000000000001	– A binary '1' used by the instruction at 55
62	STOP	

b
50	LOAD 100	
51	SUBTRACT 54	
52	BRANCHZ 200	
53	GOTO 300	
54	000000110010	– a binary '50' for use at instruction 51

5 It will be necessary for the control unit to look at the first byte during the fetch cycle, to determine if the next byte (which may be an address) is also needed. If not, the fetch cycle ends without setting the SAR by adding 1 to the SCR. If the second byte is required, the fetch cycle continues, retrieving that byte and also setting the SAR, and adding 2 to the SCR. You may prefer to think of this as two separate fetch cycles – a short one for one-byte instructions, a long one for two-byte instructions. There will be a separate execute cycle for each instruction, as before.

SOLUTIONS TO CHAPTER 7

4 When the program needs to begin execution, it takes its dummy `GOTO 0` instruction, adds the starting address (say 100) to it from `GOTO 100`, and then stores this instruction where it will be the next thing executed.

5
46	000000000001	– A binary '1'
47	000100000000	– The pattern for `INPUT 0`
48	100000000000	– The pattern for `GOTO 0`
49	000000000000	– The store used for keeping the start address
50	INPUT 49	– Get the start address
51	LOAD 49	– Put it in the accumulator
52	ADD 47	– Make it into a useful `INPUT` instruction . . .
53	STORE 54	– . . . and put it where we can use it
54	STOP	– A dummy instruction to be overwritten
55	ADD 47	– The accumulator still holds 'INPUT address', so when we add `INPUT 0` again, we get the pattern for 'LOAD address' . . .
56	STORE 57	– . . .we put this new instruction where we can use it
57	STOP	– A dummy instruction to be overwritten
58	BRANCHZ 62	– Now the accumulator has a copy of the last value loaded and we test to see if this is the special signal . . .
59	LOAD 54	– . . . if not, the `INPUT` instruction must be altered to increase the address
60	ADD 46	– This makes it into a new `INPUT` instruction . . .
61	GOTO 53	– . . . which we go back and use
62	LOAD 48	– If the last thing loaded was the signal, we get a copy of `GOTO 0` . . .
63	STORE 64	– . . . and put it where we can use it
64	STOP	– A dummy instruction, to be overwritten

9 Some possible reasons are as follows. To make especially efficient use of storage locations or to achieve an exceptionally high speed of execution. To use storage in a way that is not envisaged in a high-level language, such as storing several small numbers packed together into the space that a high-level language would use for just one number. To modify instructions by altering their address or operation-code portions. To affect locations that are deliberately not available to high-level language users to prevent accidental misuse (such as the location holding the current time, or password information). To control peripherals or to be able to switch the interrupt mechanism on and off. To write systems software!

12 a An initial program loader is used to place machine-code instructions in specified locations of main store.

b A compiler translates a source-code program into a self-contained program in object-code (usually machine code).

c An interpreter executes a source code program by translating statements, one by one, into object code and executing the object code before continuing with the next source code statement.

13 An operating system manages the operation of the computer by sharing out the resources between the users and communicating with the peripherals on behalf of users' programs.

14 a A polling routine checks each user's terminal to see if anything has been presented for input that requires the attention of the operating system.

b A command interpreter decodes the user's request for action from the operating system, and identifies which portion of the operating system or other piece of systems software is required.

c Security and accounting routines check the right of each user to have access to the computer, and to the files he requests; the share of the total resources used by each program is recorded and possibly a charge identified for the use of that share.

d A file manager keeps track of all files on-line to the computer, retrieving records requested by user programs or systems software.

SOLUTIONS TO CHAPTER 8

No exercises require solutions.

SOLUTIONS TO CHAPTER 9

No exercises require solutions.

SOLUTIONS TO CHAPTER 10

1. Verification is the checking of input data against a second copy of itself – by re-typing or re-punching, perhaps. This tests whether the data has been entered correctly, not whether it is itself the correct data.

    Validation is the checking of the data after it has been correctly entered, in order to detect any items that are in error – such as the transposition of adjacent figures, numbers too large to be realistic, and so on.

2. Both totals provide a check that no questionnaire has slipped out of the batch. The batch total is a simple count recording the fact that there are 500 documents in the batch. The hash total is a meaningless total. If a document is missing, neither the hash total nor the batch total will agree with the values that were calculated when the batch was complete. In addition, if the age field is altered or incorrectly transmitted, the hash totals will disagree. In this way, an additional check is made on one specially important field of data.

3. It is easy to switch the figures around when entering a large number to the computer; the presence of a check digit enables the computer to detect when a number is in error, although the exact error cannot be pinpointed.

    Applying the method to 123456789, we get: $(1 \times 10) + (2 \times 9) + (3 \times 8) + (4 \times 7) + (5 \times 6) + (6 \times 5) + (7 \times 4) + (8 \times 3) + (9 \times 2) = 210$.

    The next highest multiple of 11 is 220, so the check digit should be '10', for which we use the Roman numeral X, quoting the agent's number as 123456789X.

4. When a file is updated periodically, care must be taken that the updated copy is not in error. If some accident causes this new file to be corrupted, it will still be possible to recover from the accident, provided that the original file has not been damaged. To guard against this, three generations of files are kept: the Grandfather, Father and Son files. While the Son is being created from the Father, the Grandfather file plays no part in the process and hence is in no danger. After a successful update, the oldest generation is destroyed.

5. Errors detected at the vetting and validating stages (e.g. mispunched data-items, non-matching check digits, wrong type of data in a field, disagreeing control totals); errors during the update process (e.g. reconciliation errors); computer processing errors (e.g. failure of a sorting routine).

6. This solution is given opposite.

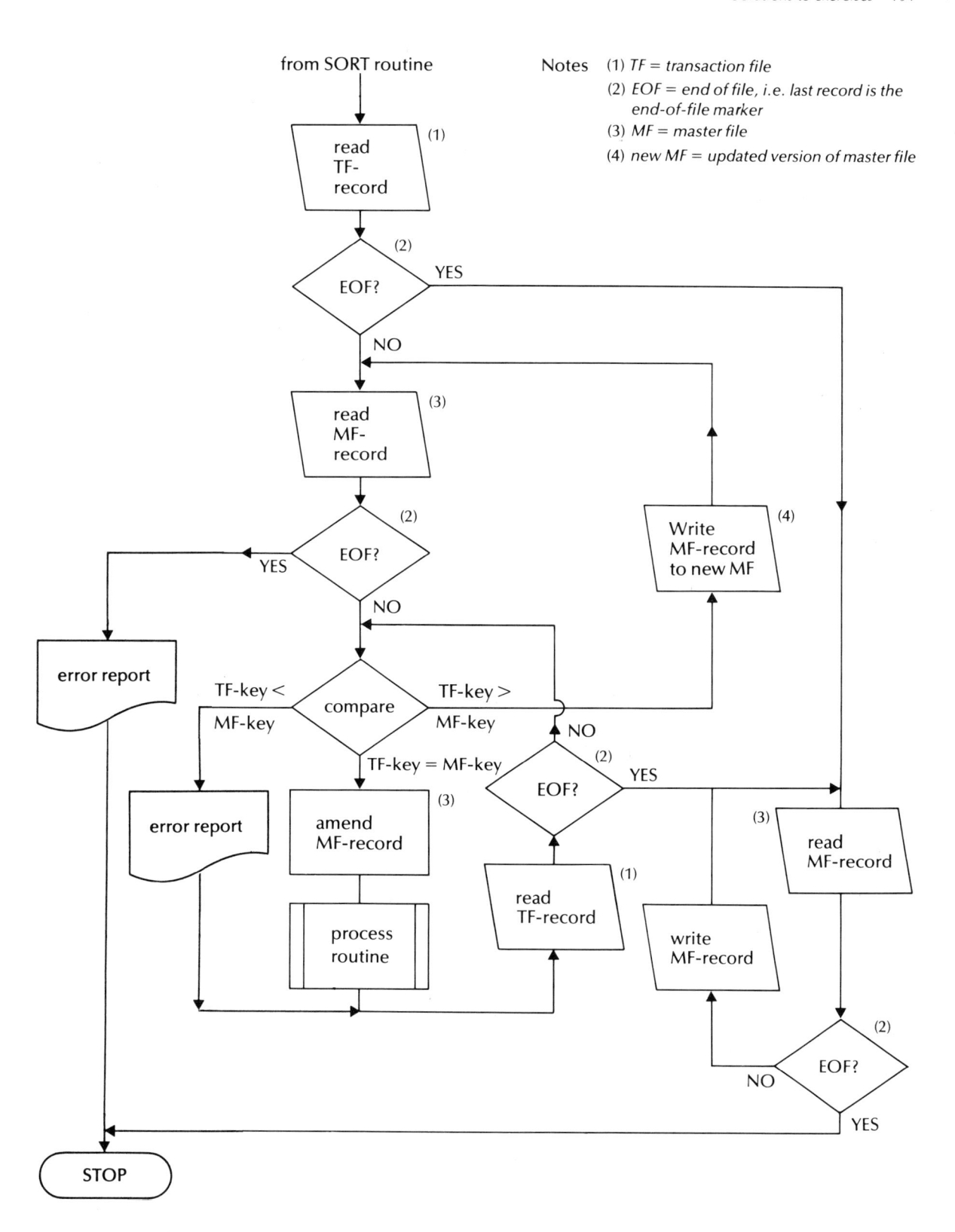

Solutions to exercises 191

Notes (1) *TF = transaction file*
(2) *EOF = end of file, i.e. last record is the end-of-file marker*
(3) *MF = master file*
(4) *new MF = updated version of master file*

```
from SORT routine
        │
        ▼
    read TF-record (1)
        │
        ▼
      EOF? (2) ──YES──────────────────────────┐
        │                                      │
        NO                                     │
        │ ◄─────────────────────────────┐     │
        ▼                               │     │
    read MF-record (3)                  │     │
        │                               │     │
        ▼                               │     │
      EOF? (2) ──YES──► error report    │     │
        │                   │           │     │
        NO                  │           │     │
        │ ◄─────────────────┼───────────┤     │
        ▼                   │           │     │
  ┌──compare──┐             │      Write MF-record
TF-key<    TF-key>          │      to new MF (4)
MF-key     MF-key           │           ▲
  │    TF-key=MF-key │      │           │
  ▼         │        │      │           │
error       ▼        ▼     EOF? (2) ──NO┘
report  amend    EOF? (2)   │
  │     MF-record    │YES   YES
  │     (3)          │       │
  │       │          ▼       ▼
  │       ▼      read     read MF-record (3)
  │   process   TF-record     │
  │   routine    (1)          ▼
  │       │       ▲         EOF? (2)
  │       │       │           │NO──► write MF-record
  │       │       └───────────┘           │
  │       │                               YES
  ▼       ▼                               │
 STOP ◄───┴───────────────────────────────┘
```

SOLUTIONS TO CHAPTER 11

1 Answered partly in the text, but you may be able to add to our suggestions.

2 At the time of writing, word processors are still relatively expensive (as compared with, say, a general-purpose microcomputer) and we couldn't afford one!

3 You will certainly get into moral and philosophical issues here, and we will not presume to lead you in this.

4 You will gain a lot from investigation of a real example at close quarters, if you can find one whose owners are willing to let you do this.

Appendix 2
EXAMINATION QUESTIONS

For many people, one purpose in studying computing will be to take an examination in the subject. In this case, it is only good sense to prepare yourself as well as possible. One way is clearly to learn as much as possible about the subject, and the rest of this book has been about gaining this knowledge; *this* section is about preparing for, and taking, examinations.

The bulk of this section is a collection of questions that have actually been set in real examinations. We suggest that you use these in a way rather different from the exercises throughout the book, as we shall shortly make clear.

No one ever sits an examination for the first time! Even if you are the very first candidate in the first year of a new examination, the examiners will have published a specimen paper, precisely so that you can see what a typical examination looks like. It is in your own best interests to study this paper, or as many past papers as you can obtain.

First: what are the instructions? How many questions are you required to answer – all or just some of those on the paper? Are the answers to be short sentences or long essays? Will the answers be written on the examination paper itself, or in a separate answer book or on paper? Knowing what the paper will look like will save you valuable thinking time on the day itself.

All examinations have a time limit, and one thing that will be tested is whether you can write down your answers in the time you are allowed. A very good way of preparing for an examination is to use the past papers as a sort of 'time trial'. Find yourself some time when you will not be interrupted, put your text books away, and begin the paper as if it was a real one. Keep a close eye on the clock and make sure that you allow yourself just as long as you will have on the day. Don't reach for your notes when you come to a question that you can't quite remember the answer for – see what you *can* manage to write down, and you may surprise yourself.

Taking a test paper like this will also be useful for your revision; it will show you exactly what it is that you can remember, and what you can't. Be careful over how you spend your time in revision. It is very easy to find a comfortable chair, open a text book or your own notebook, and begin to read. You can spend hours like this, fooling yourself that you are doing something useful! Quite often, what you read passes through your memory and straight out the other side. By far the best way of revising is to tackle questions, like those in the rest of this section, and see exactly what you can write down when you cannot rely on your notes. In this way, when you do look back at your notes to check your answer, you will either have proved to yourself that you have remembered something important about which questions may be asked, or you will have identified what it is you don't know, and you can make an effort to learn it right away.

If you are asked to choose questions in the examination, spend a little time thinking about your choice. Read all the questions carefully – it is very easy to think that you know what a question is asking, but if you have misread the question, you could well spend a considerable time writing rubbish which will score you no marks.

Examination questions 195

HOW TO USE THESE QUESTIONS

From what we have said above, it should be clear that we think that you should tackle these questions as if they were part of an exam – without books and with a strict time limit. For each of the questions (all of which are from real or specimen examinations) we have noted which examination they come from, and have tried to give you some guidance as to how long to spend. Sometimes this is our own guess, based on how many questions were on the paper, sometimes the examiners have given some indication. Certainly, you should try to get as close to our times as possible – preferably doing better!

1. How would you describe to a person not familiar with computers the difference between a *simple* calculator and a computer?

   Approximate time allowed: $4\frac{1}{2}$ minutes

   Source: Joint Matriculation Board (GCE O-level).

2. **a** Name the three components of the processor or CPU of a computer.

   b State the purpose or function of the three components mentioned above.

   Approximate time allowed: $7\frac{1}{2}$ minutes

   Source: Joint Matriculation Board (GCE O-level).

3. Complete the following passage by writing in appropriate words chosen from the list below it.

   The digital computer stores and processes data in _____ form. A group of binary digits or _____ is used to represent characters and numbers. A set of 8 bits, usually called a _____, is the unit of storage which corresponds to a character. Many computers also use a larger unit of storage called a _____ which may consist of a fixed number of bits, typically 16, _____, or 32 bits. A computer which uses 24-bit words could store _____ characters in each word. The size of a computer is often given in terms of its word _____ and the number of words in its main store. In computing, _____ of store means 1024 words. Thus a 16-bit word computer having an 8K store would have _____ words of storage which could hold 16384 _____.

word	characters
1K	byte
bits	3
24	8192
binary	length

   Approximate time allowed: 4 minutes

   Source: East Anglian Examinations Board (CSE).

4   Information is often given in coded form. The driver number on a driving licence is a 16-character string code as in the example.

R	A	Y	9	9	5	6	1	1	5	2	M	G	9	B	R
1	2	3	4	5	6	7	8	9	10	11	12	13	14	15	16

The string is made using the following rules:

Characters	Usage
1 to 5	The first five characters of the surname. If the surname has less than five characters it is padded with 9's.
6 and 11	The last two digits of the year of birth.
7 and 8	The month of birth. If the driver is a woman, 50 is added.
9 and 10	The day of birth.
11	See 6.
12 and 13	The driver's initials. If there are less than two, the second character is a 9.
14	Is always a 9.
15 and 16	Computer generated check-characters.

a Give the name, initials, date of birth and sex of the driver below.

B	E	L	L	9	5	0	9	3	0	6	P	9	9	B	T
1	2	3	4	5	6	7	8	9	10	11	12	13	14	15	16

b Fill in the driver number for Mrs Elizabeth Williamson, who was born on January 17th, 1943. Assume the check-characters to be 5T.

1	2	3	4	5	6	7	8	9	10	11	12	13	14	15	16

Approximate time allowed: 5 minutes

Source: East Anglian Examinations Board (CSE).

5   A computer file consists of records which in turn consist of fields which in turn consist of characters. Use examples and a diagram, if necessary, to illustrate what is meant by the terms

a file
b records
c fields

Approximate time allowed: 9 minutes

Source: Joint Matriculation Board (GCE O-level).

6 Give three reasons why a VDU would be used in preference to a teleprinter for a classroom demonstration in a Biology class of, say, river pollution.

Approximate time allowed: 5 minutes
Source: University of London (GCE O-level).

7 Backing storage for a computer usually consists of magnetic disk units or magnetic tape units.

  a For each of these devices, magnetic tape unit and magnetic disk unit, state the type of access and an advantage of its use.

  b With the aid of a diagram, describe briefly how a magnetic disk unit works.

Approximate time allowed: 8 minutes
Source: Yorkshire Regional Examinations Board (CSE).

8 A computer installation usually contains a number of peripherals.

  a State what is meant by 'peripherals'.

  b Give *three* examples of peripherals which you would expect to find in a *commercial* computer installation and a brief description of the particular job done by each one in the computing task.

Approximate time allowed: 8 minutes
Source: Yorkshire Regional Examinations Board (CSE).

9 Describe *one* major application of computing that you have studied. You should include in your description an outline flowchart or flowcharts of the system showing the flow of data through the system. You should also make it clear which information is held on backing store and what type of backing store is used.

Approximate time allowed: 24 minutes
Source: Joint Matriculation Board (GCE O-level).

10 The types of program listed below are examples of computer software. Describe the purpose of each:

  a assembler
  b computer
  c operating system
  d applications package
  e utility program

Approximate time allowed: 10 minutes
Source: Yorkshire Regional Examinations Board (CSE).

11 a Explain the difference between *systems software* and *applications software*.

b Give two examples of *systems software* of which you have knowledge, and briefly describe their purpose.

c Give two examples of currently used *applications packages* of which you have knowledge, and briefly describe their purpose.

Approximate time allowed: 22 minutes
Source: University of Cambridge (GCE O-level).

12 Explain the reason for including parity checks in binary codes.

Approximate time allowed: 3 minutes
Source: London Regional Examining Board (CSE).

13 a List the typical elements of program documentation.

b Why is documentation especially necessary in a commercial installation?

Approximate time allowed: 12 minutes
Source: Joint Matriculation Board (GCE O-level).

14 a ACCARD is a credit card company. The company issues cards to individuals who use them to buy goods without cash. The company sets a credit limit for each individual, pays for the goods and later recovers the money from the cardholder. All retailers offering ACCARD services to their customers have an on-line ACCARD reader connected to the ACCARD computer centre at Esshampton.
  - i) Describe two of the data files that must be housed at the Esshampton Centre.
  - ii) An individual attempts to make a purchase using his ACCARD card. Draw a systems flowchart of a system that would process his request for credit as soon as his card is inserted into the reader. (Give meaningful names to any data files that the system involves.)

b It would seem that credit card systems offer an easy and convenient way of purchasing: yet many people voice opinions against such systems because of the personal nature of the information recorded. Briefly discuss whether or not you feel that this objection is valid.

Approximate time allowed: 18 minutes
Source: University of London (GCE O-level).

15 Draw a ring round the most appropriate answer in each case.

a A teletypewriter is
  i) a high speed output device
  ii) used for input and output
  iii) a storage device
  iv) part of a lineprinter

b Peripherals are
  i) part of the CPU
  ii) part of the software
  iii) devices attached to the CPU
  iv) people

c Checking a flowchart using test data is
  i) validation
  ii) dry running
  iii) unnecessary
  iv) interpreting

d An example of a floating point number is
  i) 1.716
  ii) 171.6
  iii) 0.01716
  iv) 0.1716E−3

e A computer file is
  i) a collection of related records
  ii) a set of metal plates
  iii) a computer engineer's tool
  iv) an item of hardware

f The data preparation supervisor usually takes charge of
  i) the computer room
  ii) a data bank
  iii) the key punch operators
  iv) the programmers

g A group of instructions, which although written only once, may be called for use at a number of different places in a program is
  i) a node
  ii) a conditional jump
  iii) a subroutine
  iv) an assembler

Approximate time allowed: 4 minutes
Source: East Anglian Examination Board (CSE).

16 The following information is to be collected about each pupil in a certain secondary school: name, date of birth, sex, height (m), weight (kg).

a The information about each pupil is to be coded as a data record on to a separate 80-column computer card. Design a card layout and explain why it is suitable.

b State four of the data validation tests that it might be sensible to apply to the coded information.

c With reference to your answer to **b**, construct a program flowchart for the required data validation routine. Make it clear as to what messages would be printed out if a particular data item fails a test.

Approximate time allowed: 18 minutes
Source: University of London (GCE O-level).

17 For each job below, write the number of the person who does that job.

Person	Job
1. Computer manager	Arranging operators' shift-work
2. Systems analyst	Coding a flowchart
3. Computer operator	Loading a magnetic tape unit
4. Computer engineer	Data preparation
5. Programmer	Designing a data processing method
6. File librarian	Tracing and correcting program logic errors
7. Key-punch operator	Tracing and correcting hardware faults
	Responding to computer console messages
	Cleaning and issuing magnetic tapes
	Verification

Approximate time allowed: 5 minutes
Source: East Anglian Examination Board (CSE).

18 The Data Processing Manager of a Gas Board has called a meeting of the computer department's Chief Systems Analyst, Chief Programmer, Operations Manager and Data Preparation Supervisor. The meeting is needed in order to discuss some problems which have occurred recently. For *each* of the situations described below, explain what the manager would have to ask *each* of the four people to check so that the situation can be prevented from occurring again. In some cases you will need to explain why one or more of the four people is not involved.

  a The Smith family received a quarterly gas bill of £964.26 instead of £23.15.

  b Mr Brown received a correct bill for £19.10. He misread the amount, and sent only £19.01. When he received a computer printed letter asking for the remaining 9 pence, he ignored it, and was then sent another letter threatening to take him to court.

  c People who have been on holiday or in hospital are being threatened with being taken to court for not paying the bill which was sent while they were away.

  d People who have just moved into a house are being sued for bills run up by the previous tenants.

  Approximate time allowed: 20 minutes
  Source: London Regional Examining Board (CSE).

19 **a** List the *data-processing* requirements of a large banking system.

  b List the items of computer equipment you would expect such a system to employ and state the role(s) of each item.

  Approximate time allowed: 22 minutes
  Source: University of Cambridge (GCE O-level).

20 A *transaction file* is used to *update* a *master file*. There is a danger that the master file may become *corrupted* in this process. To allow for this possibility, various *generations of master file* are retained.

  Explain the following terms (as used above):
  a transaction file
  b update
  c master file
  d corrupted
  e generations of master file

  Approximate time allowed: 7½ minutes
  Source: Joint Matriculation Board (GCE O-level).

21 In recent years a number of retail outlets have introduced the use of computer-readable labels attached to their goods. What is the object of these labels and why do they mark a dramatic development in the computerisation of retail outlets? What kind of information are they likely to contain and to what purpose will it be put? Why has the introduction of computers made such a difference to operations in the retail trade?

Approximate time allowed: 24 minutes

Source: Joint Matriculation Board (GCE O-level).

22 Most large city hospitals use computers to aid the processing of information about their patients and the day-to-day running of the hospitals. The hospital administration department is commonly thought of as the place where patients are admitted, although much of the administrative work is carried out behind the scenes. A *visual display unit* might be used to communicate on-line with the computer. From the *visual display unit* information about patients is input into *files* on *backing storage devices*. Some files are stored on *serial access storage devices* and others on *random access storage devices*. When a doctor requires information about his patients he will study *records* from these backing storage devices.

a What is a *visual display unit*?

b Describe how a *visual display unit might be used to communicate on-line with a computer* in the hospital.

c What is a *record*?

d What is the connection between a *file* and a *record*?

e Name a *serial access storage device*.

f Name a *random access storage device*.

g List *three* tasks for which the computer could be used in the day-to-day administrative work of a hospital.

Approximate time allowed: 13 minutes

Source: Yorkshire Regional Examinations Board (CSE).

23 When a library in a particular town catalogues a book, details of the title, the author and the catalogue number of the book are recorded on a computer file.

Explain the checks that would be incorporated in a data validation program used in conjunction with the input of these data into the computer file.

Approximate time allowed: 7½ minutes

Source: Joint Matriculation Board (GCE O-level).

24 What is meant by *batch processing*?
What is meant by *interactive processing*?

  a Three applications A, B and C are described below. In each case, state with reasons whether the application would probably use batch processing or interactive processing.

  Application A: The production of gas bills for customers every three months, by a gas company.

  Application B: A reservation system which allows travellers to book seats on planes at any airline booking office.

  Application C: A supermarket company, whose 200 shops send orders to the computer centre twice a week, and which has 8 warehouses each supplying goods to the shops near them.

  b Which one of the applications *must* be a 'real-time system'?

  c What is meant by *remote access computing*?
  Which two of the three applications are most likely to use remote access computing? Give a reason for each answer.

  d Which one of the three applications is most likely to use VDUs?

  e Which application *must* hold its master files on either disk or drum?

  f Which application is unlikely to use the grandfather-father-son system for its files?

Suggest a way in which damaged files could be recreated for this application.

Approximate time allowed: 20 minutes

Source: London Regional Examining Board (CSE).

25 People often make statements about computers which are neither completely true nor completely false. Explain how this applies to each of the following statements.

  a 'Computers put people out of work.'

  b 'My bill is wrong. The computer made a mistake.'

  c 'The government has got computer files about everybody.'

Approximate time allowed: 20 minutes

Source: East Anglian Examinations Board (CSE).

INDEX

This index is designed to be helpful, not exhaustive. The entry for *disk, magnetic* will take you to the pages where the most useful references to disk storage are to be found, rather than to every occurrence of the word *disk*. Further, common words such as *computer*, *programming* and *data* tend to be omitted as being parts of many entries. Thus in searching for *programming language translator*, a page reference will be found under *T* but not under *P*. Under *L*, the entry for *language* includes such topics as *language translators* which do not form a separate entry.

This index was prepared manually; after reading this book, you should be better able to judge whether or not this is a Good Thing.

access time 67
accumulator 74
address 20, 64
address part of instruction 38
airline reservation 169–70
ALGOL 107
alphanumeric data 31
analog computer 4
analog–digital converter 174
applications software 94
archiving 176
arithmetic unit 72
array 35, 131
ASCII 31
assembler 101
assembly language 101
automatic operation 2

background 170
backing storage (same as *secondary storage*) Chapter 5 (59–69), 109
bar-code reading 86
BASIC 107, 142
batch processing 146
batch total 156
BCD 23
binary coded decimal 23
binary computer 22
binary digit 4, 22
binary point 28
bit 22
bit pattern 22
block 62
bootstrap 97
bounce (keyboard) 81
boundaries of system 115

branch instruction 76
bug 140
byte 33

calculator 2
call 143
car registration 32
cards, filing 44
cards, punched 83–4
cassette 60
central processing unit 20, 72
chain of records 51
change file 158
character machine 33
character storage 31
check digit 156–7
circuit switching 173
clock track 87
COBOL 47, 106
coding 114, 138–40
collection of data 13, 153
command interpreter 108
commercial data processing Chapter 10 (145–63)
compiler 104
complements 26, 27
computer, analog 4
computer (definition of) 1
computer, digital 3
concatenated key 47
context 11
control character 32, 63
control system 174–5
control total 156
control unit 72
core store 20
CPU 20, 72

cycle, data-processing 152–61
cycle, fetch–execute 73
cylinder 64

data 5, 11
database 170–2
database management system 171
data collection 13, 153
data file – see *file*
data flowchart 123, 149–52
data preparation 154–5
data preparation staff 161
data processing Chapter 10 (145–63)
data-processing cycle 152–61
data-processing manager 161
data structure 33, 130–1
data validation 149, 155
data vetting 139, 149, 155
DBMS 171
debugging 140
describing files 47
design of forms 14–5, 119
design of output 118
dialect 138
digit 3
digital–analog converter 174
digital computer 3
direct access 64, 67, 89
disk addressing 64
disk controller 66
disk, magnetic 63–6, 89–90
documentation 115, 121, 140–1, 148
dot-matrix printer 81
DP Chapter 10 (145–63)
Driver and Vehicle Licensing

Centre 45, 117, 168
driver number 45
drop-out ink 87
dry run 120, 132
DVLC 45, 117, 168

echoing back 79
editor 110, 177
EDSAC 19
end-of-field 62
end-of-file 62
end-of-record 62
even parity 78
exchangeable disk pack 64
execute cycle 73
executive – see *operating system*
exponent 29

Father file 159, 176
feasibility study 121
fetch cycle 73
field 45
field check 157
field length 62
file 45
file description 47
file layout 48, 119
file ordering 46–7
filing cards 44
firmware 94
fixed-length field 62
fixed-point representation 28
floating-point representation 29
floppy disk 64, 90
flowchart 122–3, 149–52
flow of information 116
foreground/background 170
form design 14–5, 119
FORTRAN 106
fractions 28
front panel 95

gap, inter-block 62
garbage 157
GIGO 157
going live 115, 121
GOTO instruction 76
Grandfather–Father–Son files 159, 176
graphics 84–5
graph plotter 82

hardware Chapter 6 (71–91), 117–8
hash total 156

header 54, 64
high-level language 102–3
high-resolution graphics 84

IAR – see *SCR*
identifier 21
immediate access storage – see *primary storage*
increment 134
incremental plotter 82
index 54, 204
information 11
information flow 116
information retrieval 166
initial program loader 94
ink-jet printer 81
instruction address register – see *sequence control register*
instruction code 38
instruction register 75
instructions, machine 38
integer 23
inter-block gap 62
International Standard Book Number *iv*, 156–7, cover
interpreter 105
interrupt 79, 109
ISBN *iv*, 156–7, cover

journal file 176

K 39
key 45–6
keyboard 80
Kimball tags 154

language 100–7
layout sheet 118
library of subroutines 110
light pen 85–6
line printer 78
link 51, 66
list 35, 131
liveware 94
loader 94
location 33
locked file 169
logical pointer 66
loop 6, 134–6
low-level language 101–2
low-resolution graphics 84

machine instruction 38
machine-orientated

language 101
magnetic disk 63–6, 89–90
magnetic tape 61–3, 87–8
magnetic tape cassette 60
main store Chapter 3 (19–41), 72
maintenance documentation 122
mantissa 29
manual procedures 119
mark sense reading 87
master file 158
'Mastermind' Chapter 9 (128–43)
matrix printer 81
media, storage 60
menu 86
module 130
monitor – see *operating system*
multiple keys 46

name table 104
network 173
next instruction register – see *sequence control register*
NIR – see *SCR*
nonsense 103–4
nonsense total 156
normalisation 30

object code 104
objectives 114, 116
odd parity 78
off-line 82
one's complement representation 26
operating system 107–10
operational documentation 121
operation code 38
operations manager 161
operators 161
ordering files 46–7
order-processing 146
outline flowchart 132
output design 118

packet switching 173
paper tape 83
parallel running 115, 120
parameter 143
parity check 78
Pascal 107
password 148
payroll 146

performance criteria 114
peripheral unit 72, 77
personnel 161–2
physical pointer 66
picture clause (COBOL) 48
pilot scheme 121
pilot survey 15
plotter 82
PNCU 166
pointer 51, 66
point-of-sale device 154
Police National Computer Unit 166
polling 108
portability 103
power-fail interrupt 79
primary key 55
primary storage Chapter 3 (19–41)
printer 81
privacy 15, 148
problem-orientated language 102–3
processing 5
program 2, 7
program counter — see *sequence control register*
program flowchart 123, 132–3
programmable calculator 2
programmer 94, 161
programming 2, Chapter 9 (127–143)
punched card 83–4
punched paper tape 83
pure binary representation 23

query langage 171–2
QWERTY keyboard 80

random access 67, 89
range check 157
reading speed 62
real number 31
real-time system 166–70
reconciliation error 159
record 45
record chain 51
record key 45–6
record structure 48
recovery procedure 121, 175–6
recursion 206
recycling paper 81
registers 73
reprogramming 3

reservation system 169–70
RETURN statement 142–3
roundabouts 55
rounding 30

sales order-processing 146
SAR 75
SCR 74, 95
secondary key 55
secondary storage (same as *backing storage*) Chapter 5 (59–69), 109
sector 64
security 148, 175
self-documenting programs 122
sequence control register 74, 95
sequential access 66–7, 88
serial access 66–7, 88
sign-and-magnitude representation 25
sign bit 25
software Chapter 7 (93–111)
Son file 159, 176
sorting 67–8, 120, 158
source code 104
spooler 110
Standard Book Number 156–7
standby arrangements 119
stock control 146
STOP instruction 76
storage Chapter 5 (59–69)
storage media 60
storage of machine instructions 38
storage, primary Chapter 3 (19–41)
storage, secondary Chapter 5 (59–69)
storage, virtual 109
store 2
store address register 75
string 34, 130
structure of data 33, 130–1
structure of information 12
sub-field 48
subroutine 142–3
subroutine library 110
subscript 131
subsystem 115
supervisor — see *operating system*
survey, pilot 15
swapping disk 109
swings 55

system boundaries 115
system flowchart 123, 149–52
systems analysis and design Chapter 8 (113–25)
systems analyst 162
systems software 94

table 35
tape librarian 162
tape, magnetic 61–3, 87–8
tape, paper 83
tender 118
test data 120, 138
testing 115, 120–1
text editor 110, 177
timesharing 108–9
time slice 109
timing track 87
touch-sensitive screen 86
trace 132, 140
trace table 136–7
track (on a disk) 64
transaction file 158
translator 100
truncation 30
turnkey system 100
two's complement representation 27
two-state system 22

uniqueness of key 46
update file 158
user documentation 121
utility program 110

validation 149, 155
variable-length field 62
variable name 21
VDU 84
verification 154
verifier 154
vetting 139, 149, 155
virtual storage 109
visual display unit 84

washing machine 7
word 33
word length 33
word processing 176–7

x–y plotter 82